Collieries, communities and the miners' strike in Scotland, 1984–85

Jim Phillips

Manchester University Press

Manchester and New York

distributed in the United States exclusively
by Palgrave Macmillan

The right of Jim Phillips to be identified as the author of this work has been asserted by him in accordance with the Copyright, Designs and Patents Act 1988.

Published by Manchester University Press
Oxford Road, Manchester M13 9NR, UK
and Room 400, 175 Fifth Avenue, New York, NY 10010, USA
www.manchesteruniversitypress.co.uk

Distributed in the United States exclusively by
Palgrave Macmillan, 175 Fifth Avenue, New York,
NY 10010, USA

Distributed in Canada exclusively by
UBC Press, University of British Columbia, 2029 West Mall,
Vancouver, BC, Canada V6T 1Z2

British Library Cataloguing-in-Publication Data
A catalogue record for this book is available from the British Library

Library of Congress Cataloging-in-Publication Data applied for

ISBN   978 0 7190 8632 8 hardback

First published 2012

The publisher has no responsibility for the persistence or accuracy of URLs for any external or third-party internet websites referred to in this book, and does not guarantee that any content on such websites is, or will remain, accurate or appropriate.

Typeset
by Action Publishing Technology Ltd, Gloucester
Printed in Great Britain
by TJ International Ltd, Padstow

To Anna, Robert and Matthew, with love and appreciation

Contents

Series editors' foreword   *page* viii
List of tables and boxes   ix
Abbreviations   xi
Acknowledgements   xiii

Introduction: rethinking the miners' strike of 1984–85   1

I: **Origins and outbreak**   19

1   Collieries, communities and coalfield politics   21
2   Closures and workplace conflict: the origins of the strike   53

II: **The strike**   81

3   The Scottish industrial politics of the strike   83
4   Communities and commitment   110
5   Ending and aftermath   143
6   Legacy and conclusion   165

Bibliography   177
Index   188

Series editors' foreword

The start of the twenty-first century is superficially an inauspicious time to study labour movements. Political parties once associated with the working class have seemingly embraced capitalism. The trade unions with which these parties were once linked have suffered near-fatal reverses. The industrial proletariat looks both divided and in rapid decline. The development of multi-level governance, prompted by 'globalisation', has furthermore apparently destroyed the institutional context for advancing the labour 'interest'. Many consequently now look on terms such as the 'working class', 'socialism' and 'the labour movement' as politically and historically redundant.

The purpose of this series is to give a platform to those students of labour movements who challenge, or develop, established ways of thinking and so demonstrate the continued vitality of the subject and the work of those interested in it. For despite appearances, many social democratic parties remain important competitors for national office and proffer distinctive programmes. Unions still impede the free flow of 'market forces'. If workers are a more diverse body and have exchanged blue collars for white, insecurity remains an everyday problem. The new institutional and global context is moreover as much of an opportunity as a threat. Yet, it cannot be doubted that, compared with the immediate post-1945 period, at the beginning of the new millennium, what many still refer to as the 'labour movement' is much less influential. Whether this should be considered a time of retreat or reconfiguration is unclear – and a question the series aims to clarify

The series will not only give a voice to studies of particular national bodies but will also promote comparative works that contrast experiences across time and geography. This entails taking due account of the political, economic and cultural settings in which labour' movements have operated. In particular this involves taking the past seriously as a way of understanding the present, as well as utilising sympathetic approaches drawn from sociology, economics and elsewhere.

John Callaghan
Steven Fielding
Steve Ludlam

Tables and boxes

Tables

1.1	NCB collieries in Scotland, October 1982	22
1.2	NUM ballot on NCB pay offer, selected areas, November 1980	42
2.1	NUM and SCEBTA ballot on NCB pay offer and pit closures, selected workplaces in Scotland, October 1982	57
2.2	Performance measures from NCB Scottish collieries, 1981–82	63
4.1	Married women in employment (part-time and full-time) and council housing density by colliery in Scotland, 1981	121
4.2	Pre-strike pit-level industrial relations and militancy index (MI) rankings	123
4.3	Pit-level potential strike endurance (PSE) rankings in the Scottish coalfields, 1984	123
4.4	Performance measures from NCB Scottish collieries, 1981–82, and pit-level economic performance (EP) rankings	124
4.5	Pre-strike employment, working miners and actual strike endurance (ASE) rankings at Scottish collieries, selected dates, June 1984 to March 1985	126
4.6	Competing NUMSA/SCEBTA and NCB back to work figures, December 1984	127
4.7	PSE, ASE and EP rankings in the Scottish coalfields, 1982–85	128
5.1	Strikers and strike dismissals, 1984–85: selected NCB holdings	152
6.1	Persons in employment, part-time and full-time combined (percentages), by colliery employment area in Scotland, 1981 and 1991	168
6.2	Women aged 16–59 as percentage of persons in employment, by colliery employment area in Scotland, 1981 and 1991	170

Box

4.1	Establishing MWE and CHD values for Scottish collieries in 1984	121

Abbreviations

ACAS	Advisory, Conciliation and Arbitration Service
ASE	Actual strike endurance
BACM	British Association of Colliery Managers
BSC	British Steel Corporation
CBI	Confederation of British Industry
CCC	Colliery Consultative Committee
CHD	Council Housing Density
COSA	Colliery Officials' Staff Association
CPA	Clyde Port Authority
EP	Economic performance
GCUA	Glasgow Caledonian University Archives
IDS	Industry Department for Scotland
ISTC	Iron and Steel Trades Confederation
KAGM	Kirkcaldy Art Gallery and Museum
MI	Militancy Index
MMC	Monopolies and Mergers Commission
MWE	Married Women in Employment
NACODS	National Association of Colliery Overmen, Deputies and Shotfirers
NAS	National Archives of Scotland
NCB	National Coal Board
NLS	National Library of Scotland
NUM	National Union of Mineworkers
NUMSA	National Union of Mineworkers Scottish Area
OMS	Output per manshift
PSE	Potential Strike Endurance
SCDI	Scottish Council for Development and Industry
SCEBTA	Scottish Colliery, Enginemen, Boilermen and Tradesmen's Association
SHHD	Scottish Home and Health Department
SMM	Scottish Mining Museum

SSEB	South of Scotland Electricity Board
STUC	Scottish Trades Union Congress
TGWU	Transport and General Workers' Union
TNA	The National Archive
TUC	Trades Union Congress
UCS	Upper Clyde Shipbuilders
UDM	United Democratic Mineworkers

Acknowledgements

My largest debts are owed to the coal industry workers and union officials who agreed to be interviewed for this book. I received help in arranging and conducting these interviews from others, including family members of some of the interviewees. So many thanks to Rab Amos, Iain Chalmers, Eric Clarke, Willie Clarke, Charlie Goodfellow, Melanie Goodfellow, David Hamilton, Alex Nicholson, David Nicholson, Lydia Nicholson and Nicky Wilson. I thank Mike Arnott of Dundee Trades Council for introducing me to Willie Clarke.

I have been helped by archive and library staff at many institutions across Scotland: Niamh Conlon at Kirkcaldy Museum and Art Gallery, when she was the Curator; Jean Crawford at the National Archives of Scotland; Carole McCallum at Glasgow Caledonian University Archives; Julia Stephen and colleagues at the Scottish Mining Museum; Donald Tait at the University of Glasgow. Colleagues at the Local History Centre in Dundee Central Library, the National Library of Scotland in Edinburgh and The National Archives in Kew were also helpful.

This book was written with the help of colleagues at the University of Glasgow, especially those in the former Department of Economic and Social History, absorbed within the School of Social and Political Sciences in a university-wide restructuring programme in 2010. Successive Heads of Economic and Social History have made available financial and time resources that enabled this book to be written: Ray Stokes, Neil Rollings and Duncan Ross. I am extremely grateful to them and to all of my colleagues in Economic and Social History who have made my own experience of employment happy and rewarding. I thank also Mike French, Head of the School of Social and Political Sciences, and Fred Cartmel.

Thanks are due to colleagues who attended a symposium on the miners' strike at the University of Glasgow in June 2007, which helped to initiate research for this book: Phil Beaumont, Terry Brotherstone, Ewen Cameron, Rob Duncan, Billy Kenefick, David Stewart and Willie Thompson. The Adam Smith Research Foundation at the University of Glasgow sponsored this event. Terry and Willie both helped greatly in other ways, Terry with generous and critical advice on the manuscript of the book, and Willie by supplying the recordings of interviews which he conducted with strike participants in 1985–86.

I am grateful to organisers of and participants at the following conferences and seminars, where I had the opportunity to discuss aspects of the miners' strike: the Economic History Society Annual Conferences of March 2008 at the University of Nottingham, and March 2010 at the University of Durham; the Modern British History Network Conference at the University of Strathclyde in June 2009; the Management History Research Group Conference at the University of St Andrews in July 2010; the Modern History Seminar at the University of York in November 2010; and the Working Class Studies Association Conference in Chicago in June 2011. I thank the editors and publishers of *Economic History Review* and *Twentieth Century British History*, for allowing me to utilise in recast form material originally published in these journals.

David Howell read the book in manuscript and gave patient and learned advice on various aspects of the strike and its politics. Chris Wrigley has offered friendly and wise assistance at various points. Andrew Perchard and Annmarie Hughes, valued colleagues both, have helped greatly, not least by reading and commenting on parts of the manuscript.

The most valuable help has come at home: from Anna Robertson, Robert Phillips and Matthew Phillips. With love, respect and thanks I dedicate this book to them.

Introduction: rethinking the miners' strike of 1984–85

On 12 March 1984, just before the afternoon shift at Bilston Glen Colliery in Midlothian, a voluble contingent of miners arrived by coach from Polmaise Colliery in Fallin, Stirlingshire. These men had been told two months before by Albert Wheeler, Scottish Area Director of the National Coal Board (NCB), that their pit was going to close, despite his guarantee six months earlier that no closure was proposed, and some £12–16 million of investment in the pit since 1980. The Polmaise workers refused to accept this, and pressed for a strike across the Scottish and British coalfields to defend their colliery, and others – in Yorkshire and South Wales – facing the same threat. Their unions, the National Union of Mineworkers Scottish Area (NUMSA), and the Scottish Colliery, Enginemen, Boilermen and Tradesmen's Association (SCEBTA), carefully constructed support for this action in Scotland,[1] although when this commenced there were considerable misgivings across the Scottish coalfields, evidenced by the reluctance of miners at some pits – notably Bilston Glen – to come out on strike. But the pickets at Bilston Glen, chiefly of Midlothian men, reinforced by the Polmaise coach-load, achieved their aim. By late afternoon the entire Scottish coalfield was at a standstill.[2]

This book is about the year-long strike that followed, in defence of jobs, collieries and communities, which was arguably the defining episode of the final quarter of the twentieth century in Britain. It embodied the painful economic and social transitions that are associated with Thatcherism and deindustrialisation, including the hardening of anti-trade union legislation and the weakening of organised labour.[3] The book focuses on Scotland, for two reasons. First, the strike across England and Wales drew much of its impetus from developments in the Scottish coalfields from the early 1980s onwards, with closures and changes in management style and policy, encompassing the bullying of union representatives and the abandonment of joint agreements. Some 50 per cent of miners in Scotland were *already* in dispute with their pit managers in March 1984, *before* the national strike began. Second, there was a distinctive Scottish narrative to the problems and tensions that prefigured the strike. The dangers and consequences of pit closures and related job losses were felt particularly keenly in Scotland, where unemployment was higher than in other parts of the UK, and the alleged benefits of Thatcherite economic restructuring much less apparent. Industrial closures across a variety of sectors, including major casualties such as the Linwood car plant in 1981, were seen by trade unionists and others as evidence of the failure of the British political and constitutional system. Scotland, or central Scotland at any rate, had different economic, social and industrial needs from the rest of the UK. This was reflected in the outcome of the 1979 and 1983 General Elections, where Scotland registered a significantly stronger vote for Labour than England, and accentuated the case for devolution of economic, social and industrial policy to a Scottish Parliament in Edinburgh. Significantly, NUMSA had in the 1960s and 1970s been one of the trade union movement's main advocates for devolution, arguing from a class perspective for a Parliament that would protect and advance the interests of workers in Scotland.[4] Thatcherism's deleterious impact on employment and social welfare strengthened the class as well as the national argument for a Parliament, 'to influence and direct our basic industries and our economy away from chaos', according to Peter Hogg of the NUMSA Executive Committee, writing in the opening weeks of the strike in 1984.[5]

'A different match': the strike and its literature

Michael McGahey, NUMSA President and Vice President of the British federal body, the National Union of Mineworkers (NUM), predicted in the strike's immediate aftermath that future histories would distort its meaning. Participants reading these histories would, like Saturday football fans puzzled by Sunday newspaper match reports, encounter the sensation of having been at 'a different match' from the writers.[6] The voluminous literature on the strike is indeed largely problematic, with many authors attempting to explain the huge and prolonged mass mobilisation of workers and their supporters as essentially a matter of high politics and personalities. This book offers an important and fresh set of perspectives, using documentary evidence and the oral testimony of participants to explain the very high level of strike commitment in Scotland. Even at Bilston Glen, sometimes characterised as a strike-breakers' bastion, the overwhelming majority of miners supported the strike for almost eight months. The book relates this commitment to the changing economic and social structure of the industry in Scotland in the 1960s and 1970s. It shows that these evolving material conditions and experiences refined Scottish coal mining's political traditions and culture, evident in the major strikes of 1972 and 1974, shaping the resistance in Scotland to pit closures in the late 1970s and early 1980s. So the book examines the strike as a social phenomenon, emphasising two inter-locking elements: its origins in colliery-level conflicts and pressures; and its year-long sustenance in community commitment and resilience.

The book thereby challenges the overwhelming emphasis – in contemporary news reporting and comment as well as labour and political history and memoir – on the importance of peak level relations between the Conservative government, the NCB and the NUM, the shifts in energy supply that decisively weakened the miners' bargaining position, and the questions of public order and 'picket-line violence'.[7] Established literature has also tended to focus on individuals, notably the ideological struggle between Arthur Scargill, NUM President, and the Prime Minister, Margaret Thatcher, with lesser although nevertheless important roles attributed to Ian MacGregor, the NCB Chairman, Peter Walker, Secretary of State for Energy, and a small number of other government ministers and officials, along with selected members of the NUM executive, including Michael McGahey.[8]

This predominant high politics emphasis connects with 'conventional wisdom' narratives of the 1970s and 1980s, to paraphrase Ross McKibbin's analysis of inter-war social relations.[9] These encompass stereotypes of industrial relations as dysfunctional and disordered, and justly 'tamed' through the processes of economic restructuring and trade union reforms that 'rebalanced' workplace authority in favour of employers.[10] In her own memoir Thatcher characterised the strike as 'Mr Scargill's Insurrection'.[11] Other accounts, including those broadly sympathetic to miners and trade unions, reinforce the primacy of high politics, presenting the strike as an ideological conflict between determined government and intransigent union leadership.[12] Defeating the miners was certainly central to Thatcherism, helping to shift the balance of the political economy from public to private enterprise, and redistributing workplace and labour market authority from employees to employers. Alastair Reid observes that after the 1982 Falklands War and the 'consolidation' of her 'regime' at the 1983 General Election, the Prime Minister turned her attention to the 'enemy within'. Thatcher's visceral anti-unionism encompassed the proscription of trade union membership at the Government Communications Headquarters at Cheltenham in December 1983, as well as her determination to humiliate the NUM. Reid writes that Scargill, one-time member of the Young Communist League, Marxist, and a veteran – along with McGahey, who remained a Communist – of the 1972 and 1974 coal strikes, was equally determined to have a 'showdown' with the government on the question of closures. But he underestimated the government's commitment to centralised policing, which inhibited the union's ability to picket working mines or stem the flow of coal to power stations or steel works. Scargill was also insensitive to the insecurity of the steel workers and the limited capacity of transport workers to help the miners, and so – Reid hints – forfeited the solidarity of the broader labour movement that enabled the miners to succeed in their 1972 and 1974 strikes.[13]

Scargill has enjoyed some support in the literature, notably from Seamus Milne, whose analysis, published ten years after the strike, refuted much of the wilder criticism of the NUM and its President, including, emphatically, allegations of financial impropriety. Milne argued that the real issue was the government's concerted and successful effort, supported by the secret services, to weaken the NUM and so diminish the strength of the organised working class.[14] Others nevertheless dwell on Scargill's egotism and intransigence, and criticise especially the decision to conduct the strike without a national ballot of union members.[15] Working miners sued the NUM under common law, focusing on the legal applicability of a 1981 vote by union members in Yorkshire for action against closures. In September 1984 the High Court in London judged that this was too remote from the on-going dispute, and restrained the NUM generally in England and Wales as well as in Yorkshire from characterising the strike as official.[16] Defiance of this restraint led to the sequestration of NUM funds in England and Wales in October 1984, although not in Scotland, where separate jurisdiction applied. There was, however, an important and contentious Scottish dimension to the anti-Scargill narrative. Jimmy Reid, one of the leaders of the 1971–72 Upper Clyde Shipbuilders (UCS) work-in, was a persistent critic of Scargill in 1984. Reid claimed that the core problem was not pit closures but 'the miners' right to vote on whether they should be on strike'. He characterised the strike as an undemocratic expression of 'Scargillism', and its 'contempt for working people who are seen as pawns to be used by an "elite" as they plan and scheme revolutionary change'.[17] The damaging nature of these interventions to the strike, comforting its opponents and dividing its supporters, and to Jimmy Reid himself, his standing diminished in some areas of the labour movement, was remembered by one obituarist, Brian Wilson, in 2010.[18]

The focus on Scargill, along with Thatcher and other national actors, and the privileging of high politics, obscures the strike's broader economic, social and cultural dimensions. For this reason, perhaps, Jonathan Meades has satirised the preoccupation with personalities in histories and memories of the strike, which he parodied in a memorable television film as a 'coiffeur clash' between 'The Barnsley Comb-over' and 'The Finchley Helmet', before outlining its true meaning: a struggle to preserve employment and dignity in industrial communities.[19] This alternative reading has been articulated elsewhere, of course, beginning with literature produced in mining communities during the strike, such as the collection from Thurcroft in Yorkshire, published in 1986,[20] and in the memoirs and recollections of socialist and trade union activists. Mark Steel, for instance, writing in 2001, ridiculed those who 'blamed' Scargill for 'calling the strike at the end of winter, when coal stocks were high. But,' Steel continued, 'the strike was in response to closures. You can't call a strike in November on the off-chance that closures will be announced the following March. Nor can you announce in March a strike to start the following November.'[21] Steel wrote within a popular agency tradition that has several important early exemplars. These examined a variety of issues and themes, from the common perspective of trying to get beneath the surface of dominant perceptions of the strike. Richard Hyman, writing in 1985, emphasised the longer history, relating the picketing and ballot controversies to the embedded tensions in mining politics between localism and centralism.[22] Raphael Samuel, introducing in 1986 an edited collection, *The Enemies Within,* looked beyond national union strategy, arguing that in the genesis and conduct of the strike 'all of the crucial initiatives came from below'.[23] David Howell likewise attempted to move understanding of the strike beyond high politics and national personalities, embedding his analysis of union politics in Lancashire's particular traditions and priorities.[24] Jonathan and Ruth Winterton focused on localised pressures too, examining how strike commitment in Yorkshire was shaped by personal variables, notably family background and occupational, political and union tradition.[25] *Digging Deeper*, a collection edited by Huw Beynon during the strike, contained a similar thrust. Its preface was written by Eric Heffer, MP for Walton and chairman of the Labour Party in 1983–84. This criticised the general characterisation of the dispute – by Tory politicians especially – as 'Scargill's strike'. Scargill was a charismatic and important figurehead, Heffer wrote, but his position was only sustainable because of the 'strength and courage' of the miners who supported him.[26] The ballot controversy was carefully dissected by Beynon. The fundamental problem in 1984, he wrote, was that miners were not affected equally by the question of pit closures. This marked a fundamental difference from 1972 and 1974, when miners won pay increases that suited them all more or less equally. In 1984 it was extremely difficult to mobilise some of those in relatively secure employment at 'economic' pits in stable coalfields for a strike to defend relatively insecure jobs at 'uneconomic' pits in coalfields perceived to be in decline. Beynon cited in this connection the words of Peter Heathfield, elected as General Secretary of the NUM early in 1984: 'it cannot be right for one man to vote another man out of a job'.[27]

Attempts to move analysis beyond national politics continued with *Miners on Strike*, by Andrew Richards, in 1996, which probed pit-level strike endurance, but only briefly in relation to South Wales while looking mainly at Yorkshire and Nottinghamshire,[28] and Keith Gildart's longer history of the North Wales miners, in 2001.[29] This popular movement historiography has been accompanied by feminist literature exploring one of the strike's principal features: the role of women. Women managing a household without male earnings encountered severe strain, but there were positive experiences too. Men not working took a greater share in domestic labour and childcare, and women shared in the organisation of the strike, forming local, regional and national support groups. The vital role of women was formally recognised by NUMSA, which unsuccessfully tried to persuade the national federation to admit female members in 1985. The particularly progressive character of gender relations in Scotland's coalfields, leavened as it was, admittedly, by a measure of unreconstructed Scottish male chauvinism, was identified although not fully explained in the feminist literature.[30] In this connection the role of Communist tradition and politics may have been significant, and is explored in Chapter 4 of this book.

The high politics literature depicts Scotland as marginal to the UK strike, or ignores it altogether.[31] This is rationalised in terms of NUMSA's supposed numerical weaknesses and internal divisions, with the Bilston Glen strike-breaking allegedly preoccupying McGahey to the extent that he was unable to concentrate on 'national' developments and moderate Scargill.[32] The popular movement literature also says little about Scotland. The specifics of the Samuel-edited collection were drawn from England and Wales, and the Wintertons scrutinise Yorkshire, with some comparative discussion of Nottinghamshire.

Beynon implies that Scotland ceased to be significant after the closure of Kinneil Colliery in West Lothian at the end of 1982.[33]

Extant literature on Scotland is limited in volume and scope. There is a study of Cowdenbeath in Central Fife by Alex Maxwell, who was a slightly unusual figure in the coalfields: a Communist activist and Councillor, he was also a manager at the NCB's workshops in the town, where colliery machinery was manufactured and repaired. Maxwell was temporarily suspended in 1984–85 by the NCB for 'actions incompatible' with his management position. His account presents this significant personal difficulty as a minor episode, focusing instead on the important details of local strike organisation, activism and endurance. It was published on the strike's tenth anniversary, as was a short collection of activist memories, edited by Joe Owens, NUM delegate at Polkemmet Colliery in West Lothian in 1984. These encompassed general and personal experiences of the strike and its aftermath, including the loss of employment, either through victimisation by the NCB or as the collieries gradually closed after 1985.[34] Greater distance of time has brought David Stewart's survey, published in *Scottish Labour History* in 2006, which highlights the picketing at the British Steel Corporation (BSC) Ravenscraig works, the failed talks to end the strike, and the slow drift back to work from August 1984 onwards. He sees the absence of a national ballot as a fundamental error. In this he is guided by George Bolton, NUMSA Vice President in 1984–85, whom he interviewed, and Eric Clarke, NUMSA General Secretary during the strike, whose frank memoir, illuminating the peculiar legalities of the dispute and the consequent financial responsibilities undertaken by NUMSA officials, was published in 2004.[35] Scargill was highly culpable in the ballot affair, according to Stewart, and committed two further strategic errors: he should have delayed the strike until the autumn of 1984; but with the strike under way from March he should have settled it by the autumn, presumably on terms approximate to those that resolved the related dispute between the National Coal Board and NACODS, the union of pit deputies and safety men, with revised procedures for consultation and agreement on pit closures.[36]

Stewart's assessment, reprised in his book on Scottish politics in the 1980s,[37] contrasts with an important short article on the origins of the strike by Terry Brotherstone and Simon Pirani, published slightly earlier, in 2005. This emphasises the primacy of popular agency and how events in Scotland shaped the strike across the UK coalfields. A national ballot was irrelevant, given the strength of workplace resistance to closures in Scotland,[38] where job losses had accelerated more rapidly than in any other NCB region. This was compounded from 1981, when Albert Wheeler, newly installed as Area Director, pursued the logic of the Conservative government's 1980 Coal Industry Act, which sought a subsidy-free, fully self-funding industry by 1983–84,[39] through closing 'loser' pits. This was challenged by the NUM with a threatened national strike early in 1981, which the government avoided by offering short-term subsidy while readying for future confrontation through stockpiling coal, satisfying the miners' immediate demands for increased production.[40] In 1982 Scargill, just elected NUM President, produced a 'hit list' of pits that he identified as earmarked for closure by the NCB. In October–November 1982 a national ballot was held, on the dual issue of the annual pay offer and closures. While the majority of miners went against the union's national executive, a big majority in Scotland – 69 per cent – voted for strike action. This reflected the steady loss of employment in Scotland: five thousand jobs were lost between 1981 and March 1984, at which point only 14,000 men were employed in twelve remaining pits.[41]

These industrial and workplace dimensions were utterly absent from mainstream media coverage of the strike's 25th anniversary in 2009. This reprised high political narratives about the inevitability of economic restructuring, the ideological struggle between Thatcher and Scargill, and public disorder arising from picketing and other forms of union protest. The involvement of communities and the role of women were generally forgotten.[42] There was an important book on South Wales, written by Hywel Francis, Labour MP for Aberavon since 2001, who in the 1980s worked in adult education and had political and personal links with coalfield trade unionism in South Wales, including through his Communist Party membership. Francis's book explored the campaign to save pits before the strike, community activism during 1984–85, and the wider industrial politics of South Wales, which, like those of Scotland, encompassed an NUM-shaped move towards devolution.[43] More broadly there was unwillingness to ask different questions about the strike, despite the serious economic and financial difficulties developing from 2008 onwards that were arguably compounded by the economic structural changes that followed 1984–85. This relative absence of historical rethinking was embodied, perhaps, in the anniversary's highest profile publication, *Marching to the Fault Line*, by Francis Beckett and David Hencke, both of the *Guardian*.[44] This was 'fatally flawed', according to David Douglass, a former member of the NUM's Yorkshire area executive, by the authors' hostility to Scargill, which prevented them from seeing the strike as a determined rank and file defence of pits, jobs and communities.[45]

Beckett and Hencke relied heavily for original insight on the diary of Bill Keys of the print workers' union, SOGAT, who was on the left of the Trades Union Congress General Council and tried to reach a negotiated settlement to the strike. In December 1984 and January 1985 Keys spoke separately to Thatcher's Deputy Prime Minister, Lord Whitelaw, and Michael McGahey, about how the strike could be settled. Hencke publicised this element of the story in the *Guardian*, implying clearly that McGahey and Whitelaw had met directly in the House of Lords, sharing 'a bottle of chablis' with Keys.[46] Scargill responded to this in over-stated but understandable terms, as a smear against McGahey and the NUM, and called for Beckett and Hencke to publish further details.[47] Beckett did so by ignoring the implication in Hencke's piece that McGahey met Whitelaw personally, recording that Whitelaw met Keys in the Lords on 13 December 1984, who then met McGahey in Edinburgh on 11 January 1985.[48] This was Beckett and Hencke's only real reference to Scotland. McGahey appeared as if from nowhere: the complex nature and role of the Communist

Party in Scotland's coal industry, explored by Alan Campbell,[49] is ignored, along with the colliery-level conflict mounting in the early 1980s. The closures of Bedlay in Lanarkshire in 1981, Kinneil in 1982, and Ayrshire's Highhouse and Sorn, along with Cardowan, the last Lanarkshire survivor, all in 1983 – which sharpened the atmosphere of conflict and suspicion, and prepared Scottish miners to fight for the remnants of their coalfield – are barely acknowledged, and certainly not as factors that shaped strike commitment. Moreover, the qualified 'militancy' of the Scottish miners, softened by a degree of demoralisation in 1983 that was cultivated by bullying management and the forced closures, is unexplored. The NUM's efforts to maintain the unity of its Scottish membership in the face of these pressures are entirely forgotten.

Collieries and communities: rethinking the strike in Scotland

This book re-examines the history of the strike. It establishes the broader significance of collieries and communities, and presents the strike as a popular and socially embedded movement. The book builds on initial investigation of the origins of the strike, its broad political, moral and material dimensions, and the economic variables that contributed to different levels of pit-level endurance.[50] Evidence is drawn from a variety of sources. Scottish Office papers, notably ministerial and official correspondence, and daily situation reports, illuminate the broad contours of the strike, the government's approach, and commitment at different collieries. Correspondence and minutes of meetings involving NCB and NUM officials explore peak-level relations in the years before the strike, illustrating the incremental dismantling of 'trust' in industrial relations. Other NCB papers, mainly relating to colliery-level joint industrial consultation and negotiations, and the origins of the strike, establish the role that these played in shaping subsequent strike commitment. Scottish Trades Union Congress (STUC) General Council papers trace the dispute's impact on the labour movement in Scotland, and efforts designed to bolster the material and moral resources of the strike. NUMSA and SCEBTA materials from the late 1970s and early 1980s – minutes of executive meetings and delegate conferences – further illuminate the origins of the strike, and NUMSA and SCEBTA strike committee minutes and daily reports illustrate vividly the dispute itself. SCEBTA had about 3,500 members in 1984, roughly a quarter of Scotland's miners, mainly the tradesmen associated with electrical and engineering work. Its politics were close to those of NUMSA. SCEBTA's President, Abe Moffat, shared Communist Party membership with McGahey, as did other leading officials and pit-level representatives in each union. This helped to maintain the cross-union organisational and political cohesion of the strike.[51] Local initiatives and community involvement are also established through miscellaneous documentary resources, including daily reports that survive from the Dysart strike centre in East Fife, and the ephemeral literature – participant memoirs, community and activist pamphlets – produced during and after the strike. The daily press provides additional perspective on the origins and character of the strike.

This documentary evidence is accompanied by analysis of two sets of interviews with strike participants. With one exception, Ella Egan, who convened the work of the women's groups in Scotland, these interviewees are all men. There is an important rationale for privileging male voices. The book examines how workplace experiences, including pit-level employment conditions and industrial relations, changed over time in ways that structured the origins, outbreak and conduct of the strike. Men, because of the gendered construction of the coal workforce, bore the weight of these experiences. The first set of interviews, including that with Egan, was conducted after the strike by Willie Thompson in 1985 and 1986, and the second between 2009 and 2011 by me. These offer different analytical challenges. Thompson's interviews, generously passed to me in June 2007, were intended for inclusion in a collection of essays on the strike, focusing on union strategy and politics, including the role of the Communist Party and how to keep the pits open.[52] Thompson completed his chapter,[53] but the volume, edited by Hywel Francis, was not published. So this group of interviewees were speaking to fairly specific temporal and political concerns in 1985–86. They nevertheless offer significant insight into the questions explored here, notably the changing character of workplace relations before the strike, and the factors shaping endurance in 1984–85, including the role of communities and women. The second set of interviews is framed by the problems and opportunities of longer perspective, and informed by theoretical insights drawn from oral history, where emphasis recently has been on the manner in which 'narratives' or 'discourses' are constructed by interview subjects, often shaped or at least mediated by their life biographies, the inter-action with their interviewer, the trajectory of subsequent events, and dominant or predominant cultural and political tropes.[54]

'Memory', writes Alessandro Portelli, in his oral history of Harlan County, in the coalfields of eastern Kentucky, 'is the ultimate site of conflict'.[55] So it is with 1984–85 in Scotland, in two distinct ways: the strike remains live for many of the participants, informing their politics and views of the world; and their testimony, while occasionally reinforcing some standard narratives, notably in relation to Scargill's leadership and the controversies surrounding picketing and the ballot, tends on the whole to jar with mainstream interpretations. This will be observable at different points in the analysis, but five elements of the Scottish 'activist' narrative are worth initial emphasis: Wheeler transformed the industry and management–worker relations for the worse; the strike was generated from within the Scottish coalfields, with miners and their supporters defending valuable collective resources; women were invaluable in sustaining the strike, as leaders and not 'just' supporters; while the strike was not 'about' – meaning not forced or created by – the union leadership, miners in Scotland were nevertheless wisely guided by McGahey; and the social costs of pit closures since the strike have been immense. These narratives challenge conventional thinking, particularly where this privileges the role of high politics and personalities, or casts miners and their supporters as relatively passive victims of the ideological conflict between government and NUM. Nicky Wilson, a former SCEBTA official at Cardowan, describes as 'nonsense' those accounts of the strike that present the Scottish miners as 'blindly' following Scargill 'like sheep', 'as if miners can't think for theirself'. They were thinking independently, and seeking to defend their jobs, collieries and communities.[56] 'I wasn't fightin for Scargill or McGahey,' recalls Iain Chalmers, a union activist at Seafield Colliery in East Fife, where the strike began 'early', in February 1984, and so lasted for thirteen months: 'I was fightin for my own pit.'[57] The activist narratives also provide cumulative evidence of what oral historians term 'composure': witnesses to the past construct internally consistent personal and political narratives about history,[58] and illustrate too the social phenomenon of the 'cultural circuit', where personal testimony is conditioned by a larger social or collective narrative. In being articulated the personal testimony then enhances the social credence or legitimacy of the collective narrative, so it will be drawn on again by other individuals seeking to recall and understand the past.[59]

These testimonies also offer a strong element of 'reconstruction', providing important qualitative evidence that is not revealed or fully conveyed in documentary sources. A good example comes with participant memories of the pre-strike colliery-level disputes in 1983, notably from Willie Clarke at Seafield and David Hamilton at Monktonhall Colliery in Midlothian, which deepens the sense of escalating conflict and crisis in the industry examined in Chapter 2.[60] Another is the manner in which internal union thinking – before and during the strike – is illuminated. Minutes of NUMSA and SCEBTA executive and delegate meetings are, by the bureaucratic standards of trade union records more generally, a rich historical resource. They relay the countervailing strands of coalfield opinion – to strike or not – that union officials were facing in 1983 and early 1984. But they do not quite capture the finer grains of strategy and tactics. McGahey's position in the autumn of 1983, for instance, rationalising the decision not to use a major crisis at Monktonhall as the 'jumping off point' for a national strike, cannot be reached through documentary evidence, but has been established through oral testimony. The daily tumults of the strike itself are recreated in these testimonies too, such as Nicky Wilson's account of his arrest at Ravenscraig in May 1984, and the long night in a Motherwell police cell that followed.[61]

The analysis develops in two parts. Part I explores the primacy of community- and colliery-level factors. Chapter 1 establishes the central and related structural factors: pit closures in the 1950s and 1960s; social changes in mining communities; shifts in trade union politics, with the re-emergence of militancy in the 1960s; and the character and meaning of the moral economy of the Scottish coalfields. This adapts E.P. Thompson's analysis of the moral economy of the eighteenth-century English crowd, the plebeian workers who intermittently resisted the economic changes associated with the emergence of free market industrial capitalism. They did so with particular force where changes confounded their collective material interests and communal customs.[62] The Scottish coalfield crowd of the late twentieth century also thought, organised and acted in a period of rapid social and industrial change, defending its material position and moral expectations against the threat of pit closures, job losses and community evisceration. The coalfield moral economy was based on two core assumptions: changes to the industry, including closures and job losses, could only be effected legitimately with the agreement of the workforce; and economic security had to be protected, so pits could only close if miners were able to secure comparably paid alternative employment. These moral economy considerations accommodated the closure from the early 1950s onwards of dozens of pits, often small or medium-size employers of between 300 and 750 or so miners, who were transferred – if they stayed in the industry in Scotland – to larger 'cosmopolitan' pits. The complex, highly contingent and fluid nature of coalfield communities is emphasised, and related to the process of industrial restructuring. This involved an erosion of community in the traditional sense, with only one 'village' pit, Polmaise, still extant in 1984, and most miners journeying by road – usually bussed by the NCB – to pits in East and West Fife, Clackmannan, Midlothian, West Lothian, Lanarkshire and Ayrshire. These were 'cosmopolitan' in that they drew their workforces from sometimes quite widely dispersed localities, with distinct political and working cultures. The miners of East and Central Fife, for example, were brought together in Seafield and Frances, on either side of Kirkcaldy, while those who worked the vast seams of the Longannet 'complex' pits of Solsgirth, Castlehill and Bogside at the junction of West Fife and Clackmannan were drawn from an even wider spatial territory. Local miners – gathered from the Cowdenbeath and Dunfermline districts to the east and the 'Hillfoot' villages around Alloa to the west – were joined in the complex by men from North and South Lanarkshire, transferred when Bedlay shut in 1981 and Cardowan in 1983, and West Lothian, including those exiled from Kinneil when it closed at the end of 1982.

There were echoes here of the earlier eastward movement of miners from Lanarkshire in the 1920s and 1930s, which had altered the politics and social relations of the Clackmannan, Fife and Lothian coalfield communities.[63] Structural changes in the industry from the 1960s were also accompanied – as they had been in the 1920s and 1930s – by a growth of workplace conflict and union militancy. Scottish miners, while characterised by numerous differences, as a body nevertheless developed a general determination to secure greater security and financial rewards, while resisting from the late 1960s further closures and job losses. These indicated that strains were being exerted on the moral economy of the coalfields, evidenced by the role of Scottish miners in the strikes of 1972 and 1974. Chapter 2 moves the analysis to the strike's origins and outbreak, with escalating workplace tension as management sought to cut production costs by closing some pits and attacking trade unionism in those that remained. Rule books detailing union involvement in daily operations were 'torn up', literally in the experience of Monktonhall's NUM delegate, David Hamilton, and figuratively elsewhere, notably at Seafield.[64] The moral economy of the coalfields, tested although not quite broken in the 1960s and early 1970s, was now explicitly transgressed, with decisions by managerial fiat, and closures and job losses damagingly felt in the context of unemployment, rapidly

escalating under the deindustrialising impact of Thatcherite economic management. Workforce resistance resulted, observable in a sequence of pit-level
disputes in 1983, as well as the outbreak of the strike itself in 1984.

Part II examines the character and conduct of the strike. Chapter 3 explores
its distinctive Scottish industrial politics. The chronological focus is mainly
from March to October 1984, when support for the strike among miners was
generally strong, but when the broader solidarity of the labour movement in
Scotland was tested by the picketing of Ravenscraig and Hunterston, the
Ayrshire coastal terminal through which strike-breaking coal passed. Against
the grain of existing literature, this picketing is presented as highly rational:
Ravenscraig represented a rare opportunity for the strikers to exert pressure on
the government, and its closure would greatly have weakened Conservatism's
already fragile position in Scotland. The head of BSC, Bob Haslam, after discussions involving government ministers, it is surmised, pressed Strathclyde Police
to disperse the pickets and ensure a steady flow of coal into the plant.

Chapter 4 moves the analysis to community level. It distinguishes between
factors that reduced the economic cost of striking and factors that increased the
social cost of strike-breaking. It utilises an innovative conceptual model to rank
pits in terms of their capacity for strike endurance. This is called Potential Strike
Endurance (PSE). It captures relative rather than absolute potential endurance,
on the basis of three potentially differentiating pit-level factors: Council
Housing Density (CHD), Married Women in Employment (MWE) and
Militancy Index (MI). Each of these is organised as a pit-level ranking and added
to produce overall PSE rankings. The CHD and MWE rankings for each pit are
calculated on the basis of data by local authority district in the 1981 Population
Census, offering quantitative perspective on the material resources available to
strikers: Labour-controlled councils deferred rents for striking miners, and
wives' wages brought valuable income into strikers' homes. 'Nobody starved,'
say several strike participants, unlike the 1926 lockout, when households generally lost all their income once the men were not working, and many miners lost
their homes, or were driven back to work by the threat of losing them.[65] The MI
rankings are the sum of two sub-factors: the vote cast in the autumn of 1982 for
strike action in pursuit of the wage claim and in opposition to closures; and the
incidence of significant pit-level conflict in 1983 and the opening two months of
1984. The PSE rankings exhibit a degree of predictive power, offering some
match with Actual Strike Endurance (ASE) rankings, based on the timing and
volume of pit-level strike-breaking between March 1984 and March 1985. There
is also a notable positive correlation between pre-strike performance – output
per manshift, costs of production and economic losses – and ASE. This runs
counter to standard interpretations of strike-breaking in Nottinghamshire, for
instance, where working miners are depicted as rational economic actors, who
refused to observe the strike because their pits were profitable and their jobs
considered safe.[66] In Scotland miners at the most 'viable' pits were those who
exhibited the strongest strike commitment. It is ventured that pre-strike
performance was in some respects a positive factor in building strike endurance,

representing a resource around which strikers could organise, to protect something valuable with perceived long-term potential.

There is a partial gap between the PSE and ASE rankings, and this is explained
in terms of moral resources. These encompassed historical and industrial tradition, and the political and cultural as well as economic role of women, along
with moral economy attitudes to pits and jobs, and raised the social cost of
strike-breaking. Chapter 4 also examines organisational features: the strike
committees and centres, the fund-raising and the soup kitchens; and the contribution of women, as both activists and breadwinners. Chapter 5 explores the
ending and aftermath of the strike at a macro-level in Scotland, from October
1984 onwards. The volume of working miners, only significant in number at
Bilston Glen before October, gradually increased in November and December,
before accelerating in January and February 1985. Key triggers here appear to
have been: the collapse at the end of October of threatened strike action by
NACODS, which might have transformed the situation in favour of the striking
miners by bringing the entire British coalfield to a standstill; the promise of
Christmas bonuses to men at work by the end of the third week in November;
the fear early in 1985 that men on strike for twelve months or more could legally
be sacked by the NCB; and the substantial attrition effects of life lived month
after month without income. In Scotland a majority of miners nevertheless
remained on strike until Monday 4 March 1985, the day after the NUM's delegate conference had voted narrowly for a resumption of work. Community- and
colliery-level factors remained paramount, with substantial resistance from
below, even as this official resumption was under way: miners at Polmaise –
where the strike in Scotland arguably began – refused to go back even as all other
Scottish pits finally did so on Monday 11 March.[67] The immediate aftermath of
the strike is then detailed, through examining the pit-level tensions and difficulties that followed, including relations between unions and management, and
former strikers and former strike-breakers. Some of the longer effects of the
strike, including the economic and social loss of employment in the coalfields,
and the limited but perceptible reconstruction of gender relations, are considered along with conclusions in the sixth and final chapter.

Union officials in Scotland had been privately seeking a return to work 'with
dignity and solidarity' at different points in the winter of 1984–85, some seeing
the inevitability of defeat as early as the lost prospect of support from NACODS
in October.[68] One of the main barriers to returning, however, was the victimisation of striking miners, 206 of whom were sacked in Scotland during the
dispute, often for fairly minor public order offences, and in some cases where
men had merely been facing charges and were – following their sacking – found
not guilty. This was the personal experience of David Hamilton, who in 2004 –
and when interviewed for this book – emphasised the disproportionate impact
of victimisation on Scotland generally and Midlothian especially, with 46
Monktonhall men and 36 Bilston Glen men dismissed.[69] Hamilton supported
the organised return to work when the matter was discussed by Scottish delegates on 4 March, but other strikers, including the dismissed men, and at the

Midlothian pits as well as elsewhere, insisted that there could be no end to the strike until those sacked had been reinstated. When the unions in Scotland voted for a return to work on 6 March there was bitterness and some violence. Hamilton was spat upon, and called a scab; McGahey was attacked and beaten on his way home.[70]

The strike was lost. But it was not – according to those who participated – a straightforward question of defeat. They were glad they chose – with tens of thousands of others – to fight, to resist the loss of their jobs and their collieries, and the diminution of their communities. 'Do mining communities still exist?', I asked Willie Clarke, still a Communist Councillor in Central Fife in November 2009. 'Aye, sort o,' was his answer. The pits, of course, are long gone. Driving me to Cowdenbeath station from his Ballingry home he pointed to two fields on opposite sides of the road: on the left, the site of his first place of employment, Glencraig Colliery; on the right, where the house of his birth had stood. But the 'ethics' of miners and mining remained, in the solidarity of people who were still electing a Communist as their Councillor. These 'ethics' – of class solidarity, workplace collectivism and commitment to community – were severely tested in Scotland's coalfields in 1984–85, but they survived, as this analysis of the strike demonstrates.

Notes

1 Scottish Mining Museum, Newtongrange (hereafter SMM), National Union of Mineworkers Scottish Area (hereafter NUMSA), Executive Committee (hereafter EC) and Minute of Special Conference of Delegates, both 20 February 1984, and NUMSA EC, 6 March 1984.

2 National Archives of Scotland (hereafter NAS), SOE 12/571, J. Hamill, Scottish Home and Health Department (SHHD), 'Miners' Strike: Picketing at Bilston Glen Colliery, Midlothian', 13 March 1984, and J.F. Laing, Industry Department for Scotland (IDS), Note for Ministers Meeting at 2 p.m., 13 March 1984; the *Scotsman*, 13 March 1984.

3 Chris Howell, *Trade Unions and the State. The Construction of Industrial Relations Institutions in Britain, 1890–2000* (Princeton, 2005), pp. 131–73; John McIlroy, Alan Campbell and Keith Gildart, 'Introduction: 1926 and All That', in John McIlroy, Alan Campbell and Keith Gildart (eds), *Industrial Politics and the 1926 Mining Lockout* (Cardiff, 2004), p. 5.

4 Jim Phillips, *The Industrial Politics of Devolution. Scotland in the 1960s and 1970s* (Manchester, 2008), pp. 37–9.

5 Peter Hogg, 'Join Crusade to Save the Nation', *Scottish Miner*, April 1984.

6 Scottish Trades Union Congress, *88th Annual Report, Inverness, 1985* (Glasgow, 1985), pp. 233–5.

7 John Saville, 'An Open Conspiracy: Conservative Politics and the Miners' Strike, 1984–5', *The Socialist Register*, 22 (1985–86), 295–329.

8 Martin Adeney and John Lloyd, *The Miners' Strike, 1984–5: Loss Without Limit* (London, 1986); Paul Routledge, *Scargill. The Unauthorized Biography* (London, 1993); David Stewart, 'A Tragic "Fiasco"? The 1984–5 Miners' Strike in Scotland', *Scottish Labour History*, 41 (2006), 34–50; Andrew Taylor, *The NUM and British*

   Politics. Volume 2: 1969–1995 (Aldershot, 2005).
 9 Ross McKibbin, 'Class and Conventional Wisdom', in Ross McKibbin, *The Ideologies
   of Class. Social Relations in Britain, 1880–1950* (Oxford, 1990), pp. 259–93.
10 Andrew Marr, *A History of Modern Britain* (London, 2007), pp. 337–43, 411–16.
11 Margaret Thatcher, *The Downing Street Years* (London, 1993), pp. 339–78.
12 Adeney and Lloyd, *Miners' Strike*, pp. 28–52; Joe England, *The Wales TUC.
   Devolution and Industrial Politics* (Cardiff, 2004), pp. 61–4; Kenneth O. Morgan, *The
   People's Peace. British History, 1945–1990* (Oxford, 1992), pp. 472–5; Hugo Young,
   One of Us (London, 1990), pp. 366–71, 373–8.
13 Alastair J. Reid, *United We Stand. A History of Britain's Trade Unions*
   (Harmondsworth, 2004), pp. 402–4.
14 Seamus Milne, *The Enemy Within: The Secret War Against the Miners* (London,
   1994).
15 W. Hamish Fraser, *A History of British Trade Unionism, 1700–1998* (London, 2000)
   pp. 239–42; Robert Taylor, *The Trade Union Question in British Politics* (Oxford,
   1993), pp. 294–8.
16 *The Times*, 2 October 1984.
17 *The Times*, 14 May and 12 October 1984.
18 Obituary, Jimmy Reid, by Brian Wilson, the *Guardian*, 11 August 2010.
19 *Jonathan Meades Off-Kilter*, 'The Football Pools Towns', originally broadcast BBC4,
   9pm, Wednesday 23 September 2009.
20 Peter Gibbon and David Steyne, *Thurcroft: A Village and the Miners' Strike: An Oral
   History* (Nottingham, 1986).
21 Mark Steel, *Reasons to be Cheerful. From Punk to New Labour through the Eyes of a
   Dedicated Troublemaker* (London, 2001), p. 139.
22 Richard Hyman, 'Reflections on the Mining Strike', *The Socialist Register*, 22
   (1985–86), 330–54.
23 Raphael Samuel, 'Preface', in Raphael Samuel, B. Bloomfield and G. Bonas (eds), *The
   Enemies Within: Pit Villages and the Miners' Strike of 1984–5* (London, 1986), p. xii.
24 David Howell, *The Politics of the NUM: A Lancashire View* (Manchester, 1989).
25 J. Winterton and R. Winterton, *Coal, Crisis and Conflict: The 1984–85 Miners' Strike
   in Yorkshire* (Manchester, 1989).
26 Eric S. Heffer, 'Preface', in Huw Beynon (ed.), *Digging Deeper. Issues in the Miners'
   Strike* (London, 1985), pp. xi–xiii.
27 Huw Beynon, 'Introduction', in Beynon, *Digging Deeper*, pp. 12–13.
28 Andrew J. Richards, *Miners on Strike. Class Solidarity and Division in Britain* (Oxford,
   1996).
29 Keith Gildart, *North Wales Miners: A Fragile Unity* (Cardiff, 2001).
30 Triona Holden, *Queen Coal. Women of the Miners' Strike* (Stroud, 2005); Vicky
   Seddon (ed.), *The Cutting Edge. Women and the Pit Strike* (London, 1986); Jean
   Stead, *Never the Same Again. Women and the Miners' Strike, 1984–5* (London, 1987).
31 Andy McSmith, *No Such Thing as Society: A History of the 1980s* (London, 2010), pp.
   137–52.
32 Adeney and Lloyd, *Miners' Strike*, pp. 101, 120, 140–2; Taylor, *NUM and British
   Politics. Volume 2*, pp. 238–9, 246.
33 Beynon, 'Introduction', in Beynon, *Digging Deeper*, p. 10.
34 Alex Maxwell, *Chicago Tumbles: Cowdenbeath and the Miners' Strike* (Edinburgh,
   1994), pp. 85–94; Joe Owens (ed.), *Miners, 1984–1994: A Decade of Endurance*
   (Edinburgh, 1994).

35 Eric Clarke with Bob McLean, 'The Mineworkers' Strike 1984–5: The Role of the Scottish Area as Banker to the Union', *Scottish Affairs*, 49 (2004), 138–50; Clarke's comments about the ballot are on p. 144.
36 Stewart, 'A Tragic "Fiasco"?', 44–6.
37 David Stewart, *The Path to Devolution and Change. A Political History of Scotland under Margaret Thatcher* (London, 2009).
38 Terry Brotherstone and Simon Pirani, 'Were There Alternatives? Movements from Below in the Scottish Coalfield, the Communist Party, and Thatcherism, 1981–1985', *Critique*, 36–7 (2005), 99–124.
39 William Ashworth, *The History of the British Coal Industry. Volume 5, 1946–1982: The Nationalized Industry* (Oxford, 1986), pp. 414–15.
40 Taylor, *NUM and British Politics. Volume 2*, pp. 155–62.
41 *The Times*, 21 February and 7 March 1984.
42 The *Guardian*, 7 March 2009; *Sunday Herald*, 8 March 2009.
43 Hywel Francis, *History On Our Side: Wales and the 1984–85 Miners' Strike* (Ferryside, 2009).
44 Francis Beckett and David Hencke, *Marching to the Fault Line. The 1984 Miners' Strike and the Death of Industrial Britain* (London, 2009).
45 David Douglass, 'Misunderstanding the Miners' Strike', *Weekly Worker*, 777, 9 July 2009: http://www.cpgb.org.uk/worker/777/misunderstanding.php, accessed 8 August 2011.
46 The *Guardian*, 9 March 2009.
47 The *Guardian*, 11 March 2009.
48 The *Guardian*, 25 March 2009.
49 Alan Campbell, *The Scottish Miners, 1874–1939. Volume Two: Trade Unions and Politics* (Aldershot, 2000).
50 Jim Phillips, 'Workplace Conflict and the Origins of the 1984–5 Miners' Strike in Scotland', *Twentieth Century British History*, 20 (2009), 152–72; Jim Phillips, 'Collieries and Communities: The Miners' Strike in Scotland, 1984–5', *Scottish Labour History*, 45 (2010), 17–35; Jim Phillips, 'Material and Moral Resources: The 1984–5 Miners' Strike in Scotland', *Economic History Review*, 65:1 (2012), 256–76.
51 Abe Moffat, Interview with Willie Thompson, 11 February 1986.
52 George Bolton, Interview with Willie Thompson, undated, but presumed late 1985.
53 Willie Thompson, 'The Miners' Strike in Scotland 1984–1985', 24 pp., unpublished essay in author's possession. Thompson interviewed McGahey and Eric Clarke, but was unable to locate these recordings when passing the material to the author in 2007. The 'surviving' interviews are listed in the bibliography of this book.
54 Luisa Passerini, 'Work, Ideology and Consensus Under Italian Fascism', in Robert Perks and Alistair Thomson (eds), *The Oral History Reader* (London, 1998), pp. 53–62.
55 Allesandro Portelli, *They Say in Harlan County. An Oral History* (Oxford, 2011), p. 192.
56 Nicky Wilson, Interview, 31 August 2009.
57 Iain Chalmers, Interview, 30 July 2009.
58 Penny Summerfield, 'Dis/composing the Subject: Inter-subjectivities in Oral History', in Tess Cosslett, Celia Lury and Penny Summerfield (eds), *Feminism and Autobiography. Texts, Theories, Methods* (London, 2000), pp. 93–108.
59 Alistair Thomson, 'Anzac Memories: Putting Popular Memory Theory Into Practice in Australia', in Perks and Thomson, *Oral History Reader*, pp. 300–10.

60 Willie Clarke, Interview, 13 November 2009; David Hamilton, Interview, 30 September 2009.

61 Wilson, Interview.

62 E.P. Thompson, 'The Moral Economy of the English Crowd in the Eighteenth Century', *Past and Present*, 50 (1971), 76–136.

63 Alan Campbell, *The Scottish Miners, 1874–1939. Volume One: Work, Industry and Community* (Aldershot, 2000), pp. 200–3.

64 Hamilton, Interview; Willie Clarke, Interview.

65 Eric Clarke, Interview, 25 August 2009; Willie Clarke, Interview; Wilson, Interview.

66 Colin Griffin, '"Notts. Have Some Very Peculiar History": Understanding the Reaction of the Nottinghamshire Miners to the 1984–85 Strike', *Historical Studies in Industrial Relations*, 19 (2005), 63–99.

67 NAS, SEP 4/6029/1, Coal Strike: 5 March, Situation Report (hereafter Sit Rep), and Sit Rep, 11 March 1985.

68 Willie Clarke, Interview.

69 Guthrie Hutton, compiler, *Coal Not Dole. Memories of the 1984/85 Miners' Strike* (Catine, 2005), p. 57; Hamilton, Interview.

70 Jocky Neilson, Interview with Willie Thompson, 19 May 1986; *The Times*, 7 and 12 March 1985.

I
Origins and outbreak

1

Collieries, communities and coalfield politics

The National Coal Board operated sixteen collieries in Scotland in October 1982, employing between 16,000 and 17,000 miners. These are listed in Table 1.1. Four closed in the ten months that followed: Kinneil, Cardowan, Highhouse and Sorn.

The twelve that remained were therefore mainly young. Seven – Seafield, Bogside, Castlehill, Solsgirth, Monktonhall, Bilston Glen and Killoch – had been established since the nationalisation of coal in 1947. Excepting Polkemmet, these were the seven largest employers in the Scottish coalfields, following the closure of Cardowan in August 1983. The age profile of these relatively large and important collieries in the early 1980s, skewed towards youth, is symptomatic of the powerful process of economic, industrial and social restructuring that took place after nationalisation. This involved multiple closures and job losses, with NCB operations concentrated in larger collieries, where mechanisation, production and output were radically increased. It also disrupted mining communities, with substantial numbers of miners and their families moving home, mainly from Lanarkshire to Fife in the 1950s and 1960s, and many others taking longer daily journeys to work. The link between community and colliery was duly weakened, although not ultimately fractured, as the 1984–85 strike would demonstrate.

The restructuring of the 1950s and 1960s reshaped the industrial politics of the coalfields, creating tensions in the new and redeveloped collieries. Workplace conflict and union militancy, key features of the pre-1947 privately owned industry, duly re-emerged, with Scottish miners prominent in major unofficial disputes in the late 1960s, and the national strikes of 1972 and 1974. These appeared to strengthen the miners politically, contributing to the defeat of Edward Heath's Conservative government and the election of a Labour government in 1974 which proposed stabilising the industry through increased investment and production. But the Conservative government subsequently elected in 1979, led by Margaret Thatcher, sought 'revenge' against the miners, to reduce the economic importance of nationalised industry and the political strength of trade unionism. Thatcher's government squeezed the miners in

Table 1.1 NCB collieries in Scotland, October 1982

Colliery	Production commenced	Approximate employment	Principal market
Seafield, East Fife	1966	1,300	SSEB[e]
Frances, East Fife	c. 1850	700	
Comrie, West Fife	1936–39	1,000	SSEB
Bogside, West Fife	1959	1,000	SSEB, Longannet
Castlehill, West Fife[a]	1969	1,300	SSEB, Longannet
Solsgirth, Clackmannan[b]	1969	1,300	SSEB, Longannet
Monktonhall, Midlothian	1967	1,600	SSEB, Cockenzie
Bilston Glen, Midlothian	1963	1,700	SSEB, Cockenzie
Kinneil, West Lothian[c]	1890	300	
Polkemmet, West Lothian	1913–16	1,300	BSC, Ravenscraig
Polmaise, Stirlingshire	1904		SSEB, Kincardine
Cardowan, Lanarkshire	1924–29	1,300	
Killoch, Ayrshire	1960	1,100	Power Stations, Northern Ireland
Barony, Ayrshire[d]	1910	900	
Highhouse, Ayrshire	1894	400	
Sorn, Ayrshire	1953	300	

Source: Miles K. Oglethorpe, *Scottish Collieries. An Inventory of the Scottish Coal Industry in the Nationalised Era*, The Royal Commission on the Ancient and Historical Monuments of Scotland in partnership with The Scottish Mining Museum Trust (Edinburgh, 2006).
[a] Castlehill employment figure provided by Tam Coulter in Interview with Willie Thompson.
[b] Solsgirth figure provided by Iain McCaig in Interview with Willie Thompson. [c] No coal was being produced at Kinneil in October 1982, where miners were employed in development work to link pit under the Forth with Bogside. In 1978, before the development work commenced, roughly 700 were employed at Kinneil. [d] Barony consisted of four shafts: the first two were sunk in 1910; the third in 1945; and the fourth in 1965; [e] South of Scotland Electricity Board.

another way. Table 1.1 also shows the principal markets for the pits surviving on the eve of the strike. This structural position, with a small number of large customers, chiefly power stations in Scotland and Northern Ireland, had helped the coal industry to adapt and survive in the 1960s and 1970s. But by the early 1980s it was becoming problematic, with the government urging electricity generators to lower consumer prices, either by turning to coal imports, or increasing the use of oil, gas and nuclear power.[1] This chapter links these various economic, social, industrial and political developments, relating the post-1947 restructuring to the reconfiguration of Scottish coalfield communities and industrial politics in the 1960s and the 1970s, which encompassed support from the miners for political devolution in Scotland. It then examines the manner in which Thatcherite analyses of political economy, trade unionism and the coal industry subsequently developed and exerted additional pressures on Scotland's surviving collieries.

Industrial and social restructuring

Longer historical explorations of coalfield industrial politics in the 1970s and 1980s tend to focus on the legacy of the great lockouts of 1921 and 1926. Alan Campbell writes evocatively about the 'genealogies of victimisation and radicalism' which these conflicts established.[2] Abe Moffat, Fife miner, trade union activist, lockout leader and Communist Party member, was sacked and did not work underground again until 1938. He served as President of NUMSA from 1942 until 1961 when his brother, Alex, succeeded him. Abe died in 1975, aged 78.[3] His son Abe, born in 1925, became a tradesman in the coal industry, and was President of SCEBTA during the 1984–85 strike, when his daughter, Ella Egan, convened the work of Scottish women's support groups.[4] Jimmy Daly, another Fife Communist, lost both job and company house in 1926, and moved to Midlothian before returning to Fife in 1938. Jimmy's son, Lawrence, born in 1924, was prominent in Fife and then Scottish industrial politics in the 1950s and 1960s, and served as NUM General Secretary from 1968 until February 1984. Jimmy McGahey, also a Communist Party member, was forced out of his job at Shotts in Lanarkshire in 1926. According to Jimmy Reid, one-time Communist Party national official, McGahey was gaoled for his lockout-related activities in 1926, and refused prison leave when one of his sons died shortly afterwards.[5] He subsequently worked in Kent and then Stirlingshire before returning to Lanarkshire, where a surviving son, Michael, born in 1925, entered the pits at the age of fourteen in 1939,[6] becoming active in workplace and industrial politics almost immediately.[7] Sacked for leading an unofficial strike at Cardowan in 1943, Michael was guided in his trade union and Communist Party politics by the elder Abe Moffat, joined the NUMSA executive in 1958, was elected to succeed Alex Moffat as NUMSA President in 1967, and then elected Vice President of the union nationally in 1973.[8] In 1984 one of those victimised was Michael's son, also Michael, a miner at Bilston Glen.[9] John Bolton, sentenced to three months' hard labour in Barlinnie for sheep rustling during the 1926 lockout, was the brother of Guy, whose son George became NUMSA Vice President in 1978, entrusted by his fellow Communist McGahey in 1985 with the job of pursuing the cases of the 206 miners sacked by the NCB during the strike. Guy Bolton, 77 years old, was arrested in 1984–85 for an 'alleged breach of the peace outside a blackleg's house'. The case was dismissed. George was elected to succeed McGahey as NUMSA President in 1987.[10] 'The victories of 1972 and 1974,' Campbell writes, 'the apocalypse of 1984–5, were not merely informed by folk memories of the great lockout; in families such as the McGaheys, the Dalys, the Moffats, the Boltons and many more, they represented a second and third generation of union militants intent on avenging the deep wounds inflicted on their forebears in 1926.'[11]

Participants in the 1984–85 strike reinforce the importance of this lineage and tradition in their memories. Iain Chalmers of Cowdenbeath, born in 1952, was a miner and union activist at Seafield. In his 'free narrative', responding to the open question, 'What are your memories?', Chalmers spoke for three or four minutes about local workplace issues and high politics. Then he said:

at a personal level, I used tae go in tae the miners' welfares at Lochore, Cowdenbeath, an, you know, the pubs and clubs, an at that time there was a whole generation of men who are sadly no longer wi us, who took part in the 1926 General Strike, an I used tae sit an listen tae them, aboot hoo they used tae steal pigs and cattle, seriously, sheep and what not, tae keep the faimlies goin, and efter the 1984–5 strike, even though we lost the strike, I gained a lot of self-respect. I could look them in the eye, no as a better but as an equal, because the fight they fought I fought, and tae me that meant a hell o a lot.[12]

Alex Nicholson was another young Seafield miner in the 1980s. Born in 1957, and raised in East Wemyss, in East Fife, he joined the industry in January 1974, weeks before the national strike. His father, Dave, was a miner too, born in 1917, with boyhood memories of the 1926 lockout, eating at a soup kitchen where his father, another miner, prepared the food. Dave retired in 1980, and, with his wife, Isabella, sustained Alex morally and materially through the strike in 1984–85.[13]

These connections between the 1920s and the 1970s and 1980s – in families, communities and personal memories – are powerful. They have a substantial bearing, clearly, on how the 1984–85 strike developed and how it is remembered, as the terminal point, perhaps, in a continuum of coalfield politics and struggles initiated in 1921 and given dramatic force by 1926.[14] There is, however, a substantial lacuna in this narrative: the mid-twentieth century, with the nationalisation of 1947, and the major restructuring of the industry that followed. This hugely influenced the industrial politics of the 1960s and 1970s, for it involved closures, job losses, and personal or 'collective biographical' discontinuities as well as continuities, with the presence in the industry by the 1960s of large numbers of men with no direct experience of the pre-1947 industry. These men, like Chalmers and Nicholson, born in the 1950s, worked and lived alongside the older men, and of course were touched and affected by their memories and politics, but surely carried their own distinct generational preoccupations and expectations. This is to be remembered when considering the trajectories of Lawrence Daly and Michael McGahey, who were elected to official positions by younger as well as older miners. The militancy of the younger men may well have been inspired by memories of the 1920s, but it was also surely shaped by the material conditions of the 1950s and 1960s. The older generation of officials who preceded Daly and McGahey tended to measure the quality and extent of the progress of life in the coalfields against the substantial workplace injustices and terrible material privations of the 1920s and 1930s. They were arguably complacent, satisfied with the general improvements arising from nationalisation, especially the invaluable asset of joint industrial regulation of the workplace, including health and safety matters, but insensitive to the different frames of social reference adopted by their younger members, who measured their existence not against the problems of the past, but the opportunities of the present. Eric Clarke, NUMSA Secretary during the 1984–85 strike, was seventeen years old when he began working in the industry in 1949, moving between older pits in Midlothian – Roslin, Lady Victoria and Lingerwood –

before a spell at the cosmopolitan Bilston Glen from the late 1960s onwards. There is a 'coming of age' quality to Clarke's testimony, emphasising, for example, the material injustices that he witnessed underground in his early working life, which turned him away from his intended career in mining management and towards union activism and Labour Party membership. It is nevertheless striking that he also speaks about the loftiness of NCB managers in the 1950s, relating this to the relatively unreconstructed nature of power under nationalisation, and the presence too in the industry of the 'officer class', former military personnel, who talked about 'goan on leave' when they 'were goan on their hoalidays'.[15]

The historical literature tends to support this narrative of limited change to authority structures arising from nationalisation,[16] although Andrew Perchard's analysis of mine managers makes important distinctions between colliery-level and Scottish Area-level management. Pit managers, he writes, tended to be 'colliers with collars', more sympathetic to workers than Area managers, whose financial priorities determined an occasionally authoritarian approach to labour questions.[17] This distinction, it will be seen in Chapter 2, was sometimes made by union officials and activists too, at least when recalling the pre-1980 position. Area-level priorities certainly shaped major pit closures and job losses, and depressed wages in the coalfields in the 1950s and 1960s, which Eric Clarke and other younger miners resented, particularly as workers in most other economic sectors were experiencing stable employment and improved living standards. This stimulated militancy, particularly among younger miners.[18] Jocky Neilson, NUM delegate at Seafield during the 1984–85 strike, but in 1962 a 25-year-old miner at Nelly in Central Fife, and spokesman of the Scottish Miners' Youth Committee, outlined the limited local prospects for young men in the coalfields in the union's Scottish monthly newspaper. The Cowdenbeath Employment Office offered only positions in the armed forces or seasonal agriculture: young men wishing to make a start in coal mining would have to move to England.[19]

Nelly was one of 206 collieries taken into public ownership in Scotland in 1947. By the end of 1962, in which year alone 19 pits closed, there were just less than a hundred. When Nelly closed in 1965 there were just over fifty, and by 1970, even with some new pits opening, there were only forty or so. Manpower requirements fell also, although not initially. At nationalisation the total NCB workforce in in Scotland exceeded 75,000, and then grew modestly, stabilising at around 80,000 for a decade or so, until a precipitous decline from 1959, to 56,000 in 1962, 38,000 in 1965, 32,000 in 1967, and 28,000 in 1972.[20] This was part of a wider process of restructuring across NCB holdings in England and Wales as well as Scotland, under the Chairmanship of James Bowman in the 1950s and Alf Robens in the 1960s. The latter was especially bullish about the urgency of concentrating resources in a smaller number of more highly capit-alised, larger collieries.[21] He was also unapologetic. 'Customers close pits,' he said in 1966, 'not managers.' This was in an NCB film, *Nobody's Face*, exhorting miners to make more efficient use of coal-cutting machinery.[22] Robens's approach – and insistence that the market rather than the NCB was responsible for closures – reflected changes in energy provision, with increased competition from other sources of electricity generation, notably oil in the 1950s, and then nuclear power in the 1960s, along with a moderate degree of hydro-electric provision in the Scottish Highlands from the 1940s onwards.[23] Coal's share of energy supplied in the UK shrank from 73.7 per cent in 1960 to 46.6 per cent in 1970. This was a smaller share of a larger market, but coal production overall fell,[24] in Scotland from its stable value of 22–23 million tonnes between 1947 and 1957 to around 18 million tonnes in 1960, just under 15 million tonnes in 1965, and 11–12 million tonnes in 1970.[25]

Labour requirements fell under the additional pressure of increased mechanisation, or power-loading, which the NCB pursued from the mid-1950s. This made production continuous, and by increments displaced semi-mechanised longwall methods, where one shift cut the coal, a second cleared it, and a third secured the face for the next advance. The coal industry's standard managerial characterisation of mechanisation, as a major and unqualified economic and social advance, feeding coal efficiently to large power stations, and reducing both energy and environmental costs, is captured in *New Power In Their Hands*, a 1959 NCB Film Unit production. Cleanliness and scientific knowledge were foregrounded, and the changing nature of the industry's labour process and requirements celebrated: future miners would be skilled technicians and engineers. The film's commentary, spoken by Ewan MacColl, the folk singer, whose Communist politics placed him closely within the traditions and culture of coal mining,[26] faced worker resistance to mechanisation by characterising manual coal-getting methods, especially shovelling at the coalface, as a 'stupid' and hazardous misuse of men's physical capacities and bodies.[27] The dangers of the industry had certainly remained clear after nationalisation. At Knochshinnoch in Ayrshire a huge inrush of peat had trapped 129 miners below ground in 1950. An epic rescue operation saved 116 of these men, but thirteen were killed. At Auchengeich in Lanarkshire a disastrous fire killed 47 miners in 1959, and four died at Barony when a shaft collapsed in 1962. On 9 September 1967 Scotland's largest pit, Michael, in East Fife, was destroyed by a catastrophic fire. Nine men were killed, although 302 others escaped.[28] These were all calamities, of course, without direct connection to production methods. But mechanisation, with its emphasis on speed and scale, created new hazards. On 10 May 1973 five miners were killed at Seafield when roof supports, which they had been advancing behind cutting machinery, collapsed. The youngest was Angus Guthrie, just twenty years old, from Cardenden; the others were James Comrie and Robert Henderson of Buckhaven, and James Holmes and Thomas 'Tom Cat' Kilpatrick of Methil.[29] Cutting and loading machinery additionally exposed face workers to elevated levels of coal dust, and so probably increased the incidence of occupational diseases. Long-term physical disabilities, such as white finger, arising from repeated and prolonged handling of vibrating machinery, also resulted.[30]

In the longer term, through strengthening managerial focus on comparative pit-level production performances, mechanisation helped to establish the 'loser' narrative that would carry such force under Albert Wheeler in the early 1980s.

Pit managers were issued with mechanisation targets, and, in 1957 at Michael and in 1961 at Kinglassie, also in Fife, removed from their positions when they failed to achieve these. Between January 1960 and May 1964 the proportion of coal power-loaded increased from 27.8 per cent of total Scottish output to 62.4 per cent, and in 1965 Scottish managers were advised by NCB national production officials that collieries unable to shift quickly to mechanisation would be closed. There would be 'no place in the economy for gross losers', the pit managers were told, in discursive terms that would be used recurrently by Wheeler in the early 1980s, and in explaining the further concentration of operations in larger pits by the early 1970s.[31]

The links between community and colliery were reconstructed, although not severed, by this process of restructuring. There were, in essence, two countervailing tendencies: the concentration of workers by workplace; and the dispersal of workers by residence. In the early 1950s there was a substantial movement of men and their families from Lanarkshire, where the number of NCB pits fell from sixty in 1947 to just ten by 1967. They shifted to Clackmannan, Midlothian, and especially Fife, clustering in the new town of Glenrothes, built to accommodate employees at Rothes, a big colliery which opened in 1957 with a projected life of one hundred years. The NCB emphasised the positive aspects of this migration, promising stable employment and modern local authority housing in Fife, itself an important and radical improvement on the single-storey, terraced 'miners' rows' that many Lanarkshire families were leaving behind.[32] The disruptions to personal and family life, and the lost bonds of neighbourhood and locality were nevertheless keenly felt,[33] and stable employment was by no means the universal experience for those who moved. Rothes closed in 1962, just five years after opening, because of geological difficulties and extreme flooding. The further major and unanticipated closure of Michael followed in 1967.[34] The miners of Rothes and then Michael – the latter from the towns of Buckhaven, Kennoway, Leven, Methil and Windygates, and the villages of East Wemyss, Coaltown of Wemyss and West Wemyss – found employment mainly at Seafield,[35] the large pit immediately to the west of Kirkcaldy, or its neighbour, Frances, to the east. There they were joined by men from the towns and villages of Central Fife: Auchterderran, Ballingry, Cardenden, Cowdenbeath, Kelty, Lochgelly, Lochore, Lumphinans. These were the Little Moscows, their militant industrial tradition, leavened by Communist Party politics, established in the workplace conflicts and austere economic conditions of the 1920s and 1930s.[36] These settlements lost their pits in the 1960s, but not their miners, who journeyed the ten miles or so to Kirkcaldy and back on a daily basis. Iain Chalmers, raised in this milieu, saw its relatively homogeneous occupational, social and political character as both strength and weakness: it united the miners, but also – and here he was thinking about the constraints on wider working-class and trade union support for the 1984–85 strike – reduced their capacity to empathise with workers and society outwith the coalfields. Chalmers also felt that the transfer of men from Lanarkshire to Fife had been managed with the ambition of diluting the mining monoculture, with the allocation of

council housing in Glenrothes placing miners in mixed occupational communities. This, he felt, was a factor, eventually, in 1984–85, where miners in
Glenrothes and points further east were slightly less committed to the strike
than those in Central Fife.[37]

The changing industrial and political character of the Scottish coalfields can
further be read in the life of Willie Clarke, born in 1935, who began his working
life in August 1950 at Glencraig Colliery in Central Fife, a few hundred yards
from his home, where more than a thousand men were employed, including
Lawrence Daly, who was the NUM delegate. The union branch committee,
which Clarke joined in 1960, was Communist-influenced, although Daly had
left the Communist Party in 1956, resenting its uncritical adherence to Soviet
policy.[38] Glencraig closed in July 1966, and Clarke transferred with many neighbours and work-mates to Seafield, starting on 26 September that year. They took
the Little Moscows Communism with them, which was still shaping the politics
and personalities of the union branch committee in the early 1980s. This
included Jocky Neilson, once of Nelly, who in the 1970s and 1980s combined his
NCB employment and union activism with service as a Communist Councillor
in Lochgelly. Neilson died in 1990, aged 53. Clarke, a year or so older, was also
a Communist Councillor of long standing, in Ballingry, remaining so in the
2000s and 2010s. To paraphrase the characterisation by some oral historians of
witness testimony, his 'composed' and so internally consistent political and
personal narrative emphasises the solidarity of labour in general and the essential unity of miners in particular, whether from East or West Fife, 'America or
the Soviet Union'. It acknowledges too that restructuring – consolidating
production into a smaller number of mechanised pits – was a 'necessary' exercise in 'retooling'. So it is striking that he also recalls the 'vast difference'
between the village pit and the cosmopolitan colliery, with miners conveyed to
work by so many coaches from the Little Moscow villages to the west, and the
settlements bereft by the loss of Michael to the east, that Seafield resembled 'a
bus garage' in the morning. At pit head and underground 'the first thing that
struck ye was the size of the place'. With separate workings at 170 and 300
fathoms, and the mechanisation-driven split shift system, the Seafield workforce
was fragmented: 'If two boys left the school and went tae Glencraig pit, even wi
twelve hundred men, they wouldae met each other, even just passin each other.
At Seafield yi could ha went and worked all yir life and never met each other.'[39]

The relatively large-scale and impersonal nature of operations at Seafield is
emphasised also in the memoirs of Ian Terris, a pit deputy who started there in
1964 after working at other pits,[40] and in the testimony of Alex Nicholson, one
of forty or so men travelling there by bus from East Wemyss before the 1984–85
strike. Alex and his father were both employed at Seafield from 1977 to 1981 but
in that time scarcely met at work.[41] In the process of industrial restructuring,
then, the social life of miners had become 'divorced', as Willie Clark puts it,
from the job. The same was true of his Glencraig 'neebors' who headed 'west' in
1966, to the Fife pits of Castlehill and Bogside and Solsgirth in Clackmannan.
These three were opened in the 1960s, connected by miles of underground

conveyer belts to the vast South of Scotland Electricity Board power station at Longannet, on the Fife shore of the Firth of Forth.[42] Those employed in the Longannet 'complex' were also drawn from West Fife, the 'Hillfoot' villages around Alloa in Clackmannan, and from further south and west, as pits closed in West Lothian, Stirlingshire and then, in the early 1980s, Lanarkshire. No 'local' recruitment, it seems, was conducted at Longannet in the five years preceding the strike in 1984.[43] The Lanarkshire men spent up to thirteen hours away from home per working day, although they were only paid, of course, for the seven hours that constituted the standard shift by 1983–84.[44]

The process of industrial concentration alongside residential fragmentation can equally be read in the testimony of David Hamilton, who left school in Midlothian in 1965, aged fifteen. He tried, unsuccessfully, to find work as an apprentice painter and decorator, and then became a miner, following his father and two elder brothers, although only up to a point, for each of these family members, spreading the risk of accident as well as unemployment, worked at separate collieries. Such was still possible in Midlothian in 1965, but by 1978 all four were either at Bilston Glen, in Loanhead, or Monktonhall, beside Danderhall, where David Hamilton became NUM delegate in 1976. His work-mates there were drawn mostly from the towns and villages of East Lothian, including Dunbar, Prestonpans and Musselburgh, with a significant minority, like the Hamiltons, 'from the hills' of Midlothian: Danderhall, Dalkeith, Newtongrange, Gorebridge. Men from these settlements worked in Bilston Glen, too, alongside residents of villages further to the west: Lasswade, Bonnyrigg, Loanhead, Bilston, Penicuick and Roslin.[45] A small number from these western Midlothian villages travelled across to Monktonhall, including Rab Amos, born in 1948, the pit's SCEBTA delegate in 1984–85, who also joined the industry from school at the age of fifteen, initially at Easthouses Colliery in Dalkeith. Amos lived in The Inch, in southern Edinburgh, before moving to Roslin in 1972. From there he travelled with about fifteen others to Monktonhall, where he had started in 1966.[46]

The workforce was even more widely dispersed, residentially, in Lanarkshire. Nicky Wilson, born in 1950, began his working life at Cardowan, near Stepps, north-east of Glasgow, in 1967, travelling from Easterhouse, boarding an NCB bus that started in Airdrie before following the old Edinburgh road to the pit. By the 1970s Cardowan was firmly established as a cosmopolitan pit, with the 'red bus' men who travelled from the Campsie Fells settlements of North Lanarkshire, notably Kilsyth and Kirkintilloch, and the 'blue bus' men of Motherwell, Hamilton and Blantyre in South Lanarkshire, plus some from North Ayrshire.[47] In South Ayrshire there were roughly twenty pits in 1964, clustered around Ayr in the west, and Cumnock and New Cumnock to the south and east. Operations thereafter increasingly focused on Killoch and Barony, large collieries to the west and east respectively of the village of Ochiltree, drawing workers from all points in the county.[48]

The concentration of miners industrially and their dispersal residentially is worthy of elaboration, in terms of the implications for community and workplace solidarity, because the sociological and historical literature on coal mining has long emphasised the connection between community and colliery as a factor in the strength and cohesion of coalfield labour. *Coal Is Our Life,* by Norman Dennis, Fernando Henriques and Clifford Slaughter, published in 1956, examined the West Yorkshire mining community of Featherstone, or 'Ashton'. It emphasised the complexity of social relations at a local level, suggesting how class identity, for example, could act as a 'dispersive' as well as 'cohesive' influence on the community. 'Miners do not live only in communities,' Dennis, Henriques and Slaughter wrote, introducing a second edition in 1969, 'but as part of their class in all its economic and political relations.'[49] With this emphasis on the socially and politically open nature of coalfield communities, *Coal Is Our Life* challenged the famous Kerr and Siegel 'isolated mass' thesis, published in 1954, which analysed strike propensity across industries and national boundaries, positioning coal miners, along with some other 'isolated mass' workers, notably dockers, as being particularly strike-prone.[50] This emphasis on the solidifying effects of unchanging homogeneity was clearly incongruent with the empirical evidence, in Britain generally and in Scotland especially, of industrial restructuring and social and human mobility after 1947. The 'isolated mass' thesis was also objectionable, David Gilbert writes, because of its essentially functionalist character, privileging the broad spatial and industrial structural features of workers, and overlooking a range of historical contingencies which would have a potentially significant bearing on strike propensity. These could include the character of the political economy, product market conditions or the immediacy of workplace politics.[51]

Gilbert's comparative study of the inter-war Nottinghamshire and South Welsh coalfields suggested a different framework for understanding strike propensity and commitment, deploying a carefully constructed critique of the concept of 'community', establishing its problematic and ambiguous character. Of the 1984–85 miners' strike it has often been said or written that 'communities' were under attack, or defending themselves, although the particular material, social and cultural characteristics of these communities were not usually scrutinised. This is important, because Gilbert observes that communities comprise a variety of experiences, relationships, structures, spaces and places, and therefore have variable 'social foundations'. Where these are strong the community-based collective interest can prevail against 'free riding' and 'rational' economic actors – like strike-avoiding or strike-breaking workers or trade unionists – who seek to profit from the collective endeavour of other economic actors, without sharing responsibility for the costs of collective action.[52] The community, in short, can exert substantial 'rational choice' social pressure on individuals who, operating on economic motives only, might resist participation in collective action. The social costs of strike-breaking are often elevated through collective or community action, encompassing ostracism or intimidation of strike-breakers. Chapter 4 of this book shows how communities achieved this in 1984–85, in highly gendered terms. Gilbert's analysis identified three community types: the first isolated village, where miners constituted a majority of the population and controlled 'popular' institutions; the second isolated village, where miners again constituted a majority of the population, but employers controlled institutions and occupied a larger role in the maintenance of authority; and towns, where miners were part of an enlarged and mixed industrial population. These were 'ideal' types, subject to the qualification of historical contingency. Urbanisation, for instance, could stimulate militancy as well as conservatism or apathy, and equally inflate or reduce the agency of community-based collective action. Gilbert nevertheless suggested that the small or localised community was 'easier to mobilize' than a larger collective of individuals or workers.[53]

The varieties of coalfield community in Scotland have been analysed by Alan Campbell, in his two-volume study spanning the 1870s to the 1930s. Campbell examined the occupational and social profile of specific mining communities through census data, taking a number of contrasting size and character from each of the four main Scottish coalfield areas: Ayrshire, Lanarkshire, the Lothians and Fife. He included industrial towns, where miners were part of a mixed industrial population, and smaller less varied settlements, recognisable as 'classic' mining villages. Studying the pre-nationalised industry, he also examined miners in different types and sizes of company and colliery. He concluded that economic setting could be as important as community type or size in shaping the character of social and industrial relations. These were more adversarial where miners worked in large pits and large firms, especially where mechanisation was advanced, with owners maximising investment returns by intensifying the labour process. Miners from mixed, larger communities could therefore be more militant than those in smaller, homogeneous communities, depending on industrial setting. Miners in smaller communities working for modest-sized local firms could be less militant, while those in large firms, with business interests beyond the locality, could be among the most militant of all, mobilising against a force that was perceived to be alien in geographical 'outsider' as well as social terms.[54]

So there are dangers, when examining the Scottish coalfields, in assuming that community cohesion is more important than industrial structures and politics in shaping labour solidarity. In the post-1947 nationalised industry workplace factors clearly remained important, with tensions arising from industrial concentration, enforced mechanisation and job transfers creating anger and resentment in the coalfields in the 1960s. These pressures were reflected in the unofficial strikes of the late 1960s and the national disputes of 1972 and 1974, and are discussed in the following section of this chapter. Yet the community, or rather the reconstructed communities, nevertheless contained important characteristics that complemented workplace factors in shaping the industrial politics of coal. These characteristics are partly revealed in Daniel Wight's ethnographic study of the working class in the 1980s in a small Scottish town, anonymised as 'Cauldmoss', but within the Scottish coalfields, near the border between West Lothian and North Lanarkshire. Wight explored the highly gendered nature of working-class attitudes, behaviour and culture in this community, with fairly rigid expectations about male and female economic and social roles being broken down only in a limited way by the increasing involvement of women in paid employment. This community attached substantial prestige to male work, particularly well-paid and physically arduous manual work, where men were able to demonstrate their social as well as economic worth through masculine endeavour and high earnings. The opprobrium, by contrast, visited on those who could but did not work, or gave work less than their full commitment, and the broader moral values of this community, were captured in Wight's acutely observed title: *Workers Not Wasters.*[55]

Charlie Goodfellow, born in 1928, and resident for much of his life in Whitburn, which, like Wight's anonymous settlement, is near the West Lothian–North Lanarkshire boundary, was a surface worker at Polkemmet in the 1950s and 1960s, before taking a job at the British Motor Corporation plant in Bathgate. His memories of working life and the coal industry are an important counterpoint to the activist narratives of some of the 1984–85 strike participants, for they are highly consistent with the moral world of Wight's community, privileging the social value of the coal industry and the pride that miners took in their work. The miners' work culture was indeed a vital element of the moral economy of the Scottish coalfields, contributing greatly to the pit-level and industry-level solidarity of the labour force. Goodfellow contrasts this with the allegedly less committed and occasionally careless approach to work at Bathgate.[56] Like Thompson's moral economy of the eighteenth-century English crowd,[57] the Scottish coalfield variant of the twentieth century rested on shared collective assumptions about economic activity. There were two of these. First, that collieries and mining jobs were social resources as well as economic units, to be managed and developed for collective benefit. Second, collieries could be closed, and jobs forfeited, only with the agreement of the workers involved and their representatives, and where the economic security of those affected was protected. For those still of working age this meant transfer to other pits, or availability of suitable employment elsewhere.[58]

The restructuring of the 1950s and 1960s, including closures, job losses, mechanisation and industrial concentration, tested but did not breach this moral economy, for the process, however fractious, was conducted through dialogue and agreement with trade union officials, and in the wider context of economic growth. Miners who left the industry, such as Charlie Goodfellow, were able to secure work in manufacturing or other comparably paid manual employment sectors. These factors did not apply in the early 1980s, when pits were closed in the face of worker and trade union opposition, and where the economic prospects of miners who lost their jobs were narrowed by heavy and prolonged manual unemployment across the economy.

Coal communities were characterised by different material as well as moral resources. In 1984–85, pit-level differences in commitment would be shaped, as Chapter 4 explains, by the variable measures in communities of married women in part-time and full-time employment and council housing density. Workplace factors would be important, as they were in the disputes of the 1960s and 1970s, but these alone could not explain, for example, the particular solidarity of the strike in West and Central Fife. This would owe much to the Little Moscows legacy, with commitment burnished by communal understanding of the injustices and struggles of the past, preserved through local oral tradition, and also, still, in 1984–85, the presence of 1921 and 1926 veterans.[59] The great crisis of 1984–85, summoning memories of the past, as well as raising questions about the future, would vividly illustrate the continuing connection between community and colliery that the restructuring of the industry in the 1950s and 1960s had only partly eroded.

Industrial politics: popular militancy and devolution

The industrial restructuring of the 1950s and 1960s altered Scottish coalfield politics, stimulating popular support for 'militant' trade unionism, meaning a more robust opposition to pit closures and job losses, and strengthening the moral economy perspective. From 1960 to 1969 a total of 112 pits closed in Scotland, but only 17 more were lost between 1970 and 1979.[60] Restructuring also contributed to a growth of coalfield trade union support for devolution in Scotland. There are clear parallels here with South Wales, where industrial changes also shaped a union-based campaign for political and constitutional reform.[61] It was hoped that a Parliament in Edinburgh would be more responsive to Scotland's particular economic, industrial and social needs, and over time help to slow or even reverse the loss of employment in coal and other manual sectors experienced since the 1950s.

At a UK level the impact of industrial restructuring 'surfaced' with the major unofficial strikes of 1969 and 1970, and then the official national strikes of 1972 and 1974. There is a substantial literature on these developments, although, as with the 1984–85 strike, it tends to focus on high politics. 'Heath and the Miners', indeed, is a familiar episode in Britain's later twentieth-century political history, and few accounts of the 1984–85 strike begin without reprising its essentials. The tale usually told is the humiliation of the Prime Minister, Edward Heath, and the Conservatives more generally, the miners exacerbating the government's already considerable difficulties in seeking to 'reform' trade unions – reducing especially the incidence of strikes – through the 1971 Industrial Relations Act.[62] The architects of this humiliation are typically presented as the 'militant' and sometimes 'politically motivated' – Heath's own characterisation – core of the national executive of the NUM. 'Moderate' voices in the union, notably its President, Joe Gormley, were drowned out by Lawrence Daly, General Secretary since 1968, Michael McGahey, Scottish President and, from July 1973, national Vice President, and Arthur Scargill, a full-time official in the Yorkshire Area of the NUM, who led the famous blockade of the West Midlands Gas Board's Saltley coke depot in 1972.[63] Margaret Thatcher, Education Secretary in Heath's Cabinet, regarded Saltley as a 'victory for violence', and the miners' behaviour during each dispute as signalling the undemocratic and bullying character of trade unionism which had to be confronted and defeated.[64] This introduces an additional element of the Heath story: the 'revenge' thesis, with Scargill, President of the NUM from 1982, along with McGahey and others, paying for temporary victories in 1972 and 1974 with heavy and unconditional defeat in 1985.[65]

Alternative accounts of 1972 and 1974 exist, privileging the significance of popular agency in the coalfields and focusing on the incremental radicalisation of miners in the 1960s under the weight of industrial restructuring and related changes in energy markets and electricity generation. In these popular agency analyses the emergence of Daly, McGahey and Scargill was neither an accidental coincidence nor a determined leftist conspiracy. Rather it reflected the impatience among a large body of miners with the willingness of 'moderate' trade union leaders to tolerate pit closures and agree wage settlements that saw miners fall behind many groups of manual workers in the wages league. Daly and McGahey were both elected to their senior union offices in the later 1960s on the basis of opposing further pit closures.[66] Their victories were evidence of a deep reservoir of discontent across the coalfields, and clearly helped to arrest the rate of the industry's decline in the 1970s. Mining communities were bolstered and emboldened as a result.[67] McGahey, it should be noted, was only narrowly defeated by Gormley in the NUM Presidential Election of 1971, winning big majorities in Kent, Scotland and South Wales, and a slight majority in Yorkshire. These four areas, plus Derbyshire, supported him when he won the Vice Presidency in 1973.[68]

The collective determination of the miners was vividly illustrated by the seven-week strike in 1972. This was a long stretch, but commitment was so strong that there was no need for picketing of pits, allowing the NUM to muster its resources elsewhere.[69] This helped to establish a particular and even distinctive Scottish narrative, with major picketing of Longannet power station in the seventh and ultimately final week of the strike, after Heath's government had appointed a Committee of Inquiry to examine the miners' pay claim under an English High Court judge, Lord Wilberforce. At this point the NUM leadership, seeking to show the NCB and the government some degree of conciliation, commanded its pickets to stand down from power stations and other energy units. More than 2,000 Scottish miners – including their officials, led by McGahey – ignored this and pressed in around Longannet, almost closing it on 14 February.[70] This coincided directly with the first Scottish Assembly on Unemployment, held that afternoon fifteen miles away in Edinburgh's Usher Hall. The Scottish Assembly was organised by the STUC, and attended by representatives of its trade union affiliates, including the miners, along with figures from local authorities, business, and the political parties, including Conservative – or Unionist – figures, such as Sir William McEwan Younger, Tory Chairman in Scotland, and Teddy Taylor, MP for Glasgow Cathcart. The Assembly articulated a position that was widely held in Scotland, from different social class and political perspectives, that slower economic growth and higher unemployment in Scotland as a whole than England as a whole were a failure of existing political and constitutional arrangements. A Scottish Parliament would

bring the management of economic, industrial and social life into closer align-
ment with Scotland's particular contingencies.[71]

Until 1972 the case for devolution had mainly been made by business leaders
and trade unionists. Business advocacy was led by the Scottish Council for
Development and Industry (SCDI), a cross-industry body, including some
union and local authority figures, but dominated by manufacturers from the
'traditional' sectors of shipbuilding and steel and the 'modernising' assemblers
of consumer goods.[72] John Toothill of Ferranti electronics, among the latter,
chaired the committee that authored the 1961 report outlining the basic position of the SCDI, that economic growth in Scotland, including the development
of new enterprises, was retarded in two ways by Whitehall and Westminster
stewardship. First, controlling inflation in higher growth regions of southern
and central England involved periodic public spending cuts or increased indi-
rect taxes or interest rates. These choked off Scottish growth. Second, regional
policy, the various carrots to guide business, especially in consumer goods, to
regions that were over-reliant – as Scotland certainly was – on a narrow range of
mature, or 'declining' heavy industrial sectors, such as shipbuilding and steel,
was allegedly failing. It focused on diminishing unemployment in particular
localities rather than encouraging growth more broadly. Public investment was
therefore attracted to the declining sectors, chiefly in west central Scotland,
rather than the higher added value consumer goods sectors. Modernising businessmen like Toothill were unable to transform regional policy and transfer its
administration, as they wished, in devolutionary terms, from the Board of Trade
in Whitehall to the Scottish Office in Edinburgh.[73]

Consumer goods industries – electronics, principally, along with electrical
goods and clothing – nevertheless continued to grow in the 1960s and 1970s,
with overseas firms, chiefly from the USA, clustering in West Lothian, around
the new town of Livingston, and Midlothian, and stretching west and south into
Lanarkshire and Ayrshire, and north and east into Fife and Tayside. This inward
investment gradually established Scotland as a 'branch-plant' economy with
low-skilled 'screwdriver' jobs. Research, development and strategic investment
decisions were usually taken elsewhere,[74] with a small number of exceptions,
notably IBM in Greenock, where some diversification into new product development and consumer care was effected.[75] The majority of US firms continued
to focus on low-cost assembly, and duly left Scotland from the late 1970s and
then especially in the 1980s and 1990s, usually for lower wage cost environments
in Asia. But for more or less the span of one human generation's working life
these firms provided reasonably stable industrial employment, which was experienced by significant numbers of women as well as men. In the coalfields the
earnings of women employed in these firms, and married to miners, would help
to sustain the strike in 1984–85, as Chapter 4 illustrates.[76]

The modernising businessmen in Scotland, while thwarted over regional
policy, won other battles, most notably when Harold Macmillan's Conservative
government compelled Colvilles to establish a rolling strip mill at Ravenscraig
in 1958. The steel maker knew this would be a heavy loser financially, but the

government wanted in effect a subsidised supply of steel to the consumer goods industries, including car assembly, with the Midlands motor assembly firm Rootes directed to Linwood under regional policy terms, opening in 1963. Ravenscraig also provided a stable market for high quality Scottish coking coal, and so helped to sustain mining in Lanarkshire and then West Lothian in the 1960s and 1970s.[77] So Ravenscraig was a powerful emblem of the Conservative Party's commitment in the 1950s and 1960s to the economic and social integrity of the UK. It therefore became an apt target in 1984 for miners intent on explaining their strike at least partly in terms of the Conservative government's insensitivity to Scotland's particular problems.

Labour movement support for devolution had been present in the 1900s and 1910s. But from the 1920s until the 1950s the emphasis was on advancing working-class living standards within a centralised UK state, transferring resources progressively across regions as well as wealth and income groups.[78] This position was altered by deindustrialisation in the 1960s, and the intervention of NUMSA was decisive. McGahey pushed the STUC towards its settled position as an unambiguous advocate of legislative devolution for Scotland within the UK. McGahey and NUMSA supported devolution on the grounds that the interests of Scottish workers were damaged by the remote administration of economic and political power from London. This had resulted in declining industrial activity and inhibited the growth of working-class living standards. Restructuring in the Scottish coalfields illustrated this. The closures and job losses were devised in narrow economic terms by the NCB in London, with insufficient reference to the wider social costs, with miners and their communities 'forgotten', in Willie Clarke's estimation.[79] A Scottish Parliament would correct what in the 1980s became known as 'the democratic deficit': the unresponsive nature of extant UK political mechanisms that contributed to human neglect in Scotland. This was devolution from a working-class rather than a national or nationalist perspective: McGahey wanted government in Scotland to be more accountable to workers in Scotland, while emphasising the essential unity of workers across the UK.[80]

Class and devolutionary politics were also blended in industrial affairs on the Clyde, with the 1971–72 UCS work-in, whose leaders, notably Jimmy Reid, Sammy Barr and James Airlie, blamed the company's liquidation in June 1971 on the 'faceless men' in Whitehall who decided to end operating subsidies. Reid was especially successful in subverting established discourses in industrial politics by characterising the Conservative government as the irresponsible 'wrecker' of the dispute. The workers, by comparison, were behaving responsibly, building ships and so supporting communities and the broader regional economy of west central Scotland. The work-in's impact was strengthened by the deteriorating economic picture in Scotland in 1971–72, with Heath's economic management geared to eliminating 'lame duck' concerns and leading to a sharp escalation of unemployment. This worried Tory figures and business leaders as well as trade unionists in Scotland, and contributed to the cross-party nature of the Assembly in February 1972. The Heath government duly conceded defeat, reversing the decision on subsidies and shipbuilding was preserved on the Upper Clyde.[81]

The UCS stewards and NUMSA officials were allies, Reid addressing a miners' rally in Edinburgh in November 1971, and linking their separate campaigns to the common source: a remote Conservative government out of sympathy with the social needs of workers.[82] The UCS workers and the miners were brought together through industrial and class solidarity, but the close nature of the alliance also reflected the Communist Party membership that Reid, Airlie and Barr shared with NUMSA officials, including McGahey, who joined the Communist Party's national executive in 1971. The Communist Party itself supported a Scottish Parliament, and this consolidated its political ascendancy in the coalfields. David Hamilton, like many other union activists, joined the Party in the early 1970s at least in part because of the manner in which it related developments in the coal industry to broader political questions, including the structures of power in the UK.[83]

The broader class politics of NUMSA and SCEBTA were articulated in support for other workers beyond the coalfields, including the Grunwick photo-processors of West London, who unsuccessfully sought union recognition from their employer in a lengthy dispute between 1976 and 1978. Literature on Grunwick usually makes reference to the presence of Arthur Scargill and Yorkshire miners. But Scottish miners reinforced the Grunwick picket lines in abundant numbers too, travelling in busloads from Fife, Midlothian and Stirlingshire. Willie Clarke and Rab Amos, Communists both, were among them, as was John McCormack, the non-Communist NUM delegate at Polmaise.[84] McGahey, Eric Clarke and other NUMSA officials were frequently there too, captured in a sequence of memorable photographs by Homer Sykes.[85] Their appearance alongside the Grunwick workers, many of whom were women of Asian origin, suggests that industrial politics in the 1970s, particularly those of the coalfields, were more outward-looking than popular memory typically admits.[86]

The 1972 strike culminated in a wage agreement reached in Downing Street, based on the Wilberforce committee recommendation that the miners receive a substantial increase, including an 'adjustment factor' component to raise their pay relative to that of other manual workers.[87] This was a victory for the miners, and owed more – in McGahey's pithy terms, recalled by Willie Clarke – to 'picket force than Wilberforce'.[88] It brought them up to 'where we should have been', in the words of Eric Clarke.[89] Popular support for the strike in the coalfields, rooted in the long-running process of restructuring, was not readily understood by Heath and his colleagues, who sought instead to explain developments in terms of the conspiratorial and 'politically motivated' behaviour of Communists and their sympathisers in the NUM. This highly ideological misapprehension was pursued by Tory sympathisers and supporters in the daily and business press, including Nigel Lawson, who would influence the origins and conduct of the 1984–85 strike as Thatcher's Secretary of State for Energy and then Chancellor of the Exchequer.[90]

The militant 'conspiracy' was an important element in Thatcherite discourse, in the later 1970s and 1980s, exploring how the supposedly inefficient nationalised coal industry had become prisoner of monopoly and politicised trade union power. This would place additional pressure on the Scottish coalfields. Yet there was in fact little evidence that large-scale industrial unrest was 'caused' by Communist Party activists. Even the secret service, detailed by Heath to uncover the extent of subversion in the 1972 strike, concluded that the Communist Party had not guided events in any significant way.[91] But the government remained preoccupied with the notion of conspiracy, unable to comprehend the importance of popular attitudes and actions in the subsequent coal dispute, in the winter of 1973–74. Heath's Prime Ministerial papers include notes highlighting the public statements of McGahey and other Communists.[92] These reprised the essence of McGahey's comments in Downing Street on 28 November 1973 about his desire to drive the Tory government from office. McGahey's meaning, that this be achieved through politicising the electorate via mass industrial mobilisation, was misinterpreted as a call to subvert the democratic process. As such it was excoriated by Heath and others in his government, along with a number of right-wing Labour MPs, including Reg Prentice, the party's employment spokesman. McGahey stood by his position, saying that he was speaking for the miners of Scotland,[93] whose gains in 1972 had been eroded by rapid price inflation. This was the source of the coal dispute, which was then shaped by OPEC's four-fold oil price increase in October, greatly improving the miners' bargaining position. The NUM called an overtime ban on 25 October, and the government responded by declaring a State of Emergency on 13 November.[94] On 13 December Heath declared a three-day industrial week, to conserve energy supplies, and either side of the Christmas and New Year holiday fruitless talks were held between NUM representatives and William Whitelaw, the Employment Secretary. Whitelaw sought progress by indicating that the industry's post-OPEC price jump would lead to a review of future pay arrangements, so long as the NUM settled the immediate dispute within the terms of the government's anti-inflationary pay policy.[95] At this point the Trades Union Congress leadership intervened, its General Secretary, Len Murray, advising Heath that the miners were seen by constituent unions as 'distinctive and exceptional'. No others, Murray pledged, would use any settlement reached in the coal industry outwith the pay policy 'as an argument in negotiations for their own settlement'.[96]

The government saw this as an uncertain promise. Heath wrote instead to Gormley on 23 January 1974, asking the NUM to avert a strike that would worsen the most dangerous economic situation since 1945.[97] The union's national executive ignored this and on 31 January and 1 February balloted members for a strike, commencing on 9 February. The vote for strike action was an overwhelming 81 per cent. The government responded by securing the dissolution of Parliament and a General Election on 28 February. Heath wrote to Gormley again, asking the NUM to suspend its overtime ban and the strike so that the election could be held 'in as undisturbed an atmosphere as possible'.[98]

The strike was not averted. Heath, still unable to come to terms with the broad mood of the miners, restated the militant 'conspiracy' view: 'I know that the miners are democrats. It is therefore especially disappointing that the politically motivated arguments of some of their leaders should have prevailed.'[99]

The February 1974 election resulted in a minority Labour government, which then secured a very narrow majority of five seats in the House of Commons at a second election in October 1974. Labour settled the coal dispute. The miners received terms more generous than those allowed under the outgoing government's pay policy, explicitly designed to restore the miners' relative position.[100] In partnership with the NCB and mining unions the Labour government also developed the *Plan For Coal*, a long-term programme of investment in the context of the uncertain energy economics and politics that had unfolded in the oil crisis of 1973.[101] In Scotland 1975 was the highest production year since 1968, and employment remained fairly stable, exceeding 20,000 until 1979.[102] Valleyfield, a large West Fife colliery operating since before the First World War, closed in 1978, but Jimmy Cowan, the outgoing Scottish NCB Area Director, was in 1980 nevertheless optimistic about mining's future in Scotland. The eighteen remaining collieries would be joined by a new pit, Castlebridge in West Fife, which would feed Longannet power station, and further scale economies would be secured through underground link-ups between Bogside and Kinneil, and Seafield and Frances in East Fife.[103]

The changing political economy of coal

Cowan was succeeded as Scottish Area Director by Albert Wheeler, whose initiatives precipitated significant workplace tensions, which are examined in the next chapter. Wheeler's policy resembled in exaggerated form the earlier NCB emphasis on production costs, pit closures and job losses. This strained but did not rupture the moral economy of the coalfields, with its assumptions of joint industrial regulation and income security. In this respect Wheeler's initiatives were a radical departure, pushed through against union and workforce opposition, and in the context of major economic and industrial instability.

Wheeler operated within a political economy of coal greatly altered by the election in 1979 of Thatcher's Conservative government. Conservative thinking was not uniform, as Peter Dorey's study of the party's policy-making between 1974 and 1979 has shown, with some Heath supporters still favouring a conciliatory approach to trade unions and the management of industrial disputes.[104] But the humbling of Heath's government stimulated a powerful Thatcherite analysis of the coal industry and trade unionism that became the predominant influence after 1979, conditioning the anti-union policy agenda of the 1980s and into the 1990s.[105] Two initiatives are of note: the 'Ridley Plan', written in June 1977, and leaked to *The Economist* in May 1978, and the 'Stepping Stones' political and communications strategy, developed after 1974. Nicholas Ridley was Industry Minister in the 1970–74 Conservative government, and his proposals for minimising the effects of public sector strike action – appended to a Tory document on nationalised industries – were geared to negating the type of industrial unrest that had embarrassed Heath. Ridley recommended four measures: massive stockpiling of coal reserves, converting power stations to dual coal/oil firing, recruiting non-union road haulage firms to convey coal if a miners' strike was supported by rail workers, and establishing mobile police units to outmanoeuvre flying pickets. Each of these measures was encouraged by the government after 1979, and contributed to the outcome in 1984–85, as Chapter 3 demonstrates, with the strikers' efforts, at Ravenscraig especially, foundering on Ridley's combination of stockpiled coal, road haulage labour (although the drivers were union members) and mobile policing, with electricity generation from non-coal energy sources extending the government's capacity to endure lost coal production.[106]

The 'Stepping Stones' strategy, developed in 1977–78, was, in characteristically Thatcherite fashion, highly 'declinist', offering what some economic historians see as an ideological exaggeration of Britain's economic and industrial difficulties.[107] The ideological purpose of Thatcherite 'declinism' was clear: rebalancing economic power from labour to capital, and in the workplace from employees to employers. With 'Stepping Stones' this involved relating Britain's supposed economic decline to trade union behaviour, with strikes and other forms of industrial action allegedly lowering productivity, preventing technological innovation, and inhibiting entrepreneurial enterprise. This required determined remedial actions by government, to counter the tyranny of collectivist socialism and restore individual autonomy along with business freedom. Coal miners – along with printers – were singled out as embodying the worst elements of abusive, monopoly trade unionism.[108]

This anti-union discourse was sharpened during the 'Winter of Discontent', a sequence of industrial disputes from October 1978 to March 1979. These involved various groups of workers in different employment and industrial settings, although most revolved around a common theme: the reluctance of manual workers to accept the Labour government's anti-inflationary wage controls. These weighed most heavily on the low paid by admitting only a flat rate increase of five per cent in 1978–79.[109] The Labour government was brought down by a vote of no confidence in the House of Commons, after its proposals for devolution in Scotland and Wales had foundered in referendums held at the beginning of March. Leading the vote of no confidence, Thatcher claimed that Labour had failed to reverse economic decline, and connived in the collapse, as she put it, of law and order. Significantly, in terms of future industrial politics, she said this was not just the escalation of criminality and violence, but also encompassed the refusal of people to accept authority and direction, including in the workplace.[110]

Thatcher's government did not initiate an immediate transformation of industrial politics. The Employment Secretary, Jim Prior, like others in the Cabinet, was an associate of Heath, and keen to maintain dialogue with trade union as well as business leaders. Changes in industrial relations law emerged only slowly, therefore, although the incremental process of reform was nevertheless consistent with the Thatcherite 'Stepping Stones' strategy. There was separate legislation in 1980 and 1982, defining controls on numbers of pickets, and then narrowing the legality of strike action to those directly engaged in an industrial dispute with their immediate employer. This made it potentially very difficult to pursue 'sympathetic action', and was followed by legislation obliging unions to hold ballots of members in advance of strikes, and adhere to tighter regulation of internal union matters, including the election of union leaders and the administration of political funds. This passed through Parliament in the summer of 1984, during the miners' strike.[111]

But while changes in industrial relations law emerged only gradually, shifts in economic conditions – shaped by deliberate government policy – were immediate and had a direct bearing on industrial politics. The budgets of 1979 and 1980, squeezing the money supply and inflation, involved a substantial slowing in economic activity, and accelerated the increase of unemployment. Public expenditure savings contributed to the first major industrial dispute of the Thatcher years, in the nationalised steel industry. Thatcher's government had appointed Ian MacGregor to chair the BSC, and in 1980 it announced the loss of 52,000 jobs, roughly one-third of employment in the sector. A national strike by members of the Iron and Steel Trades Confederation (ISTC) ensued in the first three months of 1980, which was settled with an offer of improved wages but little prospect of saving the jobs. The ISTC leadership was cowed partly by the escalation of unemployment, which continued to rise in 1980 and 1981.[112] 'Rationalisation' in steel continued relentlessly, with employment in the industry reduced from roughly 166,000 in 1980 to just 71,000 in 1983.[113] This would have a substantial bearing on the reluctance of steel workers and their union officials to support the miners in 1984–85.

Unemployment crept upwards, peaking above 4 million in 1984–85. The costs of maintaining the unemployed were by this time roughly equivalent to revenues derived by the UK government from oil production in the North Sea, which had been coming onshore since 1975.[114] The North Sea bounty was also eliminating rather than creating manufacturing jobs, because increased government revenue boosted the relative international value of sterling in currency markets, thereby reducing the price competitiveness of UK exports.[115] In this way oil, already a major energy rival to coal, placed additional pressure on the miners, with joblessness – stimulated and financed by the North Sea developments – a key labour-disciplining instrument. The miners voted nationally not to strike for improved wages and against closures in November 1982. 'Fear of the dole queue', concluded The Economist, which supported the government's shackles on unions, was 'forcing miners and others to toe the line'.[116]

Job threats in the coalfields arose from the 1980 Coal Industry Act, which effectively replaced the 1974 Labour government's expansionist Plan For Coal. This illustrated the new position by establishing the desired objective of ending state subsidy by 1983–84.[117] This, the industry's official historian writes, was 'almost impossible' to achieve. Revenues were dropping with the recession-induced fall in industrial demand for coal, but the NCB still had to invest heavily to modernise capital stock. Rising unemployment, especially in manufacturing, made it more difficult to remove 'surplus' NCB labour through redundancy,[118] a problem accentuated by the relatively young age profile of the workforce with ever fewer miners aged 50 and over remaining by the early 1980s. Aligning production with demand would therefore be expensive, to the NCB and the government, in terms of significantly enhanced redundancy terms to younger miners, and to the coalfield communities denuded of well-paid employment.[119]

The social costs of the Coal Industry Act were strongly criticised by Labour's parliamentary spokesmen, David Owen and Alex Eadie, in private talks with the NCB and in the House of Commons,[120] and by mining unions in discussions with the NCB, the NUM stating its absolute opposition to pit closures on market or economic grounds.[121] McGahey, at the Scottish Miners' Gala in Edinburgh in June 1980, and the NUMSA Conference that followed at Rothesay, promised that closures would be resisted by a 'mass campaign in the coal-field'.[122] Conflict duly mounted in the autumn and winter of 1980–81, through the conduct of annual pay negotiations. When the NCB admitted that large-scale pit closures were being considered, McGahey and other NUMSA officials denounced the NCB's pay offer as 'Tory wage restraint', and criticised the union national executive's recommendation that it be accepted as a 'sell-out'. In a ballot of NUM members 56 per cent of votes cast were in favour of accepting the offer. This result encompassed substantial area variations, outlined in Table 1.2, which might be interpreted as the outcome of new area-based pay incentives introduced by the NCB in 1977–78, against union opposition in Kent, South Wales, Yorkshire and Scotland. This weakened the potential for cross-coalfield union solidarity and action on wages, as the NCB intended and union dissenters predicted. It should be noted, however, that area differences on the value of incentives were in themselves a reflection of contrasting area political cultures, which the differential ballot result further illustrated.[123]

Table 1.2 NUM ballot on NCB pay offer, selected areas, November 1980

Area	Percentage against
Scotland	73.0
South Wales	67.2
Yorkshire	64.6
Kent	59.3
Nottinghamshire	22.7
Midlands	21.3
NUM Aggregate	44.0

Source: Scottish Miner, December 1980.

The NCB's response to the Coal Industry Act and falling demand for coal then provoked a major crisis in February 1981. Money for continued capital investment would be found through increased sales, achieved by lowering unit costs and more competitive marketing, but to match supply with demand ten million tonnes per annum of capacity would be removed,[124] equating perhaps to fifty pit closures and 30,000 job losses over the next five years. In Scotland those pits endangered included Cardowan, along with Highhouse and Sorn in Ayrshire,[125] but there were unofficial protest strikes at all Scottish pits, and many in England and Wales too. McGahey said that pithead meetings would be convened to make the Scottish strike official, after Wheeler told him that Cardowan, Sorn and Highhouse would definitely close.[126] With the NUM executive agreeing unanimously to ballot for a national strike, pushed by the determined popular militancy of the coalfields,[127] the government announced a surprise change of direction. This reflected the scale of the potential crisis, with railway workers and steel workers intimating their intention to support the miners. In Scotland a meeting of the 'Triple Alliance' – union representatives of coal miners, rail and steel workers – was convened on 16 February, with Andy Barr of the National Union of Railwaymen (NUR) indicating that his members would not cross NUM and SCEBTA picket lines, and Clive Lewis of the ISTC pronouncing his members' '100 per cent' support for the miners.[128] This would have been an early major test of the secondary action and picketing provisions of the 1980 Employment Act. Thatcher detailed David Howell, Secretary of State for Energy, to hold talks with the NCB and the NUM, after which it was announced that cash limits, including the requirement to break even by 1983–84, would be reviewed, and coal imports reduced. The unofficial strikes ended within two days.[129]

Michael McGahey, reflecting, perhaps, on his own family history, with his father victimised after the 1926 lockout, counselled against interpreting this outcome as a victory. He likened Thatcher's retreat to the 'Red Friday' episode of 1925,[130] when Stanley Baldwin's Conservative government prevented a national coal strike by financing extant wages for twelve months. During this period the government then organised the emergency apparatus that broke the lockout and General Strike that followed the termination of the subsidy.[131] NUMSA acted on the assumption that a crisis had been postponed rather than averted, formalising shortly afterwards the Triple Alliance with the railway and steel workers in Scotland.[132] Meetings of relevant union officials were duly held every three months or so in the course of 1981 and 1982. Addressing one of these, in June 1981, McGahey said that the NCB and the government wished to dispense with the coalfields of Scotland, Wales and Kent, and concentrate operations on Yorkshire, Nottinghamshire and Derbyshire. The Scottish coalfields had to be protected, through investment, especially in the Kincardine area, and the combined 'vigilance' and combativity of the Triple Alliance.[133]

McGahey was right about the Thatcher government's motives in 1981. While the Coal Industry Act's break-even goal was moderated by further legislation in 1982 and 1983,[134] the 'Ridley Plan'-inspired policing initiatives were developed and the movement of coal, including increased imports, by non-union road haulage firms planned. The process of stockpiling coal, to weaken a future strike, was accelerated after the 1981 crisis by a new Secretary of State for Energy, Nigel Lawson.[135] Lawson further increased pressure on miners, detailing the state-owned power-generating firms to secure cheaper electricity. The trend to increase coal imports was accentuated, together with the pursuit of non-coal electricity generation.[136] The NCB, meanwhile, quietly pursued pit closures at Area level. In the two years from March 1981 twenty were shut, the largest number of closures in a two-year period since 1973–74.[137] The most notable Scottish casualty was Kinneil in West Lothian. This episode, examined in Chapter 2, would mark a very clear breach by NCB management in Scotland of the moral economy of the coalfields, with the pit – in an area of high and rising male unemployment – closed against concerted workforce and union opposition.

The government's interest in securing radically lower costs in the coal industry was then pursued by another route, with the Monopolies and Mergers Commission (MMC), which had a role in scrutinising nationalised industry, appointed to investigate the NCB in March 1982. This investigation, and the report that followed after the 1983 General Election, gave further credence to the increasingly predominant narrative of the industry, articulated, for example, by the Institute of Economic Affairs in 1981, as a high-cost drain on public expenditure, in thrall to politicised and monopolistic trade unionism.[138] The NUM, including McGahey in discussion with Triple Alliance partners in Scotland, correctly anticipated that the MMC Inquiry would strengthen the political pressure for closures on economic grounds.[139] The MMC duly asked the NCB for detailed pit-level data on labour costs, production costs and output. This material, showing losses at numerous pits, especially in Scotland, Northumberland, Durham, South Wales and Kent, was leaked to the NUM, just when it was conducting the strike ballot over predicted closures and the annual pay offer in October 1982. There was a decisive national majority of 61 per cent against strike action, although this encompassed majorities in favour in four areas: Kent and Scotland, both with 69 per cent, South Wales, with 59, and Yorkshire, with 56. The position in Scotland is explored in more detail in Chapter 2. Scargill, recently elected NUM President, argued that the leaked MMC papers amounted to a closure 'hit list'. The NCB tried to de-emphasise the significance of the data, describing it in talks with the NUM as 'research material' rather than strategic planning.[140] Norman Siddall, NCB chairman, had nevertheless asked Area Directors before this meeting to comment on the position, and Wheeler replied by arguing for the closure of Highhouse, Sorn and Killoch – also in Ayrshire – and Cardowan, all 'heavy losers'.[141] The NUM then obtained and published a new 'hit list', of 55 pits, which in Scotland included Kinneil along with the four identified by Wheeler.[142] NUM officials protested by boycotting the industry's National Consultative Council from November 1982 to March 1983,[143] and union representatives across the coalfields likewise refused to attend pit-level consultative committees.

The MMC findings, submitted to the government before Christmas 1982,[144] were eventually published after the General Election – won by the Conservatives with a substantially increased majority – in June 1983. A 10 per cent cut in capacity was recommended, through closing pits with the highest losses per tonne.[145] Rising labour costs were described as worsening the industry's unprofitability. Wages as a proportion of production costs had been increasing since the early 1970s, with miners making full use of the market advantages conferred by the escalating cost of oil relative to coal.[146] This can be understood as rational economic behaviour, combined with the desire within the NUM and among miners generally to make good the remembered injustices of falling relative wages and closures in the 1960s.[147] But the MMC related these wage movements to the structure and composition of NCB management, with too many 'home-grown mining engineers' allegedly crowding out the potentially liberating presence of cost-controlling business executives from private industry.[148] Perhaps this especially is why Ian MacGregor described the report as his 'bible'.[149] MacGregor's appointment coincided more or less directly with the publication of the MMC report, in the summer of 1983, and embodied the radical changes to the political economy of coal. His authoritarian and anti-union approach to industrial politics, shaped by the pre-Second World War mentoring influence of Sir James Lithgow, the Clydeside shipbuilder, and honed by thirty years in US business, had become more immediately evident in the early 1980s with his chairmanship of BSC.[150]

The MMC report emphasised – as McGahey had forecast – the particularly uncompetitive nature of the 'peripheral coal-mining Areas'.[151] The NCB's Area-incentive schemes, unpopular as they were in Kent, South Wales, Yorkshire and Scotland, had not secured an overall improvement in productivity. Incentive earnings tended to be greater in areas where productivity was already higher, notably in Nottinghamshire. To the industry's official historian this suggested that 'low productivity may encourage habits and practices that tend to prolong it even when opportunities for change arise'.[152] But critics of the incentive schemes observed that area bonus differentials essentially reflected the comparative ease of coal-getting in more 'productive' areas, rather than the efforts expended, say, by Scottish as opposed to Nottinghamshire miners.[153] The authors of 'The Aberystwyth Report on Coal', published in 1983 by the University College of Wales's Economic History Department, reinforced this perspective. They related variable pit-level productivity to differential rates of investment and the relative difficulty of geological conditions.[154]

An even more fundamental academic challenge to the new political economy of coal was provided by Andrew Glyn, of Corpus Christi College, Oxford. His central argument, published by the NUM during the strike, was that NCB data on costs and losses were fundamentally misleading. They included several large items that were not connected to the ongoing economic cost of producing coal. There were high interest payments to the government on capital loans, which at 6.3 per cent per annum were twice the average rate for nationalised industry; and there were 'transfer payments' associated with past activities, notably compensation for subsidence and pensions to retired employees, along with 'social costs', mainly redundancy payments. These swallowed up more or less the entirety of the government's £1.3 billion subsidy to cover NCB 'losses' in 1983–84. Glyn further challenged the economic case for closures by pointing to the broader social costs of 'non-production', with redundancy payments followed by unemployment maintenance, coupled with lost multiplier effects in coalfield areas.[155]

Glyn's analysis, adapted slightly and applied to the Scottish industry by George Kerevan and Richard Saville,[156] was against the tide of predominant thinking about the coal industry and, of course, the broader, politicised economic discourse of the 1980s, which emphasised the virtues of competition, industrial and labour market restructuring, trade union 'reforms' and a slimmer role for state enterprise.[157] The domination of the Thatcherite narratives, encompassing the equation – as Glyn put it – of 'unprofitable' with 'uneconomic',[158] was such that economic arguments against coal closures had little impact on public and media opinion during the strike.[159] At pit level, however, at least in Scotland, these narratives unexpectedly and positively influenced strike commitment, as Chapter 4 will demonstrate in detail. The pits where production was most 'economic', or 'least unprofitable', were those which fed the Longannet power station. They would also be the pits where strike commitment was strongest, suggesting that good – or in a Scottish context, relatively good – economic performance amounted to a solid material resource, with long-term value, in defence of which strikers could be mobilised.

Conclusion

Coalfield communities and industrial politics in Scotland evolved substantially from the late 1940s to the early 1980s. The process of industrial restructuring in the 1950s and 1960s, concentrating production in a smaller number of larger collieries, had loosened the connection between community and workplace. There was only one 'traditional' village pit in Scotland by 1982, Polmaise in Fallin, Stirlingshire, with the great majority of miners travelling within – and sometimes between – extended and reconstructed mining communities, to work mainly in the 'cosmopolitan' collieries opened by the NCB since nationalisation in 1947. This may have indirectly reduced the neighbourly solidarity of the coalfields. But wider processes of economic and social change were at work also, and these included the development in coalfield communities of local authority housing and the provision of wider employment opportunities for women. These material resources, embedded in communities, would prove vital in building pit-level strike endurance in 1984–85. Restructuring resulted, moreover, in changes in industrial politics that strengthened industrial 'militancy' and encouraged workplace solidarity. In Scotland a new generation of trade union officials emerged in the coalfields in the 1960s, elected by miners who were disaffected by declining wages, and the related sequence from the late 1950s of pit closures, transfers and job losses. These officials, of whom the most noteworthy was Michael McGahey, NUMSA President from 1967, were more 'militant' than their immediate predecessors, in that they were not prepared to tolerate the further retrenchment of the coal industry. They campaigned in devolutionary as well as class terms, seeing the managed decline of their industry from NCB headquarters in London as symptomatic of a broader deficiency in UK life, the remote administration of power. A Scottish Parliament would make government in Scotland more accountable to the workers in Scotland.

Closures and job losses created tensions in the coalfields, shaping the national disputes of the early 1970s as well as the unofficial disputes of the 1960s and the emergence of the McGahey generation of union officials. It is important to remember, however, that restructuring before the 1980s was generally secured by joint industrial agreement. It also resulted in no permanent loss of economic security. Miners at pits that closed were able to find alternative employment, within the industry, or in relatively well-paid manual employment elsewhere. This meant that the moral economy of the coalfields was tested but not broken before 1980. The opposite was true thereafter, with closures by unilateral managerial decision, and in the context of rapidly escalating manual unemployment. The transformed political economy of coal had special implications for the industry in Scotland, with its particularly 'marginal' and 'loser' components. The Thatcherite analysis grossly offended the moral economy of Scottish miners, but found a willing adherent in Albert Wheeler, the NCB's Area Director in Scotland from 1980. Wheeler's cost-controlling and anti-union initiatives, and the resistance they encountered at pit- and Area-level, shaped the outbreak of the 1984–85 strike, and are analysed in the following chapter.

Notes

1 Adeney and Lloyd, *Miners' Strike*, pp. 15–20, 78–9.

2 Alan Campbell, 'Scotland', in McIlroy, Campbell and Gildart, *Industrial Politics*, pp. 179, 184–7.

3 *Scottish Miner*, April 1975.

4 Ella Egan, Interview with Willie Thompson, 28 October 1985.

5 Jimmy Reid, Obituary of Michael McGahey, the *Herald*, 2 February 1999.

6 Terry Pattinson, Obituary of Michael McGahey, the *Independent*, 1 February 1999; Arthur McIvor and Hugh Paterson, 'Combating the Left: Victimisation and Anti-Labour Activities on Clydeside, 1900–1939', in Robert Duncan and Arthur McIvor (eds), *Labour and Class Conflict on the Clyde, 1900–1950* (Edinburgh, 1992), pp. 129–54; McGahey's experience is noted on p. 140.

7 John McIlroy and Alan Campbell, 'Beyond Betteshanger: Order 1305 in the Scottish Coalfields during the Second World War, Part 1: Politics, Prosecutions and Protest', *Historical Studies in Industrial Relations*, 15 (2003), 27–72, and 'Part 2: The Cardowan Story', *Historical Studies in Industrial Relations*, 16 (2003), 39–80.

8 Obituary of Michael McGahey, *The Times*, 1 February 1999; John McIlroy and Alan Campbell, 'McGahey, Michael (Mick), (1925–1999)', in Keith Gildart and David Howell, *Dictionary of Labour Biography. Volume XIII* (Houndmills, 2010), pp. 242–51.

9 Mick McGahey, Penicuik, in Owens, *Miners*, pp. 82–3.

10 Campbell, 'Scotland', in McIlroy, Campbell and Gildart, *Industrial Politics*, pp. 179, 184–7.

11 Alan Campbell, 'Reflections on the 1926 Mining Lockout', *Historical Studies in Industrial Relations*, 21 (2006), 181.

12 Chalmers, Interview.
13 Alex Nicholson, Interview, 8 March 2011.
14 John McIlroy, 'Finale: A View from a New Century', in McIlroy, Campbell and Gildart, *Industrial Politics*, pp. 308–9.
15 Eric Clarke, Interview.
16 Andrew Taylor, *The NUM and British Politics. Volume 1: 1944–1968* (Aldershot, 2003).
17 Andrew Perchard, *The Mine Management Professions in the Twentieth-Century Scottish Coal Mining Industry* (Lampeter and Lewiston, 2007).
18 Taylor, *NUM and British Politics. Volume 2*, pp. 1–12.
19 *Scottish Miner*, June and November 1962.
20 Miles K. Oglethorpe, *Scottish Collieries. An Inventory of the Scottish Coal Industry in the Nationalised Era* (Edinburgh, 2006), pp. 20, 316.
21 Alf Robens, *Ten Year Stint* (London, 1972), *passim*, but especially 'Battling for Business', pp. 58–87, and 'Getting the Coal', pp. 88–108.
22 *Nobody's Face*, NCB Film Unit, 1966, produced by Francis Gysin, directed by Peter Pickering, commentary by Ewan MacColl. The film is preserved by the BFI National Archive, and features on the DVD two-disc set, *National Coal Board Collection, Volume One, Portrait of a Miner* (London, 2009).
23 Martin Chick, 'Time, Water and Capital: The Unintended Contribution of the North of Scotland Hydro-Electric Board to the Application of Welfare Economics in Britain, 1943–1967', *Scottish Business and Industrial History*, 25 (2009), 29–55.
24 Ashworth, *British Coal Industry*, pp. 38–9, 678–9.
25 Oglethorpe, *Scottish Collieries*, p. 20.
26 Robin Denselow, 'MacColl, Ewan (formerly James Miller), (1915–1989)', in H.C.G. Matthew and Brian Harrison (eds), *Oxford Dictionary of National Biography* (Oxford, 2004), pp. 138–9.
27 *New Power In Their Hands*, NCB Film Unit, 1959, written and produced by David Alexander, directed by Alun Falconer, visualised and edited by Kitty Wood, commentary by Ewan MacColl. The film features on *Portrait of a Miner*.
28 Oglethorpe, *Scottish Collieries*, pp. 70–1, 83–4, 153–4, 159, 170–1.
29 Fife Pits: www.users.zetnet.co.uk/mmartin/fifepits/starter/east/pits/s/pit-6.htm, accessed 7 February 2011.
30 Arthur McIvor and Ronald Johnston, *Miners' Lung: A History of Dust Disease in British Coal Mining* (Aldershot, 2007), pp. 151, 244 and 249; Andrew Perchard, 'The Mine Management Professions and the Dust Problem in the Scottish Coal Mining Industry, c. 1930–1966', *Scottish Labour History*, 40 (2005), 87–110.
31 Andrew Perchard and Jim Phillips, 'Transgressing the Moral Economy: Wheelerism and Management of the Nationalised Coal Industry in Scotland', *Contemporary British History*, 25 (2011), 395.
32 'Replanning a Coalfield', *Mining Review*, 2nd Year, No. 10 (1949), directed by Peter Pickering, produced for Data Film Productions, sponsored by NCB, with commentary spoken by John Slater. The film features on *Portrait of a Miner*.
33 Hazel Heughan, *Pit Closures at Shotts and the Migration of Miners* (Edinburgh, 1953).
34 Oglethorpe, *Scottish Collieries*, pp. 133–4, 153, 167.
35 Ian Terris, *Twenty Years Down the Mines* (Ochiltree, 2001), pp. 111–12.
36 Stuart Macintyre, *Little Moscows: Communism and Working-class Militancy in Inter-war Britain* (London, 1980), pp. 48–78.
37 Chalmers, Interview.

38 William Thompson, 'The New Left in Scotland', in Ian MacDougall (ed.), *Essays in Scottish Labour History* (Edinburgh, 1978), pp. 208–9.

39 Willie Clarke, Interview.

40 Terris, *Down the Mines*, pp. 24–93.

41 Nicholson, Interview.

42 Guthrie Hutton, *Fife – the Mining Kingdom* (Ochiltree, 1999), pp. 6–8.

43 Tam Coulter, Interview with Willie Thompson, 28 January 1986.

44 Iain McCaig, Interview with Willie Thompson, 12 March 1986.

45 Hamilton, Interview.

46 Rab Amos, Interview, 23 February 2011.

47 Wilson, Interview.

48 Oglethorpe, *Scottish Collieries*, pp. 65–6.

49 Norman Dennis, Fernando Henriques and Clifford Slaughter, *Coal Is Our Life. An Analysis of a Yorkshire Mining Community* (2nd edition, London, 1969, originally 1956), pp. 10, 17.

50 Clark Kerr and Abraham Siegal, 'The Inter-Industry Propensity to Strike – An International Comparison', in A. Kornhauser, R. Dubin and A.M. Ross (eds), *Industrial Conflict* (New York, 1954), pp. 189–212.

51 David Gilbert, *Class, Community and Collective Action. Social Change in Two British Coalfields, 1850–1926* (Oxford, 1992), pp. 10–16.

52 Mancur Olson, *The Logic of Collective Action. Public Goods and the Theory of Groups* (Cambridge, Mass., 1965), pp. 66–97

53 Gilbert, *Class, Community and Collective Action*, pp. 33–8, 43–6.

54 Campbell, *Scottish Miners. Volume One*, pp. 159–212.

55 Daniel Wight, *Workers Not Wasters. Masculine Respectability, Consumption and Employment in Central Scotland* (Edinburgh, 1993).

56 Charlie Goodfellow, Interview, 12 August 2009.

57 Thompson, 'Moral Economy'.

58 *Scottish Miner*, April 1967.

59 Chalmers, Interview.

60 Oglethorpe, *Scottish Collieries*, pp. 317–18.

61 England, *The Wales TUC*, *passim*, especially pp. 6–16.

62 Robert Taylor, 'The Heath Government and Industrial Relations: Myth and Reality', in Stuart Ball and Anthony Seldon (eds), *The Heath Government, 1970–1974: A Reappraisal* (London, 1996), pp. 161–90.

63 Ashworth, *British Coal Industry*, pp. 289–315; Andy Beckett, *When the Lights Went Out. What Really Happened to Britain in the Seventies* (London, 2009), pp. 53–87; Edward Heath, *The Course of My Life. My Autobiography* (London, 1998), pp. 325–53; Kevin Jefferys, *Finest and Darkest Hours. The Decisive Events in British Politics from Churchill to Blair* (London, 2002), pp. 162–85; Morgan, *People's Peace*, pp. 325–56; Taylor, *NUM and British Politics. Volume 2*, pp. vii–viii, 50–72.

64 Margaret Thatcher, *The Path to Power* (London, 1995), pp. 201–22.

65 Routledge, *Scargill*, pp. 78–9.

66 Robert Taylor, 'McGahey, Michael (Mick), (1925–1999)', in Matthew and Harrison, *Oxford Dictionary of National Biography*, pp. 390–1; *Glasgow Herald*, 20 November and 2 December 1968; *Scottish Miner*, October and November 1967.

67 Tony Hall, *King Coal: Miners, Coal and Britain's Industrial Future* (Harmondsworth, 1981), pp. 166–96; Dave Lyddon and Ralph Darlington, *Glorious Summer. Class Struggle in Britain in 1972* (London, 2001) pp. 31–74; Malcolm Pitt, *The World on our*

Backs: The Kent Miners and the 1972 Miners' Strike (London, 1979).

68 *Scottish Miner*, May 1971; *The Times*, 25 April and 4 July 1973.

69 Willie Clarke, Interview.

70 Jim Phillips, 'The 1972 Miners' Strike: Popular Agency and Industrial Politics in Britain', *Contemporary British History*, 20 (2006), 187–207.

71 Phillips, *Industrial Politics of Devolution*, pp. 38–9, 104–5.

72 John Foster, 'The Twentieth Century, 1914–1979', in R.A. Houston and W.W.J. Knox (eds), *The New Penguin History of Scotland* (London, 2001), pp. 467–72.

73 Committee of Inquiry appointed by the Scottish Council (Development and Industry) under the Chairmanship of J.N. Toothill, *Report on the Scottish Economy* (Edinburgh, 1961).

74 W. Knox, 'Class, Work and Trade Unionism in Scotland', in A. Dickson and J.H. Treble (eds), *People and Society in Scotland. Volume III, 1914–1990* (Edinburgh, 1994), p. 111.

75 Pavlos Dimitratos, Ioanna Liouka, Duncan Ross and Stephen Young, 'The Multinational Enterprise and Subsidiary Evolution', *Business History*, 51 (2009), 401–25.

76 Ian MacDougall, *Voices From Work and Home* (Edinburgh, 2000), pp. 134–7.

77 Peter L. Payne, *Colvilles and the Scottish Steel Industry* (Oxford, 1979), pp. 374–83.

78 David Howell, *A Lost Left. Three Studies in Socialism and Nationalism* (Manchester, 1986), pp. 7–13.

79 Willie Clarke, Interview.

80 Phillips, *Industrial Politics of Devolution*, pp. 104–5.

81 John Foster and Charles Woolfson, *The Politics of the UCS Work-In: Class Alliances and the Right to Work* (London, 1986).

82 *Scottish Miner*, December 1971.

83 Hamilton, Interview.

84 Amos, Interview; Willie Clarke, Interview; John McCormack, Fallin, in Owens, *Miners*, p. 115.

85 Homer Sykes: http://homersykes.photoshelter.com/gallery/GRUNWICK-STRIKE -STOCK-IMAGES-PHOTOS-PHOTOGRAPHY-LONDON-1977–1970s-UK /G0000MmrftXBGUt0, accessed 7 February 2011.

86 Beckett, *When the Lights Went Out*, pp. 358–403.

87 Phillips, *Industrial Politics of Devolution*, pp. 136–7.

88 Willie Clarke, Interview.

89 Eric Clarke, Interview.

90 *The Times*, 24 May 1972.

91 Phillips, *Industrial Politics of Devolution*, pp. 137–9.

92 The National Archives, Kew (hereafter TNA), PREM 15/2127, Prime Minister's Office, notes, no date.

93 John Campbell, *Edward Heath. A Biography* (London, 1993), pp. 574–97; Jefferys, *Finest and Darkest Hours*, pp. 168–78; Morgan, *People's Peace*, pp. 346–9; Routledge, *Scargill*, pp. 90–5; McIlroy and Campbell, 'McGahey', 246; Vic Allen, Obituary of Michael McGahey, the *Guardian*, 1 February 1999.

94 Beckett, *When the Lights Went Out*, pp. 130–50.

95 TNA, PREM 15/2126, Note of Meeting between Secretary of State for Employment and Representatives of the NUM, 20 December 1973, and Note of Meeting between Secretary of State for Employment and the NUM National Executive, 9 January 1974.

96 TNA, PREM 15/2126, Lionel Murray to Edward Heath, 10 January 1974.

97 TNA, PREM 15/2127, Heath to Gormley, 23 January 1974.

98 TNA, PREM 15/2128, Heath to Gormley, 7 February 1974.

99 TNA, PREM 15/2128, Statement by the Prime Minister, 8 February 1974.

100 Phillip Whitehead, *The Writing on the Wall. Britain in the Seventies* (London, 1985), pp. 110–15, 123–33.

101 Taylor, *NUM and British Politics. Volume 2*, pp. 113–7.

102 Oglethorpe, *Scottish Collieries*, p. 20.

103 Perchard and Phillips, 'Transgressing the Moral Economy'.

104 Peter Dorey, 'Conciliation or Confrontation with the Trade Unions? The Conservative Party's "Authority of Government Group", 1975–1978', *Historical Studies in Industrial Relations*, 27/28 (2009), 135–51.

105 Howell, *Trade Unions and the State*, 131–73.

106 Saville, 'An Open Conspiracy', 295–301.

107 David Edgerton, 'The Decline of Declinism', *Business History Review*, 71 (1997), 201–7; Jim Tomlinson, *The Politics of Decline: Understanding Post-war Britain* (Harlow, 2000).

108 Andrew Taylor, 'The "Stepping Stones" Programme: Conservative Party Thinking on Trade Unions, 1975–9', *Historical Studies in Industrial Relations*, 11 (2001), 109–25.

109 Taylor, *Trade Union Question*, pp. 250–62.

110 *Parliamentary Debates, Fifth Series, Commons*, 965, 463–9, 28 March 1979.

111 Taylor, *Trade Union Question*, pp. 299–302.

112 Steel, *Reasons to be Cheerful*, pp. 73–80.

113 M.W. Kirby, 'MacGregor, Sir Ian Kinloch (1912–1998)', in Matthew and Harrison, *Dictionary of National Biography*, pp. 433–5.

114 Christopher Harvie, *Fool's Gold: The Story of North Sea Oil* (Harmondsworth, 1994); Theo Nichols, *The British Worker Question. A New Look at Workers and Productivity in Manufacturing* (London, 1986), p. 237.

115 G.C. Peden, 'The Managed Economy: Scotland, 1919–2000', in T.M. Devine, C.H. Lee and G.C. Peden (eds), *The Transformation of Scotland: The Economy Since 1700* (Edinburgh, 2005), 261.

116 'Pit Ponies Don't Jump Fences', *The Economist*, 6 November 1982, pp. 21–2.

117 Routledge, *Scargill*, pp. 103–5.

118 Ashworth, *British Coal Industry*, pp. 414–15.

119 Ned Smith, *The 1984 Miners' Strike. The Actual Account* (Whitstable, 1997), pp. 12–15.

120 TNA, COAL 30/615, Note of Discussion between Sir Derek Ezra, NCB Chairman, and Labour Party Representatives, 3 June 1980; *Parliamentary Debates, Fifth Series, Commons*, 986, 1387–93, 1455–61, 17 June 1980.

121 TNA, COAL 31/262, Minutes of a Meeting between the NCB and the National Executive Committee of the NUM, Hobart House, 18 June 1980.

122 *The Times*, 2 June 1980; *Scottish Miner*, June–July 1980.

123 Winterton and Winterton, *Coal, Crisis and Conflict*, pp. 15–17.

124 Ashworth, *British Coal Industry*, pp. 416–17.

125 *The Times*, 11 and 19 February 1981.

126 *Scottish Miner*, February 1981.

127 SMM, NUMSA, Minute of Conference of Delegates, 20 February 1981.

128 *Scottish Miner*, February 1981.

129 'How the Coalmen Defeated the Government', *The Economist*, 21 February 1981, pp. 35–6.

130 *Scottish Miner*, February 1981.
131 McIlroy, Campbell and Gildart, 'Introduction', in McIlroy, Campbell and Gildart, *Industrial Politics*, pp. 1–11.
132 National Library of Scotland (hereafter NLS), Acc. 9805/263, Eric Clarke, General Secretary, NUM (Scottish Area) to J. O'Connor, NACODS, 26 February 1981.
133 NLS, Acc. 9805/263, Minute of Meeting of Triple Alliance held in the Board Room of Edinburgh Trades Council on Friday 26 June 1981.
134 Winterton and Winterton, *Coal, Crisis and Conflict*, pp. 20–2.
135 Taylor, *NUM and British Politics. Volume 2*, pp. 155–62.
136 Adeney and Lloyd, *Miners' Strike*, pp. 78–9.
137 Ashworth, *British Coal Industry*, pp. 418–19.
138 Colin Robinson and Eileen Marshall, *What Future for British Coal? Optimism or Realism on the Prospects to the Year 2000* (London, 1981).
139 NLS, Acc. 9805/263, Minute of Meeting of Triple Alliance, NUMSA offices, Edinburgh, Tuesday 4 May 1982.
140 TNA, COAL 31/264, Statement to be made by Mr Siddall to the meeting with the NUM on 23 November 1982 on Mr Scargill's 'Disclosures' on Colliery Closure.
141 TNA, COAL 31/824, Wheeler to Siddall, 16 November 1982.
142 *The Times*, 24 and 27 November 1982.
143 TNA, COAL 74/4783, CINCC, 9 November 1982, 11 January 1983, 1 February 1983, 8 March 1983, 10 May 1983.
144 TNA, COAL 74/4783, CINCC, 1 February 1983.
145 The Monopolies and Mergers Commission (hereafter MMC), *National Coal Board. A Report on the Efficiency and Costs in the Development, Production and Supply of Coal by the National Coal Board. Cmnd. 8920, Volume One* (HMSO, 1983), pp. 363–6.
146 Robinson and Marshall, *British Coal*, pp. 23–8, 51–2.
147 Eric Clarke, Interview.
148 MMC, *National Coal Board, Volume One*, pp. 380–2.
149 Adeney and Lloyd, *Miners' Strike*, pp. 23, 27.
150 Ewen A. Cameron, *Impaled Upon a Thistle. Scotland Since 1880* (Edinburgh, 2010), p. 329; Kirby, 'MacGregor'.
151 MMC, *National Coal Board, Volume One*, p. 178.
152 Ashworth, *British Coal Industry*, pp. 371–3.
153 Winterton and Winterton, *Coal, Crisis and Conflict*, pp. 15–17.
154 T. Cutler, C. Haslam, J. Williams and K. Williams, 'The Aberystwyth Report on Coal', in D. Cooper and T. Hopper (eds), *Debating Coal Closures: Economic Calculation in the Coal Dispute, 1984–5* (Cambridge, 1988), pp. 161–94.
155 A. Glyn, 'The Economic Case Against Pit Closures', in Cooper and Hopper, *Debating Coal Closures*, pp. 57–94.
156 G. Kerevan and R. Saville, 'The Economic Case for Deep-Mined Coal in Scotland', in Cooper and Hopper, *Debating Coal Closures*, pp. 119–60.
157 Will Hutton, *The State We're In* (London, 1995), pp. 89–110.
158 Glyn, 'Economic Case Against Pit Closures', p. 75.
159 Adeney and Lloyd, *Miners' Strike*, pp. 24, 252–3; Saville, 'An Open Conspiracy', 317–21.

2

Closures and workplace conflict: the origins of the strike

The deep roots of the 1984–85 strike were located in the long process of industrial and social restructuring that was examined in the previous chapter. The pressures on Scottish miners arising from this, with increased managerial control in pursuit of cheaper production, intensified further in the early 1980s, and resulted in a sequence of pit-level disputes. These were the more immediate origins of the 1984–85 strike. Miners facing pit closures, and troubled by managerial incursions on established joint industrial regulation of daily mining operations, pressed their unions to adopt an assertive collective response. This chapter establishes the significance of this workplace conflict, mounting in 1982 and 1983, and subverts the predominant view in the literature that the strike was forced on the workforce by the NUM's 'politically-motivated' leadership. Scottish developments in this respect were crucial, shaping the national strike constructed on workforce resistance to the closure of 'uneconomic' pits. Collieries in Scotland were highly vulnerable on these grounds. At the peak level joint industrial talks on 6 March 1984 that immediately preceded the strike, the NCB presented unions with materials purporting to forecast an overall deep-mining loss of £105.4 million on the 97.4 million tonnes of coal to be mined in the financial year 1984–85. In excess of half of this deficit – £55.1 million – would arise from extracting just 5.15 million tonnes of coal in the Scottish Area.[1] Market uncertainty shaped a highly adversarial pattern of industrial relations: 50 per cent of miners in Scotland were already engaged in pit-level disputes in March 1984 when the national strike began. These disputes were caused by cost-reducing managerial initiatives that offended the moral economy of the coalfields, encompassing pit closures in the face of workforce opposition, and the abandonment of existing joint industrial procedures. The strike is presented here as a legitimate and roughly democratic union response to the NCB Scottish Area's managerial style and strategy. It was not imposed on the Scottish industry from outside, via the ideological conflict between Conservative government and NUM leadership. Quite the opposite is in fact the case: the strike developed much of its national – that is, UK-wide – momentum from the dispute between management and workers in the Scottish coalfields.[2]

This managerial strategy, shaped by the NCB's Scottish Area Director, Albert Wheeler, was designed to 'test' the miners' militancy. It was developed within the high political context examined in the previous chapter, with the move towards a self-funding industry shaped by Thatcherite coal industry discourses and policies, through the 1980 Coal Industry Act, followed by the 1983 Monopolies and Mergers Commission report on the NCB.[3] The outcome was a strengthening emphasis, encouraged by market changes in energy supply, on reducing costs and tightening managerial control. Scottish pits with relatively expensive production records were targeted by Wheeler, who disturbed existing workplace management–union relations by rotating colliery managers. In 1983 the arrival of new managers at Seafield and Monktonhall was followed very shortly afterwards by a major dispute at each pit. Across the coalfields, including at Monktonhall, stoppages were provoked, sometimes where pre-shift emergency union meetings were discussing managerial attacks on existing agreements. Men who reported several minutes late for work after attending these meetings were locked out and sent home without pay. The established right of union delegates to conduct union business on NCB premises and in working hours was also challenged. This pattern of conflict, which included managerial allegations at several large pits of workforce indolence, absenteeism and declining morale, was instrumental in the outbreak of the strike in March 1984.

Attempts to block Wheeler's strategy – to resist closures as well as managerial authoritarianism – were initiated by workplace activists at various points between December 1982 and March 1984, but could not be converted into official strike action because of divisions among union members. A significant minority of miners were demoralised, and not prepared to risk open conflict. These included a sizeable number of men – perhaps even a majority – at Bilston Glen and the Ayrshire pair of Killoch and Barony. The position was complicated, with NUMSA and SCEBTA officials pushed forward and held back by competing strands of workplace opinion, before eventually securing collective support for a strike against closures. This complexity is immensely important, challenging the standard interpretation of the strike as a top-down phenomenon, forced on miners by their officials, with little or no distinctive Scottish narrative.[4] The strike, it will be shown here, began in Scotland, triggered by the careful union response to the workplace conflict. The chapter develops and extends an earlier analysis of the strike's origins,[5] utilising a wider range of pit-level archive materials and oral history testimonies. It proceeds in two parts, exploring Wheeler's broad approach and the 1980–83 closures, followed by the intensification of workplace tensions and the outbreak of the strike in 1983–84.

Closures and 'Wheelerism', 1980–83

Albert Wheeler became the NCB's Scottish Area Director in 1980. His approach, closing pits and micro-managing pit-level affairs, was not unprecedented in the nationalised coal industry. Scottish Area management recurrently emphasised production imperatives and costs, and over-rode colliery managers and localised interests where these competed with the NCB's broader strategic goals. This was particularly evident, as Chapter 1 indicated, from the late 1950s, when the NCB responded to competition in energy provision with a major programme of closures, halving the size of the workforce, and concentrating production in a small number of larger collieries. The restructuring was accompanied by mechanisation and productivity drives, exerting considerable strain on colliery managers as well as workers.[6] It is important to reiterate, however, that these processes were managed within the terms of the moral economy of the Scottish coalfields: changes, including closures, were generally undertaken with the agreement of union representatives, and economic security was guaranteed for displaced miners, either through transfers to other pits, or with the availability of work elsewhere in the economy. Wheeler's approach, by contrast, transgressed this moral economy: closures from 1982 were driven through against the opposition of NUMSA and SCEBTA; he wanted, indeed, to downgrade the role of unions in managing the industry; and jobs were lost in coal mining just as unemployment was rising steeply across the economy. This approach angered many miners and their supporters, but it was consistent with the ascendant ideological concepts of political economy in the 1980s: the privileging of market competition, diminished public enterprise, and trade union 'reforms' to strengthen managerial agency.[7] In 'management style' terms this encouraged the adoption by managers of what Alan Fox called unitary practices as well as attitudes,[8] with diminished collective bargaining and consultation mechanisms, especially at industry and company level, highly notable features of the post-1979 economic environment. This process is usually understood in terms of private sector developments, particularly in manufacturing,[9] but the analysis here indicates its presence in large measure also in the nationalised coal sector in Scotland under Wheeler.

Wheeler was a personable individual, 'a hand shaker', according to David Hamilton, the NUM delegate at Monktonhall before the strike. He would enter a room and shake hands with all those present, engaging in eye contact and offering words of greeting. This combination of personal courtesy and abrupt managerial directness left a lasting impression on Hamilton, who was elected Labour MP for Midlothian in 2001, succeeding Eric Clarke. In this capacity Hamilton voted against British participation in the US-led invasion of Iraq in March 2003,[10] and says that Wheeler was 'like George Bush', another 'hand shaker'. Hamilton remembers especially an early encounter where a smiling Wheeler shook his hand and said, 'I'm going to break you', meaning the union, in order to drive down costs and enhance profitability in the NCB's Scottish Area.[11]

Similar anti-Wheeler narratives emerge from other trade unionist memories. These are indicative of what oral historians term 'composure', where witnesses construct internally consistent personal and political narratives about the past,[12] in this case to make sense of the decline of Scottish coal mining in general, and the character and outcome of the strike in particular. In this connection, emphasising the culpability of confrontational management, personified by Wheeler, these testimonies also recall Alistair Thomson's 'cultural circuit', where personal memory seems to draw upon a collective narrative. In the process the personal memory then strengthens the persuasive force of the collective narrative.[13] Eric Clarke, NUMSA Secretary during the 1984–85 strike, first met Wheeler, 'a wee insignificant fella fae Leith', at training college in Midlothian. Wheeler had sustained a disability, a 'gammy hand', after an accident underground at Lady Victoria Colliery in Midlothian, before working for the NCB elsewhere, notably as the Deputy Director (Mining) for North Derbyshire.[14] Clarke says that when Wheeler returned to Scotland in 1980 he was tougher, 'flingin his weight about', and unfavourably different from 'old style' senior managers, including his predecessor as Scottish Director, Jimmy Cowan.[15] A similar narrative was articulated in 1986 by Tam Coulter, a NUMSA executive member and union branch secretary at Castlehill. Wheeler was initially 'Mr Nice Guy personified', shaking hands and being verbally pleasant at meetings and social gatherings, before exhibiting his 'true colours'.[16] Nicky Wilson discusses the closure in 1983 of Cardowan, where he was the SCEBTA delegate, in the same discursive manner, emphasising Wheeler's departure from established collaborative customs and social priorities. Cardowan's manager, John Fram, was 'a real Coal Board man', with a sense of obligation to the workforce and local community. He tried to save the pit from closure, and as a result was removed by Wheeler from his post and 'stuck in a Doocot at Green Park', the NCB's Scottish headquarters, until his retirement. Other 'old managers' like Fram, 'good mining engineers', were similarly squeezed out. In their place, to execute his cost-controlling strategy, Wheeler promoted the 'ruthless bastards'.[17] These were a mixture, it might be surmised, of opportunists who sought personal advance by pursuing Wheeler's strategy, and those whose inclination to confront joint industrial control and cost reduction was emboldened by the new position.

Wheeler's strategy was developed in the larger context of the changing political economy of coal, examined in the previous chapter. In the second half of 1982, it will be remembered, the NUM and its new President, Arthur Scargill, averred the existence of an NCB 'hit list' of threatened pits, including several in Scotland. At a meeting with the NCB on 23 September Scargill indicated the union's intention to negotiate simultaneously on pay, pit closures and job losses. This irritated the NCB, which had already prepared an offer in response to an initial claim presented by the NUM in July which was not linked to closures or redundancies.[18] Union pressure on these related issues was advanced by a national overtime ban, commencing on 5 October 1982, agreed by the national executive, which also resolved to ballot the members on a strike on 28 and 29 October.[19]

Pairing closures with the pay claim was designed to maximise support for strike action,[20] and it had a clear logic. Huw Beynon, writing two years later, during the strike, noted that the NCB itself saw the issues as linked, willing to boost earnings of miners in 'profitable' pits on the condition that 'unprofitable' pits were closed. But the union's approach was unsuccessful. Many miners, especially in the English Midlands where closures were not an immediate threat, resented the prospect of losing wages during a strike to protect employment elsewhere.[21] Earnings, moreover, had been temporarily squeezed by the overtime ban. NCB officials saw this as material to the high 'no' votes on the ballot in Nottinghamshire, Leicestershire and Staffordshire, which shaped the national picture, declared at the start of November, with 61 to 39 per cent against industrial action. This outcome closely resembled that of the national ballot in November 1980, with substantial majorities favouring industrial action in Kent, with 69 per cent, Yorkshire, with 56, South Wales, with 59, and Scotland, with 68.4 per cent.[22] The result in Scotland, where slightly over two-thirds of those eligible to vote did so, is expressed in Table 2.1.

Table 2.1 NUM and SCEBTA ballot on NCB pay offer and pit closures, selected workplaces in Scotland, October 1982

Colliery	Yes	Percentage yes	+ or – Scots Area average yes	No	Percentage no
Seafield	965	72.5	+4.1	360	27.0
Frances	276	71.1	+2.7	112	28.9
Comrie	334	70.0	+1.6	143	30.0
Bogside	440	72.5	+4.1	163	26.9
Castlehill	507	71.4	+3.0	201	28.3
Solsgirth	586	68.3	−0.1	229	26.7
Monktonhall	994	74.2	+6.2	324	24.2
Bilston Glen	858	56.5	−7.9	657	43.3
Kinneil	194	94.0	+25.6	12	6.0
Polkemmet	628	69.0	+0.6	282	30.9
Fallin (Polmaise)	146	99.3	+31.9	1	0.7
Cardowan	526	76.0	+7.6	168	24.0
Killoch	824	60.4	−8.0	536	39.2
Barony	299	58.5	−9.9	212	41.5
Highhouse	178	63.1	−5.3	102	36.2
Sorn	100	76.0	+7.6	32	24.0
Scottish aggregate	8059	68.4		3631	30.8

Source: *Scottish Miner*, December 1982. Notes: Yes means support for industrial action, including strike action, to secure an improved pay offer and a guarantee that pits would not be closed on grounds other than through exhaustion of coal reserves; Scottish aggregate includes other branches, attached to NCB workshops.

The pit-level data in Table 2.1 is highly significant, anticipating the differential pattern of strike commitment that materialised in 1984–85. Clearly Bilston Glen, Barony and Killoch stand out with the largest minorities against industrial action in 1982. The strongest potential strike commitment in 1982 was expressed at Polmaise, Kinneil and Cardowan, where the dangers of closure

were particularly acute, and Seafield and Monktonhall, where workplace
tensions – examined later in this chapter – were mounting. Such tensions,
however, were also apparent at Bilston Glen and in Ayrshire, although perhaps
with different results, in terms of pit-level politics.

The pressures at Bilston Glen can be read in the minutes of its joint industrial
Colliery Consultative Committee (CCC) from 1981 onwards. J. Pettigrew,
colliery manager, was preoccupied with output levels that from month to
month were scarcely sufficient, he alleged, to make the enterprise 'viable'. He
told union representatives that cost control was the 'top priority at all times'.
This was compromised, he claimed, by poor worker effort and job commitment,
encapsulated in allegedly high absenteeism levels, particularly on Mondays and
Fridays.[23] The NCB Scottish Area's Production Manager, D. Paterson, attended
Bilston Glen's CCC in June 1981. Paterson was one of the 'ruthless bastards' of
collective union memory, new to his senior role, and combining the same blend
of personal geniality and managerial menace as Wheeler. He had been at a func-
tion for retired miners on the night before the CCC meeting, and 'wished to
express his thanks' for a pleasant evening. This had been organised with care and
dedication by miners and their unions. Then, shifting his emphasis, Paterson
asserted that miners and their unions had to dedicate the same commitment to
the work of the pit, to make it 'viable'. If outputs 'budgeted' – or demanded –
by management were not met, jobs would be lost, and the colliery's existence
threatened.[24] In 1982 Pettigrew's successor at Bilston Glen, T. Clarke, repeatedly
articulated the same narrative: the pit was falling 'deeper into the mire', and this
– with 'no geological or technilogical [sic] reason' – was the consequence of
workforce 'apathy'. Wheeler visited the pit in the summer of 1982, and could
'see no reason' for the alleged production shortfall. Colliery managers held
direct meetings with employees, in groups of sixty or so, detailing – with an
overhead projector and slides – the output position and future requirements,
but no immediate improvement was secured.[25] There was no perceptible change
in the production position at the colliery in 1983, with managers continuing to
issue dire warnings about the future.[26]

This precarious and adversarial situation at Bilston Glen is enormously significant, for in 1984–85 it was the only pit where significant numbers of men
returned to work in the first eight months of the strike. This is examined in
detail in Chapter 4, but it is worth stating here that relatively weak strike
commitment at Bilston Glen is usually attributed in historical literature to the
pit's status as a high performing 'superpit', or a 'mighty complex'. Strike-breakers appear as economically rational men, going to work to dig up 'profitable'
coal.[27] This may reflect the successful impact of NCB dissembling in 1983 and
1984. Despite the CCC evidence of cost-related pressures, and the relatively
downbeat evidence of the MMC report, exhibited below, in Table 2.2, senior
NCB managers publicly argued that Bilston Glen had a big future. Their intention, clearly, was to construct rivalries between different pits, and weaken the
solidarity of trade unionism across the coalfields. This is certainly the memory
of those involved in the strike.[28] They remember the visit in September 1983 of

Ian MacGregor, newly installed as NCB Director, to Bilston Glen, explored in more detail later in this chapter, where he praised the successes of the men and criticised the 'second division' miners at nearby Monktonhall.[29] In this connection it is highly significant that in June 1981 Wheeler's Production Manager, Paterson, had made the opposite allegation, threatening Bilston Glen miners by telling them that they measured poorly against Monktonhall.[30]

The type of economic and industrial relations problems evident at Bilston Glen from 1981 onwards were present also in Ayrshire. CCC minutes from Killoch and Barony document prolonged tension between local management and union officials, arising from anxieties about production levels and costs, and allegedly plummeting employee morale. These problems were partly aggravated by management attempts to cajole older miners into redundancy or retirement, in order to absorb younger men after the closures of Sorn and Highhouse early in 1983. At both Barony and Killoch the discourse of non-viability arising from poor worker effort was trenchantly articulated by colliery managers. At Barony there was 'room for vast improvement' in production terms, according to Tam Gaw, colliery manager, in August 1983, and in areas of the pit the men's 'performance was unacceptable'. The mine, if such continued, 'would be stopped'. In the same month J. Lawson, pit manager at Killoch, told union representatives about the Area Director's distinction between 'acceptable and unacceptable losses'. Without immediate improvement Killoch's losses would be regarded as constituting the former, and it would go the same way as Cardowan, which had just been closed.[31]

Cardowan's closure was preceded in December 1982 by that of Kinneil. This was a major episode in the development of tensions across the Scottish coalfields. The threat to Kinneil, announced by Wheeler in September 1982, explains the huge majority for industrial action among its miners in the ballot that followed in October–November, detailed in Table 2.1, as well as the large majority more generally across Scotland. The colliery was in Bo'ness, near the south bank of the Forth. It was the oldest survivor in the Scottish coalfields, opened in 1890, but substantially renovated by the NCB in the 1950s.[32] Coal production had been intermittent since 1979, and ceased in May 1981,[33] with operations concentrating instead on what the NCB styled as an experimental attempt to tunnel under the Forth and through to the giant Longannet mining and electrical power generation complex on the opposite shore.[34] Once this tunnelling was completed it was intended that employment at Kinneil would greatly increase, manpower having dropped temporarily from more than 600 to about 340.[35] But there were difficulties: faulting stopped the drivages from Kinneil, and the upward gradient towards Bogside on the Fife side was steeper than envisaged. This worried the NCB's Chief Major Project Engineer, D.N. Simpson,[36] who discussed the position with Wheeler and Scottish Area officials in May 1982.[37] Wheeler duly persuaded the NCB to abandon the development work,[38] asserting that the financial costs – £14 million already spent and another £12 million just to complete the final fifth of the road to Longannet – had become unacceptably high. Officials at NCB headquarters agreed that Kinneil should be closed, with its miners offered redundancy terms or transfers to other pits. This decision was communicated to mining union officials by the NCB on 17 September.[39] Wheeler used a form of words that would become grimly familiar over the next eighteen months, indicating his unwillingness to 'throw good money after bad'.[40]

Kinneil's miners, along with NUMSA and SCEBTA officials, community leaders and representatives of Central Regional Council, opposed the closure in moral economy terms. First, they pointed to the vast reserves of coal accessible from Kinneil, an estimated 160 million tonnes. These were public assets that the community could not afford to abandon. Second, the proposed voluntary redundancies and transfers were criticised as a base forfeiture of jobs that were themselves also highly valuable community or public assets: 'We will not trade jobs for money,' Michael McGahey told reporters.[41] Third, these assets were all the more precious given the context of chronic economic insecurity, with a very uncertain local employment situation in Bo'ness and West Lothian more broadly.[42] NUMSA and SCEBTA officials pledged to fight the closure, invoking industry procedures to appeal against the area decision before the NCB in London.[43]

The NUM was refused a meeting with the NCB in London, on the basis that joint procedures had not been exhausted at a 'local level' in Scotland,[44] Wheeler having invited representatives of the various industry unions and associations to discuss the future of Kinneil at the Scottish Area's Edinburgh headquarters on 12 November. Representatives of NUMSA, SCEBTA, and the Colliery Officials' Staff Association (COSA), the white collar workers' union, stayed away, awaiting an appeal to the NCB in London. Wheeler said this contravened the industry's tradition of resolving its own difficulties internally in Scotland, with dialogue producing 'sensible solutions'.[45] Representatives of NACODS, the union of pit safety men, and the British Association of Colliery Managers (BACM), were present. Wheeler used slides to illustrate the 'very heavy and erratic pattern of faulting' confronting the Kinneil development, which rendered remaining reserves 'unworkable'. Closure would finance development of the Forth workings from Bogside. BACM representatives accepted this, but NACODS were opposed, defending Kinneil's 'individual identity'. Wheeler was not persuaded that the NCB should preserve the pit as a central pillar of community life in Bo'ness, and focused determinedly on the economic aspects, which made closure inevitable: the pit was 'costing' the NCB £500,000 each month.[46]

Wheeler's decision was endorsed by the NCB's Mining Committee on 25 November, and his recommendation that the NUM be granted a meeting at the NCB's London headquarters, Hobart House, as soon as possible – to hasten the closure – was accepted.[47] This took place at on 14 December, chaired by L.J. Mills of the NCB, accompanied by eight other national officials, and Wheeler, G. Gillespie and M. McDonald of the Scottish Area. National and Scottish Area officials of the mining unions were present, including Scargill, McGahey, Lawrence Daly, Eric Clarke and Kinneil's NUM and SCEBTA delegates, Jim

McCallum and Bill Sneddon. McGahey observed that all pits had geological problems of some kind, and these could be overcome – as they had been in recent times at the Longannet complex – by the type of skilled men employed at Kinneil. But the NCB supported Wheeler's argument about the limited 'workability' of the pit's reserves, amounting to an emphasis on cost and market value, which Scargill characterised as an admission that the board was being 'influenced by economic considerations in deciding Kinneil's future'. He saw this as a departure from an undertaking apparently given to the NUM by the NCB during recent joint talks – on 23 November – that, while economic closures would be considered in the future, there was no 'present intention' of bringing such proposals forward.[48]

McGahey and Scargill told reporters afterwards that Kinneil was being shut on economic rather than geological grounds, and that to prevent such precedent being established a national strike across the British coalfields might take place.[49] The Kinneil men had demonstrated their willingness to fight in the October–November ballot, and a dozen miners, including Jim Frater, NUM branch chairman, and Bill Sneddon, began a stay-down strike at 7 a.m. on Tuesday 21 December, the morning after Albert Wheeler had come to the pit to confirm its immediate closure. The stay-down protest ended five days later, on Christmas Day, the Kinneil men predicting that their proposed strike on Monday 27 December would be made official at a NUMSA delegate conference in Edinburgh on 28 December, and supported across Scotland.[50] Local and Scottish Area union officials certainly attempted to muster a Scotland-wide strike, through the established bureaucratic instruments of Area executive, delegate and pithead meetings.[51] But this effort failed, with only a handful of pits coming out in support of Kinneil. This belied the large majority support – 68.4 per cent, remember – for industrial action against closures in Scotland in the October–November ballot, demonstrating in stark form the difficulty of defending endangered collieries through collective action.[52] Brotherstone and Pirani attribute this to the overly cautious and even temporising role of the Communist Party in Scottish coalfield politics.[53] A competing interpretation, offered at the time by the NUMSA executive, was that significant numbers of men were pessimistic and feared isolation, doubting that action in defence of Kinneil would receive support beyond Scotland. There were also miners who resented the support being mounted for Kinneil when the union had recently accepted the closure of other pits, although on the basis that their coal reserves were 'exhausted',[54] notably Valleyfield in West Fife in 1978 and Bedlay in Lanarkshire in 1981.[55] This reinforces the complexity of the position. The movement towards strike action in Scotland was not a straightforward consequence of managerial aggression and threatened closures; it had to overcome the fatalism of a significant number of miners – at times a significant minority and at some pits perhaps a majority – who viewed resistance as futile.

The Kinneil miners accepted the position, with understandable anger, and returned to work on Wednesday 29 December.[56] The NCB immediately began removing machinery and equipment from the pit, and announced a final closure date in April.[57] Beynon comments that this was when the NUM in Scotland 'caved in', accepting the NCB agenda of closures without any further meaningful opposition.[58] Brotherstone and Pirani broadly concur, pointing to the alleged defeatism of NUMSA officials, which encouraged the NCB to initiate further closures, although they emphasise also the continued commitment of rank and file miners to the fight.[59] There is evidence, however, that union leaders shared this willingness to resist, and in this sense the interpretations of Beynon on the one hand and Brotherstone and Pirani on the other hand should be qualified. The activity of union officials was accompanied by workplace political effort, although this may have varied from pit to pit. Rab Amos, SCEBTA delegate at Monktonhall, saw Kinneil's outcome as evidence of 'depoliticisation' among Scottish miners. He and other union representatives at Monktonhall recognised the need to argue the case 'day and daily' with their members for collective, cross-coalfield action against closures. The same union leadership analysis and effort was adopted elsewhere, he adds, but not at Bilston Glen, which he links to the pit's relatively weak strike commitment in 1984–85.[60]

Renewed area- and pit-level determination to resist closures in Scotland was observable in late February 1983, in McGahey's response to events surrounding the closure of Tymawr-Lewis Merthyr colliery in South Wales, which was to call for a rolling strike, as in February 1981. Challenged to justify the legitimacy of a national strike without a national ballot, McGahey averred that such a mechanism was unnecessary. 'I don't think constitutionality will be the deciding factor,' he said, anticipating his famous maxim on the eve of the 1984–85 strike that miners would not be 'constitutionalised' out of their jobs. NUMSA's executive and a special delegate conference both voted unanimously for a stoppage from Monday 7 March.[61] McGahey elaborated on the changing position since December, when English and Welsh miners were on holiday and the Scots potentially isolated. Now he said that Kinneil – where 230 men were still employed, salvaging equipment and materials – could be 'resurrected' through a national strike against closures.[62]

Pithead meetings at Castlehill, Solsgirth, Bogside, Polmaise and Cardowan elected to respond to the strike call for 7 March, but meetings at Highhouse, Killoch, Polkemmet and Monktonhall went the other way. Meetings at Frances and Bilston Glen were scheduled but postponed when the NUM's national executive decided to hold a national ballot before the strike could begin in Scotland.[63] This yielded a decisive anti-strike majority of 61 to 39 per cent.[64] In Scotland the rank and file militancy that Brotherstone and Pirani identify was tempered by the caution evident in some of the pithead meetings, and reflected further in the roughly 50–50 outcome of the ballot, a marked shift from the 68.4 per cent majority for action just four months earlier.[65] This diminished confidence in collective action against closures may, admittedly, have been partly the effect rather than the cause of the leadership's caution, but Kinneil's hopes were in any case now expunged. On 24 March NCB officials finalised details of the procedures to cap the shafts and demolish the surface buildings. This work was undertaken, at a cost approaching £100,000, over the subsequent four months.[66]

Wheeler's strategy was further emboldened by the Scottish-level findings of the MMC report on the coal industry, explored in Chapter 1, which were being readied for publication early in 1983. These revealed substantial variances in pit-level performance in Scotland, as Table 2.2 indicates, and explain Wheeler's approach to closures in 1983, as well as the workplace tensions evident at several pits since 1981.

Table 2.2 Performance measures from NCB Scottish collieries, 1981–82

Colliery	Saleable output (000s tonnes)	Output per manshift (Tonnes)	Operating costs (£ per tonne)	Operating Loss (£ per tonne)
Bilston Glen	892	2.06	42.70	4.60
Monktonhall	895	2.31	38.30	8.20
Polkemmet	390	1.39	54.50	9.00
Cardowan	267	1.30	69.90	38.30
Seafield	848	1.98	44.10	8.70
Frances	254	1.85	53.10	17.80
Killoch	698	1.58	49.00	16.70
Barony	227	2.00	50.20	13.80
Highhouse	118	1.81	47.30	7.40
Sorn	57	1.33	58.10	21.50
Solsgirth[a] Castlehill Bogside	1955	3.19	31.20	1.50
Comrie	374	1.61	48.30	16.60
Polmaise[b]	N/A	N/A	N/A	N/A
NCB Average		2.4	39.48	

Source: Monopolies and Mergers Commission, National Coal Board, Volume Two, Appendix 3.5 (a), NCB Deep Mines. Operating Results 1981–82 – Scottish Area. [a]Figures for Solsgirth, Castlehill and Bogside are composite for Longannet complex; [b]Polmaise was classed as a Development Pit in 1981–82, not producing coal.

The fractious exchanges in the Bilston Glen, Killoch and Barony CCCs, examined earlier in this chapter, can be more readily understood on the basis of these measures, indicating below coalfield average output per manshift (OMS) performance at the large Midlothian pit, and both large financial losses and weak OMS performance at the Ayrshire pair. The contested nature of NCB finances – especially when measuring purported operating losses – was noted in Chapter 1, along with the importance of seeing output as the result of a welter of economic, social and technological factors, including the degree of mechanisation, geological conditions and level of investment. But Wheeler was impervious to these complexities, and closed two small Ayrshire pits, Highhouse and Sorn, before turning to Cardowan, the biggest financial 'loser', with the lowest OMS. The workforce comprised 1,100 men, with an average age of just 39. Alec Hogg, NUM delegate, described the men's commitment to the pit in vivid terms: 'This is our Alamo.' Wheeler was kicked and punched by infuriated miners after making the closure announcement – which emphasised significant financial losses, exacerbated by allegedly acute geological difficulties – at a nearby community centre on 13 May. He also had an ice-cream cone pressed into his clothing.[67] Cardowan miners were offered transfers to Polkemmet, Polmaise and the Longannet complex, with inducements of up to £1,500 each. McGahey, who had worked at Cardowan in the 1960s,[68] said the closure and the transfers would be resisted, with the impending General Election offering a glimmer of hope. John Smith, the opposition energy spokesman, sharing a platform with McGahey at a rally following Wheeler's visit to Cardowan, said the pit would be kept open 'after' Labour won the election and Ian MacGregor would not, as scheduled, become chairman of the NCB.[69]

The Tory landslide of 9 June negated these prospects, and at the start of July the NCB announced that 240 Cardowan men had accepted redundancy.[70] Other pits were drawn into the dispute as the NCB attempted to weaken the 'Alamo' by dispersing its workforce. Transfers were resisted at 'receiving' collieries, starting at Bogside and Polmaise on 6 July,[71] largely because this process – like the closure of Kinneil – transgressed the moral economy of the coalfields, and on two grounds. First, the NCB acted unilaterally, abandoning the time-consuming joint industrial procedures for managing closures. McGahey told reporters that the NCB in Scotland 'no longer believe in having consultations with the unions'.[72] Second, those seeking transfers were regarded within the NUM as 'renegades' for abandoning their pit, selling resources – jobs – which belonged to the community and were not theirs.[73]

Wheeler – further exhibiting his attachment to unilateral managerial agency – described workplace opposition to these transfers as unwarranted interference in the affairs of the board, whose 'job it is to manage the collieries', and where he encountered it the cessation of work was ordered.[74] A lengthy lockout ensued at Polmaise, where Wheeler confronted an angry crowd of miners and their supporters, including a voluble company of women. He 'lost the place', according to Tam Coulter, NUM branch secretary at Castlehill, threatening the Fallin crowd that the Lanarkshire men would become unemployed if they were not taken on at Polmaise. Local union officials fought back, taking the NCB through the full official disputes procedures, and the men were paid for each of the shifts that they missed because of the lockout between 6 July and 8 August.[75] There were brief stoppages too, in the summer of 1983, at Bogside and Frances, arising from difficulties with the transfers,[76] and then at Polkemmet, where 300 of the pit's 1,340 workers were offered early retirement, their jobs to be taken one-for-one by Cardowan men.[77] Wheeler's approach was nevertheless effective, gradually securing the voluntary departure – by transfer or redundancy – of 300 Cardowan men by 25 August, when the pit's immediate closure was announced. The remaining 750 voted by a majority of 3 to 2 against industrial action to save Cardowan.[78] McGahey saw this in terms of management 'duplicity', the transfers in particular diminishing efforts to save Cardowan, and the macro-economic environment. 'Miners did not live in isolation,' he advised comrades on the Scottish Area executive, 'and their morale had been affected by 4 million unemployed.'[79]

Workplace conflict and the outbreak of the strike, 1983–84

Wheeler has been described as pioneering MacGregor's anti-union, job-shredding methods.[80] This was true of his approach to closures, and even more so in his emphasis on deconstructing joint industrial regulation, which only emerged in full force in England *after* the 1984–85 strike.[81] Nationalisation in 1947 established the principle and formal structures of joint industrial consultation. Workforce representatives were duly engaged in the management of various operational matters, including the design and execution of work, transferring miners between pits, especially where closures were projected, and health and safety questions.[82] Worker and union involvement in operational management was partly diminished in the 1950s and 1960s by the development of mechanised coal-getting, and in the 1970s by advanced technology mining (ATM) forms, notably remote operated longwall faces (ROLF) and then the mine operating system (MINOS), with operational management provided by centrally compiled data and forecasts.[83] In the coal industry workers' representatives nevertheless retained an unusual degree of influence in the management of the workplace when measured against 'employee involvement' in other sectors.[84] Wheeler sought to subvert these established arrangements and destabilise workplace trade unionism in pursuit of reduced labour and production costs. At two collieries, Seafield and Monktonhall, new pit managers were appointed, apparently briefed to undermine union representatives and diminish joint industrial regulation. At other pits union representatives reported being harassed or bullied by management. A sequence of serious pit-level disputes resulted, many of which were still live when the Scottish Area-wide and 'national' strikes commenced in March 1984.

The escalation of workplace tension was particularly marked at Seafield, the third largest producer in Scotland – after Monktonhall and Bilston Glen – but in the NCB's 'bottom 30' in performance terms each year since 1976.[85] Seafield's CCC minutes show that union–management relations were positive in the late 1970s and very early 1980s despite the entrenched difficulty of the production position. In March 1980, for example, a combined meeting of the Seafield and adjacent Frances CCCs discussed rumours that Frances men were to be transferred to Seafield. Both sides – union and management – declared a willingness to work hard to secure the future of deep mining in East Fife. In July 1981, moreover, with output continuing to fall below target, it was agreed that a joint industrial team be established to explore the best means of optimising production. 'This,' the minutes read, 'would not be a fault finding exercise but a genuine attempt to improve the current situation.'[86] Iain Chalmers, a union activist at Seafield, remembers that joint industrial consultation in this period was 'genuine', but a radical change to 'autocratic' management was then effected as part of Wheeler's 'main game plan'.[87] The same narrative features in Willie Clarke's testimony, and was also articulated in 1986 by Jocky Neilson, NUM delegate at Seafield before the strike, who told Willie Thompson that managers launched an 'attack' with 'vengeance' on working conditions and union rights.[88] Alex Nicholson, a face worker at Seafield, also recalls a major escalation in tension before the strike, initiated by apparently trouble-making managers, including new faces introduced 'jist out o university'. This is significant, for Nicholson was neither a union official or activist, presenting himself as a 'quiet supporter' of the 1984–85 strike, which he observed to the end, but without picketing or even regularly attending the local strike centre. His testimony is, admittedly, conditioned by a sense of loss: he mourns the disappearance of the coal industry's work culture, which he inherited from his grandfather and father. But it is not shaped by what McIvor and Johnston characterise as a 'heroic', working class-consciousness,[89] and because of this it renders the similar narrative of former officials and activists – who were guided by a politicised working class identity – all the more convincing.[90]

The deterioration in relations at Seafield was accelerated from May 1983, when George Caldow arrived as colliery manager from Comrie. Caldow and his staff, notably Willie Miller, deputy manager, and Max Meharry, personnel manager, adopted an increasingly abrasive position, explaining the pit's historic output shortfall in terms of the workforce's low work ethic, manifested in a refusal to operate 'diligently' and high levels of absenteeism. This claim had some basis in fact, with a moderate increase in absenteeism, from around 13 per cent of all employees in 1981 to around 14 per cent in 1982 and 1983,[91] this exceeding absolute absenteeism across NCB holdings, and at odds with the modestly decreasing national trend, from 12.4 per cent in the financial year 1980–81 to 10.8 per cent in the six months to October 1981 and then 10.1 per cent in 1982–83.[92] Union representatives claimed that Seafield's problems, including low motivation and absenteeism, arose from employee anxieties about the future and 'poor communication' between managers and workers. These anxieties were ignored or ridiculed by managers, who increasingly dominated consultative meetings with lectures – assisted 'by use of the blackboard' – on the damaging implications of allegedly poor worker effort.[93]

Willie Clarke recalls that Caldow's confrontational approach involved dividing the workers, 'creating argumentation', and attacking 'the credibility' of union negotiators, sometimes by reneging on joint industrial agreements. He abandoned a provision where miners engaged in development work, and so unable to access bonuses enjoyed by production workers, were paid additional compensation. Development workers lost money and were angry, and a small jealousy between the different work groups had been cultivated, which union representatives had to repair.[94] Caldow kept pushing. In the autumn of 1983 there was a problem with new cutting machinery: face workers were hampered by steep gradients, according to Nicholson.[95] Union representatives suggested that more dialogue with the men would improve results, but Caldow adopted what Fox would have characterised as an utterly 'unitary' managerial position, intent on eliminating workforce involvement in planning and organising the labour process.[96] 'Talking was not the answer,' Caldow said, and when the problem persisted into November he declared his intention to state 'precisely what he wanted done and if it was not carried out there would be dismissals'.[97]

McGahey, Eric Clarke and other NUMSA officials were surprised, even slightly 'disbelieving', when Willie Clarke and Jocky Neilson first told them about Caldow's behaviour.[98] But the managerial attack on workers and union rights was being adopted elsewhere from the late summer of 1983, most notably at Monktonhall, resulting in a seven-week stoppage of work from 14 September to 7 November. The production position at Monktonhall, detailed in Table 2.2, was reasonably favourable. Operating costs were lower than any other pit in Scotland outside the integrated Longannet complex, and the OMS in 1981–82 was very close to the NCB average. In the spring of 1983 its CCC was able to reflect on two and a half years of 'excellent results'.[99] But there were difficulties developing in the second and third quarters of 1983, mainly relating to output,[100] and these shaped a dispute which was provoked by William Kennedy, who moved from Polkemmet to become Monktonhall's manager in the summer of 1983. Kennedy was respected by union officials at Monktonhall as a 'good mining engineer, who knew how to extract coal safely and work in a disciplined manner'. But they understood too that he arrived with a brief from Wheeler to downgrade joint industrial regulation.[101] In his first meeting with union officials at the colliery Kennedy wielded the document outlining various local agreements, ripped it up, and – symbolically as well as literally – threw its remnants into the bin.[102] Ensuing developments resembled those at Seafield. In early August Kennedy suspended development work, including roads into the Peacock seam that unions and management had seen in May as vital to the pit's long-term future.[103] Drivage equipment was broken up and removed from the pit, angering the SCEBTA men who had assembled and maintained it.[104] Kennedy told union delegates that development work would resume only when output increased to the point where losses were reversed and the pit was breaking even. David Hamilton, NUM delegate, replied that halting development was wrong, and in any case should not have been announced before consultation with the workers, whose morale was greatly shaken by the apparent dwindling of the pit's future prospects. Kennedy responded in the same terms used by Caldow at Seafield. With 'major surgery' required to make Monktonhall 'viable', it was 'time for action not words'.[105]

Kennedy, echoing Caldow once more, and recalling too the managerial explanations for disappointing performance at Bilston Glen, Barony and Killoch, asserted that the main problem at Monktonhall was poor worker effort. Output was falling, he said, due to 'lack of urgency, bad workmanship, supervision and attitudes'.[106] This was a particular feature, he alleged, at the pit's newest face, L43, which had started in March 1983, with 'good results' initially reported, before problems emerged in June.[107] There developed, essentially, a struggle between management and labour over control of mechanised production methods, and existing joint industrial procedures. Hamilton suggested that a more flexible deployment of cutting machinery along the face – at the workers' discretion rather than in accordance with management's preconceived demands – would improve production.[108] Monktonhall managers resisted this, intent on tightening their control of labour and production processes, and – again like

Caldow at Seafield – further eroding worker and union involvement in operational matters. Kennedy then sent eight men home from the day shift on Monday 15 August when the face was not ready for production after the preceding night shift, because, he claimed, the union was applying a weekend overtime ban. Hamilton said that weekend overtime shifts were arranged, but only a handful of men actually attended. This did not constitute an overtime ban, and he asked Kennedy why he had broken from normal practice by sending the eight men home – causing them to lose earnings – instead of directing them to work elsewhere.[109]

Kennedy spent the entire night shift that followed on L43 with Hamilton, in accordance with existing procedures, before accepting that work was being conducted normally. But on 25 August he told union officials that a 'Ca' canny situation prevailed' on the face,[110] meaning that workers were deliberately rationing their effort. He inspected again that day, although only for part of a shift, and without the NUM delegate present. This contravened agreed procedures, which required that the full shift be inspected – with the relevant union delegate present – prior to any disciplinary procedures being initiated.[111] Kennedy nevertheless accused 63 face workers by letter of withholding effort and threatened their dismissal unless improved output ensued in the following two weeks. NUMSA officials were not surprised by Kennedy's behaviour, as they had been initially by developments at Seafield. The *Scottish Miner* interpreted the threatening letter to the L43 face workers as an attempt to 'drive a wedge' between groups of men at Monktonhall as well as between Monktonhall and other pits. This reflected the NCB's more generally divisive and confrontational approach to workers and unions in Scotland.[112]

Kennedy's next provocation was to offer voluntary redundancies to men aged 50 and over, seeking 300, with no transfers available. This was made over the heads of union representatives, and so again broke agreed procedures. It also contradicted an assurance given three months earlier by management that workers younger than 55 would only be offered redundancy where agreement had first been reached with the unions.[113] Before the 7 a.m. shift on Wednesday 14 September Hamilton called a meeting of NUM members to discuss the crisis. Many of the 150 men attending were then several minutes late for work. Management stopped them from going underground. This was a lockout, deliberately forced by managers seeking confrontation, according to Robbie Dinwoodie of the *Scotsman*, writing a few weeks later.[114] Those already below, on hearing the news, came back up and walked out. The subsequent back and night shifts voted not to work in protest.[115]

Monktonhall union officials recommended an indefinite strike, which the men agreed to support on 15 September.[116] On the same day Ian MacGregor made his first visit to Scotland as NCB chairman. After an underground inspection of Bilston Glen he agreed to meet a group of Monktonhall union representatives, including Rab Amos. 'Understand,' he told them, 'I'm visiting the jewel in the crown. And you, at Monktonhall, are the Second Division.' MacGregor, described by Amos as 'the coldest man I have ever, ever, seen', with 'dead carp's eyes',[117] left cans of beer in the Bilston Glen canteen, telling reporters that it was his birthday and he wanted to buy these valued men a drink to celebrate. He repeated the 'Second Division' criticism of Monktonhall miners, whose alleged inability to use machinery effectively suggested shameful comparisons with workers at mechanised pits in the USA.[118] There was, it will be recalled, little difference between Bilston Glen and Monktonhall, in terms of the NCB's own narrow view of performance measures, as Table 2.2 indicates. 'Losses' per tonne were lower at Bilston Glen, but 'costs' per tonne were also higher. It will be remembered too that in 1981 the NCB's Scottish Production Manager compared the efforts of Bilston Glen miners unfavourably with those at Monktonhall. So MacGregor's intervention can only be read as a deliberate attempt to construct rivalries and jealousies between pits, and weaken the solidarity of Midlothian's miners.[119]

In private discussions with Triple Alliance steel and rail transport union allies in late September McGahey emphasised that the Monktonhall crisis was part of the NCB's larger anti-union approach in Scotland.[120] He made the same point at a rally in Edinburgh before a one-day Scottish Area strike in support of Monktonhall on 17 October, referring to managerial bullying at Killoch, where thirty miners had been threatened with dismissal unless productivity improved in the next fortnight.[121] These threats were counterproductive, as Killoch's managers privately acknowledged in a meeting with Wheeler early in September: workers believed their pit 'was next for closure' and so refused to respond positively when asked to work harder.[122]

The Monktonhall strike was made official by the NUMSA executive on 27 September.[123] Brotherstone and Pirani suggest that this was the time to launch a national strike, with mounting anger in Scotland, and winter's imminence pressurising energy reserves.[124] The 'punch up' strike in the Barnsley coalfield in the final week of September added further potential momentum in this direction, with 15,000 men at sixteen pits out after a miner, George Marsh, was sacked for hitting his overseer, Michael Guest, who the NCB conceded had been bullying and provocative.[125] David Hamilton also sees this as an opportunity missed, but remembers McGahey's rationale for desisting. Monktonhall was large, relatively well-resourced and efficient. Its closure on 'economic' grounds, even in the changing political economy of coal in 1983–84, was not easy for management to justify. McGahey knew that other pits were significantly more vulnerable than Monktonhall on 'economic' grounds, and wanted to preserve the weapon of the national strike for their defence.[126]

There were, in any event, doubts about whether the anger of miners across the coalfields could be transmitted into support for an all-out strike in defence of Monktonhall, even in Scotland. The low morale at Killoch was a sign of possible apathy – defeatism, even – among miners that NUMSA officials recognised as an obstacle to action in defence of pits and jobs. On Tuesday 11 October a special union delegates' conference at the North British Hotel in Edinburgh agreed unanimously to call for a one-day strike the following Monday across the Scottish coalfields in support of Monktonhall.[127] But some Monktonhall men were sceptical about the support of miners elsewhere, telling reporters, 'Nowadays it's every pit for itself'.[128] Rab Amos asked for a cash contribution of £1 per miner across Scotland for the Monktonhall strikers. It was important, he says, that this came from miners individually, and not through branch funds, for this would reinforce solidarity between miners at separate pits. But the response of some at Bilston Glen, sending photocopies of bank notes, including pesetas, was 'embarrassing', and illuminated the difficulty of constructing a collective coalfield response to closures and managerial incursions on union rights.[129] At Monktonhall some miners told reporters that they now regretted not coming to the aid of Kinneil at the end of 1982, having thought their pit would be protected. 'We didn't listen to Scargill,' the *Scotsman*'s Sarah Nelson was told by one of them, Dougie Collins, who continued, 'We voted him in with a huge majority, then kicked him in the face.' Collins and others at Monktonhall had relatives and friends at Bilston Glen who were refusing to see the logic of the NCB's apparent step-by-step approach to the targeting of pits for disinvestment, closure, job losses or altered working practices. 'They have their eyes shut,' Nelson learnt, 'and their heads in the sand. They're scared. Everyone's scared.'[130]

The one-day Scottish Area strike went ahead, nevertheless, after pithead meetings across the coalfields,[131] halting production entirely in Scotland. The NCB claimed that between 10 and 30 per cent of the 14,000 workforce had reported for work. The largest picket was at Bilston Glen, where a crowd ten deep in places prevented cars from entering.[132] The strike at Monktonhall lasted until the first week of November, ending when Wheeler agreed to discuss the pit's future with unions at Area level.[133] On the first day back Hamilton was refused permission to catch up with the significant backlog of union work that had accumulated during the stoppage. He told Kennedy that the union regarded this as coming close to 'victimisation', complained about management's 'hard, unrelenting attitude', and said that 'blind obedience from the workforce could not be expected'. Kennedy rejected Hamilton's request for an additional two weeks under existing 'time allowance' arrangements to conduct official business on NCB premises. 'All persons,' he said, were to be 'gainfully employed'. Hamilton defended his ground, stating that his job was to represent the miners as the NUM delegate at the pit. Kennedy replied that this was not what the NCB paid Hamilton to do, and 'from today' his job was underground, salvaging materials from an exhausted face. Hamilton accepted this position, under protest.[134]

Anti-union activities had been seen elsewhere as workers at other collieries mobilised in support of Monktonhall. At Frances on 23 September the branch delegate, John Mitchell, was sacked after organising a cash collection for the Monktonhall strikers. There was an immediate walk-out by 400 men, and Mitchell was reinstated only after senior NUM and NCB officials intervened.[135] At Polmaise 130 men were sent home without pay on 28 September after arriving several minutes late, having attended a union meeting to collect cash for Monktonhall. This was another lockout, according to John McCormack,

Polmaise union delegate, engineered by Donald Cameron, pit manager, as revenge for the 'row in July', when the workforce had opposed the Cardowan transfers.[136] Hamilton's experience at Monktonhall was replicated at Polmaise, with McCormack compelled to work underground, inhibiting his conduct of normal union duties.[137]

Polmaise then assumed a central position in the coalfield crisis that developed in the winter of 1983–84. Like Kinneil in 1982 it was a 'development' pit. No coal was being mined but it contained substantial reserves, employed 400 men, and had received investment amounting to £22 million since 1980. Wheeler proposed writing this off and closing the pit, citing substantial geological difficulties, and offering transfers to the Longannet complex from where the Polmaise reserves could reputedly be more easily accessed.[138] The problems at Polmaise surfaced in the context of the NUM overtime ban, starting in November 1983, which aimed to pressurise the NCB on the annual wage claim and the potential threat of pit closures. Among other things, this reduced weekend safety cover: the labour required to operate fans, pumps and other items of equipment that kept underground workings free from flooding.[139] In Scotland the position was complicated by Wheeler's response to the ban. Other Area chairmen detailed colliery managers, members of the BACM, to provide cover for absent NUM men.[140] Wheeler acted differently. BACM members were instructed not to operate machinery normally handled by NUM and SCEBTA members, which enabled the safety men, members of the NACODS union, to run underground pumps and fans. At Monktonhall more than a thousand gallons of water per minute came down the pit's two shifts. The resulting post-weekend recovery effort needed each Monday was a major strain, not least on men's earnings, because it cost them a day's shift each week. Few men, indeed, at Monktonhall earned a full weekly wage from the start of the pit-level strike in September 1983 until the end of the national strike in March 1985.[141] Flooding was a problem elsewhere, notably over the last weekend in November at Frances, Barony and Killoch as well as Polmaise, after management had switched off unmanned fans and pumps. These were switched on again only where emergencies had been declared and NUM and SCEBTA members agreed to come in.[142] At Barony the pit manager, Tam Gaw, spoke of the 'irresponsibility' of union officials, who asked why managers had switched the machinery off. Gaw responded tersely that operating this machinery was not management's job. Written warnings were sent to miners at Barony,[143] Killoch and Polmaise, advising that they would not be summoned if flooding occurred again, once managers had switched off unmanned pumps: the pits would simply be lost.[144] Over the next weekend NUM and SCEBTA members provided full safety cover at all pits in Scotland except Polmaise, which flooded again, at which point the NCB informed the press that the pit's closure was likely owing to geological difficulties.[145]

The NCB told NUMSA, SCEBTA and local officials on 13 January 1984 that the pit was to close. McCormack and others at the pit reminded reporters of Wheeler's promise in May 1983, announcing the end of Cardowan: no further closures were envisaged in Scotland, and NCB investment guaranteed 'long-term' job security at Polmaise.[146] McCormack added that the NCB knew about the geological difficulties three years earlier when the development plans had been agreed, and so the closure could only be interpreted as Wheeler's revenge against the Polmaise men for refusing to accept the Cardowan transfers the previous summer. McCormack also made demands of the NUM, asking that its Scottish leadership 'lead the way' in protecting Polmaise, and not just 'say they will back the men at the pit in whatever they decide'. The following week Arthur Scargill visited Polmaise, accompanied by McGahey, and spoke about the need to defend every colliery in Scotland endangered by the NCB's bullying and dishonesty.[147] Wheeler and his officials came several days later, on 26 January, and confirmed the decision to shut the pit, speaking to the men about the geological difficulties, and offering them employment at the Longannet complex. He did not receive much of a hearing, and was 'jostled and spat on'.[148] On 6 February the NCB ratified Wheeler's decision, and communicated this in writing to the various unions involved, which then exercised their right to a final appeal under the board's Colliery Review Procedure. This was scheduled for 14 March, but not heard, with the outbreak of the strike on 12 March.[149]

Problems were escalating elsewhere. In East Fife the continuing tension was illustrated at Seafield, where Caldow suspended joint industrial practices alto-gether in January 1984.[150] Pit-level stoppages ensued, again in the context of the overtime ban, with management demanding additional early Monday shifts to offset lost weekend operations. There were intermittent lockouts in February, and the adjacent Frances men were drawn into the conflict. A permanent stop-page was in place from mid-February, the immediate origins of which are contested. Press reports stated that the NUM delegate had been sacked. The delegate himself, Jocky Neilson, told Willie Thompson in 1986 – only two years later – that the strike arose because thirty men were sent home after reporting one minute late for work.[151] In any event the broader issue – and the real source of the strike – was the managerial drive against working conditions and union rights. This was exemplified by Caldow's behaviour when he prevented the NUM branch from holding a discussion of the crisis in the colliery canteen, which he occupied and refused to leave. The stoppage was continuing in March, when the national strike began.[152] The difficulties in Ayrshire, meanwhile, were culminating in frequent and protracted work stoppages. In the week ending 18 February an industrial dispute at Killoch cut the intended seven-day production target of 14,227 tonnes to just 166 tonnes.[153] Disputes were also under way at Comrie, over the allocation of jobs, and at Solsgirth, Killoch and Monktonhall, arising from the absence of weekend cover. There was a major crisis too at Bogside, after three men were disciplined on 26 January for not undertaking tasks requested by management. A short sit-in followed. Management summoned the police, who made no arrests. Without safety cover over the following weekend the pit flooded, and within days its closure was announced by the NCB.[154] Jim McCallum, former NUM delegate at Kinneil, and now in the same role at Bogside, told reporters that the board had engineered this position deliberately. The 850 Bogside men agreed to accept temporary transfers, but also decided in a pithead meeting to fight to preserve the colliery. McCallum indicated that this would involve collaboration with Polmaise.[155]

This widespread pattern of pit-level conflict contributed to the growing pressure on the NUMSA leadership, especially from Polmaise, to engineer an official Area-wide strike against closures and confrontational management. NUMSA executive and delegate meetings were held on 13 February, but these faced a countervailing strand of workplace opinion. Cautious, and to an extent demoralised by the apparent difficulties of mounting effective collective action, this strand initially prevailed. There were angry scenes in the North British Hotel, on Princes Street in Edinburgh, where the meetings were held. Polmaise miners especially were highly critical of what they saw as official prevarication, but immediate strike action was nonetheless rejected.[156] A positive response to the crisis was nevertheless being carefully staked out, with pithead meetings across the coalfields and then Area executive and delegate meetings on 20 February securing 'absolute' authority for the Scottish Area executive to call any action deemed necessary to halt closures.[157] Similar measures were taken within SCEBTA, early in March, providing its leadership with the same executive powers.[158]

These meetings formed the basis for the legitimacy of the subsequent strike in Scotland. It will be remembered from the introductory chapter that the legal position in England and Wales was different. During the strike a number of working miners in England sued the NUM over the legal applicability of a 1981 vote in Yorkshire for action against closures. This had formed the basis for the NUM's claim that the strike was official in Yorkshire, and underpinned the calling for a national strike, on an area by area basis, at an NUM special delegate conference on 19 April. The High Court in London ruled in September that the 1981 vote was too distant in time to be applicable in 1984, and restrained the NUM nationally and in Yorkshire from characterising the strike as official.[159] When Scargill and other officials defied this ruling, affirming the official nature of the strike, NUM funds in England and Wales were sequestered in October 1984. In Scotland the legality of the strike was tested in a case taken by strike-breakers, led by a Bilston Glen miner, Harry Fettes. In the High Court in Edinburgh on 25 September Lord Jauncey ruled that the strike was lawful under NUMSA rules. These required the agreement of members through pithead, branch and delegate meetings, which the union had made provision for: a ballot was not necessary. Moreover, the Scottish strike preceded the special delegate conference of 19 April, and the Edinburgh High Court judgment therefore was that the legality of NUMSA's action was not affected by any invalidity that might be attached to the national strike call.[160]

The NUMSA leadership's careful construction of support for collective action against closures, gradually winning a majority, secured the legitimacy of the 'national' strike in Scotland, which commenced on 12 March. Standard interpretations generally settle on two key 'triggers' in the first week of March: the surprise announcement of the closure of Cortonwood, which led to an official

Area-wide strike in Yorkshire, resembling developments in Scotland, and the peak-level talks in London between the NCB and industry unions.[161] Here the NCB produced a proposed budget and production target for 1984–85 which indicated a reduction in capacity roughly equivalent to twenty pit closures, with perhaps 20,000 job losses. The burden of these cuts would fall in the 'heavy losing' areas of South Wales, Durham, Kent and Scotland. Herrington and Bullcliffe Wood, both in Durham, and Snowdon, in Kent, were facing immediate closure along with Cortonwood and Polmaise.[162] McGahey's famous words about miners not being 'constitutionalised' out of their jobs, which feature in David Peace's novel, GB84, were uttered to reporters after these talks, along with his declaration that a 'domino'-effect strike would develop. This would start in Scotland and Yorkshire on 12 March, and be joined incrementally by the NUM's other federal areas until the entire coalfield was out.[163] This was a circuitous route to a national strike, but obviated the requirement for a national ballot. Eric Clarke and others who supported this strategy later came to regret it, thinking that greater labour movement and indeed wider social support for the strike might have been forthcoming had a ballot first been taken.[164] This is probably now the predominant view in the Scottish literature on the strike too,[165] but it remains highly vexatious. Pit closures, it must be emphasised, did not affect all miners equally, and a ballot on this question was potentially highly divisive. In any case, more than 50 per cent of miners in Scotland were already in dispute with pit-level management,[166] and their majority demand for a militant response against closures and Wheeler's anti-unionism would now be met.[167]

NCB officials were nevertheless optimistic, according to information they fed to the press, that a substantial proportion of NUMSA and SCEBTA members – perhaps even half – would work normally on Monday 12 March.[168] Over the preceding weekend miners at Bilston Glen, Comrie, Polkemmet, Killoch and Barony resolved, again according to NCB intelligence, to work on Monday. At Bilston Glen there were miners who felt that a strike was only now being advocated nationally because Arthur Scargill's Yorkshire 'stronghold' was directly affected by closures, whereas Scottish pits had been abandoned with no support from the union nationally since 1982. Paradoxically, perhaps, at Polkemmet the men indicated that they could support the strike if it was observed across the UK coalfield, this being likely to have more impact than action confined to Scotland.[169]

During the first shift on Monday some 2,000 miners – roughly, as predicted by the NCB and the Scotsman, half the normal day shift workforce in Scotland – entered the pits at Bilston Glen, Comrie, Polkemmet, Killoch and Barony. Matters were apparently turned, however, by the arrival of one hundred Polmaise miners in two buses at Bilston Glen at noon. They doubled the size of the existing picket, which 350 miners had crossed at 6 a.m. for the beginning of the early shift. Less than 100 – insufficient to keep the pit working – crossed the reinforced picket line for the afternoon shift at 2 p.m., with the police cordon temporarily breached under the weight of the strikers. The Polmaise men

planned to return to Bilston Glen for the 2 p.m. shift change on 13 March, but
this was unnecessary. The Midlothian colliery, along with the rest of the Scottish
coalfields, had been closed by the middle of Monday afternoon. The 'rebellion'
against the NUM in Scotland had 'fizzled out' and production, Scottish Office
officials noted, was 'at a standstill'.[170]

Conclusion

The peak-level and Yorkshire developments in the first week of March 1984
were clearly significant in shaping the outbreak of the strike. But it is important
also to reflect on the evidence examined in this chapter of escalating workplace
tension and conflict in the coal industry in Scotland from 1980 onwards. This
counters the view generally expressed in the literature on the strike that its
origins are located chiefly in high politics, the ideological tensions between
Conservative government and NUM leadership, and particularly the ambitions
of Scargill and his allies on the national union executive. High industrial politics
and events outwith Scotland were clearly important to the strike in Scotland: the
national 'rolling' strike, for example, provided the broader mobilisation that
many – such as the wary miners of Polkemmet – regarded as a prerequisite of
the defence of endangered Scottish pits. Yet the strike was nevertheless in large
part rooted in Scotland. It drew impetus from the longer history of the industry
in Scotland, with the moral economy of the coalfields challenged but in fundamental aspects strengthened by the post-1947 restructuring that was analysed in
Chapter 1, culminating in the full contribution that Scottish miners made to the
strikes of 1972 and 1974. The moral economy was overtly transgressed after
1979 by the manner of the pit closures, and managerial attacks on workplace
trade unionism. The 1984–85 strike was the result of this, with a militant
response carefully articulated and channelled by union representatives and officials in Scotland. Wheeler's strategy greatly worried miners and their union
officials in England and Wales, who feared its emulation in their own areas and
pits, and so Scottish developments directly prefigured the strike across the
British coalfield.

The particular cases of Seafield and Monktonhall demonstrate the various
elements of managerial strategy, and its contribution to the serious deterioration in industrial relations that eventually resulted in the strike. At both
collieries managers undermined employee and union involvement in the planning and organisation of production. This management assault on joint
consultation and regulation, broadened to encompass pits elsewhere in the
Scottish coalfields, provoked a sequence of disputes, including the lengthy strike
at Monktonhall in the autumn of 1983, and the intermittent strikes and lockouts
at various collieries in the opening months of 1984. These pit-level conflicts
were unresolved when the national strike began on 12 March. This strike would
be a defence of the pits, and the wider moral economy of the Scottish coalfields
which Wheeler's approach had plainly transgressed. Closures had been forced
through against the opposition of workers and unions; jobs had been lost in a

climate of increasingly chronic economic insecurity; and the consultative role of labour – an embedded and from the workforce's perspective an invaluable feature of the industry since nationalisation in 1947 – had been crudely compromised. The NUMSA leadership's careful response to this attack, supported by confederates in SCEBTA, slowly constructing a majority for strike action, allowed the union to demonstrate the legality as well as the legitimacy of its actions in Scotland, and protected it against the humiliation and sequestration of assets experienced in England and Wales in the High Court in London. This enabled both unions in Scotland to enter the strike warily, but with some confidence, concentrating initially on pressurising the Conservative government by inhibiting the supply of coal to the industrially and politically significant BSC plant at Ravenscraig, which is examined in the following chapter.

Notes

1 TNA, COAL 74/4783, Coal Industry National Consultative Council Minutes (hereafter CINCC), 6 March 1984.
2 Brotherstone and Pirani, 'Were There Alternatives?'
3 MMC, *National Coal Board.*
4 Keith Aitken, *The Bairns O' Adam. The Story of the STUC* (Edinburgh, 1997), pp. 273–81.
5 Phillips, 'Workplace Conflict and the Origins of the Strike'.
6 Perchard, *Mine Management Professions*, pp. 216–64.
7 Hutton, *The State We're In.*
8 Alan Fox, *Industrial Sociology and Industrial Relations. Royal Commission on Trade Unions and Employers' Associations, Research Papers, 3* (HMSO, 1966).
9 Neil Millward and Mark Stevens, *British Workplace Industrial Relations, 1980–1984* (Aldershot, 1986), pp. 36–53, 151–65.
10 'Iraq – Declaration of War – 18 March 2003 at 22.00': www.publicwhip.org.uk /division.php?date=2003–03–18, accessed 17 June 2010.
11 Hamilton, Interview.
12 Summerfield, 'Dis/composing the subject'.
13 Thomson, 'Anzac Memories', 300–10.
14 Perchard and Phillips, 'Transgressing the Moral Economy'.
15 Eric Clarke, Interview.
16 Coulter, Interview with Thompson.
17 Wilson, Interview.
18 TNA, COAL 26/1049, Daly to Cowan, 15 July 1982, and COAL 31/261, Cowan to Daly, 29 September 1982.
19 *The Times*, 18 October 1982.
20 Routledge, *Scargill*, p. 118.
21 Beynon, 'Introduction', in Beynon, *Digging Deeper*, pp. 9–10.
22 *The Times*, 30 October and 3 November 1982.
23 NAS, CB 229/3/1, NCB Scottish Area, Bilston Glen Colliery, Minutes of Colliery Consultative Committee (CCC), 14 January 1982, 22 April 1981.
24 NAS, CB 229/3/1, Bilston Glen CCC, 3 June 1981.
25 NAS, CB 229/3/1, Bilston Glen CCC, 31 March, 26 May, 26 July, 11 August and 8 September 1982.

26 NAS, CB 229/3/1, Bilston Glen CCC, 7 September, 4 October and 2 November 1983.
27 Andrew Newby, 'Scottish Coal Miners', in Mark A. Mulhern, John Beech and Elaine Thompson (eds), *Scottish Life and Society. A Compendium of Scottish Ethnology. Volume 7: The Working Life of the Scots* (Edinburgh, 2008), p. 593; Stewart, *Path to Devolution and Change*, pp. 96–7; Taylor, *NUM and British Politics. Volume 2*, p. 189.
28 Eric Clarke, Interview; Hamilton, Interview.
29 *Glasgow Herald*, 21 September 1983.
30 NAS, CB 229/3/1, Bilston Glen CCC, 3 June 1981.
31 NAS, CB 221/3/4, NCB Scottish Area, Barony Colliery Consultative Committee, 11 January , 5 April, 23 August 1983; CB 328/3/4, NCB Scottish Area, Killoch Colliery Consultative Committee, 14 June and 4 October 1983.
32 Oglethorpe, *Scottish Collieries*, pp. 262–3.
33 TNA, COAL 89/222, D.G. Brandrick, Secretary, NCB, to Department of Energy, and the various coal industry trade unions, 10 June 1981.
34 *Glasgow Herald*, 22 December 1982.
35 NAS, CB 335/3/3, NCB Scottish Area, Kinneil Colliery Consultative Committee, 20 January 1981 and 26 January 1982.
36 TNA, COAL 89/222, D.N. Simpson, Chief Major Project Engineer, NCB, to A. Ludkin, Deputy Chief Mining Engineer, Scottish Area, 11 January 1982.
37 TNA, COAL 89/222, D.N. Simpson, memo to R.J. Price, 21 May 1982.
38 TNA, COAL 89/222, P.M. Moullin, Deputy Secretary, NCB, to M. McNamara, Secretary, Scottish Area, 17 September 1982.
39 NAS, CB 335/14/1, Deputy Press Officer, Scottish Area, NCB, to Chief Press Officer, NCB, 17 September 1982.
40 *The Times*, 4 October 1982.
41 John Lloyd, 'Scottish Pit Closure Move Angers Miners', *Financial Times*, 20 September 1982, clipping in NAS, CB 335/14/3.
42 NAS, CB 335/14/3, Percival W. Buchanan, Director of Administration and Legal Services, Central Regional Council, to the Secretary, NCB, Scottish Area, 14 October 1982.
43 *The Times*, 4 October 1982.
44 TNA, COAL 89/222, R.H. Thompson to Lawrence Daly, 28 October 1982.
45 TNA, COAL 89/222, NCB Scottish Area Press Statement, 12 November 1982.
46 NAS, CB 335/3/3, NCB, Scottish Area, Draft Minutes of a Consultative Meeting held at Scottish Area HQ, Green Park, Edinburgh, in Room D. 217 at 10.45 a.m., on Friday 12 November 1982.
47 TNA, COAL 89/222, Secret Annex No. 31 to Mining Committee 'Minutes, 25 November 1982.
48 NAS, CB 335/14/1, 'Kinneil Colliery: Note of an informal meeting with the NUM held on Tuesday 14 December 1982 in the Board Room, Hobart House' (NCB head-quarters).
49 *Glasgow Herald*, 15 December 1982 and *The Times*, 15 December 1982.
50 *Glasgow Herald*, 21, 22, 24 and 28 December 1982.
51 SMM, NUMSA, EC, 20 December 1982.
52 *Glasgow Herald*, 28 and 29 December 1982.
53 Brotherstone and Pirani, 'Were There Alternatives?', 107.
54 Bolton, Interview with Thompson.
55 SMM, NUMSA, EC, 27 December 1982, and Joint Conference of Mining Unions, 28 December 1982.

56 *The Times*, 3 January 1982.
57 NAS, CB 335/14/3, M. McNamara, NCB, Scottish Area Staff Manager and Secretary, to various recipients, including Scottish Economic Planning Department, Tam Dalyell, MP, COSA and BACM officials, 28 December 1982.
58 Beynon, 'Introduction', in Beynon, *Digging Deeper*, p. 10.
59 Brotherstone and Pirani, 'Were There Alternatives?', 107–8.
60 Amos, Interview.
61 *The Times*, 2 March 1983.
62 *Glasgow Herald*, 2 March 1983.
63 *Glasgow Herald*, 4 March 1983.
64 *The Times*, 9 March 1983.
65 *Glasgow Herald*, 11 March 1983.
66 NAS, CB 335/14/1, A. Ludkin, Acting Chief Mining Engineer, NCB Scottish Area, to various officials, regarding meeting at Kinneil Colliery, scheduled for 24 March 1983 at 2.30 p.m., and various other materials.
67 Wilson, Interview.
68 McIlroy and Campbell, 'McGahey', p. 244.
69 *Glasgow Herald*, 14 May 1983 and *The Times*, 14 May 1983.
70 The *Scotsman*, 2 July 1983.
71 The *Scotsman*, 7 July 1983.
72 The *Scotsman*, 9, 11 and 12 July 1983.
73 SMM, NUMSA, EC, 12 July 1983 and Minute of Special Conference of Delegates, 12 July 1983.
74 The *Scotsman*, 7 July 1983.
75 Coulter, Interview with Thompson.
76 The *Scotsman*, 7–9 and 11–15 July 1983.
77 The *Scotsman*, 9, 11 and 12 July 1983.
78 The *Scotsman*, 26 and 27 August 1983.
79 SMM, NUMSA, EC, 29 August 1983.
80 Adeney and Lloyd, *Miners' Strike*, pp. 52, 85–8.
81 Taylor, *NUM and British Politics. Volume 2*, pp. 235–80.
82 Adeney and Lloyd, *Miners' Strike*, pp. 3–4.
83 Jonathan Winterton and Ruth Winterton, 'Production, Politics and Technological Development: British Coal Mining in the Twentieth Century', in Joseph Melling and Alan McKinlay (eds), *Management, Labour and Industrial Politics in Modern Europe: The Quest for Productivity* (Cheltenham, 1998), pp. 122–44.
84 Jim Phillips, 'Industrial Relations, Historical Contingencies and Political Economy: Britain in the 1960s and 1970s', *Labour History Review*, 21 (2007), 215–33.
85 *The Times*, 2 November 1982.
86 NAS, CB 398/3/2, NCB Scottish Area, Seafield Colliery Consultative Committee, 14 March 1980 and 14 July 1981.
87 Chalmers, Interview.
88 Neilson, Interview with Thompson; Willie Clarke, Interview.
89 McIvor and Johnston, *Miners' Lung*.
90 Nicholson, Interview.
91 NAS, CB 398/3/2, Seafield CCC, 1981–83: author's calculations on the basis of absenteeism levels reported to Seafield CCC at the mid-point of the months of February, April, June, August, October and December in each year.
92 TNA, COAL 74/4805, CINNC, 10 March 1981 and 10 November 1981, and COAL

74/4806, CINNC, 8 March 1983.

93 NAS, CB 398/3/2, Seafield CCC, 24 May, 28 June and 12 July 1983.

94 Willie Clarke, Interview.

95 Nicholson, Interview.

96 Fox, *Industrial Sociology*, pp. 6–7.

97 NAS, CB 398/3/2, Seafield CCC, 27 September and 8 November 1983.

98 Willie Clarke, Interview.

99 NAS, CB 363/3/3, NCB Scottish Area, Monktonhall Colliery Consultative Committee, 4 May 1983.

100 NAS, CB 363/3/3, Monktonhall CCC, 15 June 1983.

101 Amos, Interview.

102 Hamilton, Interview.

103 NAS, CB 363/3/3, Monktonhall CCC, 4 May 1983.

104 Amos, Interview.

105 NAS, CB 363/3/8, Monktonhall CCC, 10 August 1983.

106 NAS, CB 363/3/8, Monktonhall CCC, 24 August 1983.

107 NAS, CB 363/3/3, Monktonhall CCC, 2 March, 16 March, 13 April and 15 June 1983.

108 NAS, CB 363/3/8, Monktonhall CCC, 27 July 1983.

109 NAS, CB 363/17/8, Monktonhall Colliery, Minute of Meeting between Management and Trade Union Representatives, 15 August 1983.

110 NAS, CB 363/17/12, Monktonhall Colliery, Minute of Meeting between Management and Trade Union Representatives, 25 August 1983.

111 The *Scotsman*, 14 October 1983.

112 *Scottish Miner*, November 1983.

113 NAS, CB 363/3/3, Monktonhall CCC, 1 June 1983.

114 The *Scotsman*, 14 October 1983.

115 *Glasgow Herald*, 15 September 1983.

116 SMM, NUMSA, EC, 10 October 1983.

117 Interview, Amos.

118 *Glasgow Herald*, 16 and 21 September 1983.

119 Amos, Interview; Eric Clarke, Interview; Hamilton, Interview.

120 NLS, Acc. 9805/263, Minute of Meeting of Triple Alliance, 29 September 1983.

121 *Glasgow Herald*, 27 September 1983.

122 NAS, CB 328/3/4, NCB, Killoch CCC, 6 September 1983.

123 SMM, NUMSA, Special EC, 27 September 1983.

124 Brotherstone and Pirani, 'Were There Alternatives?', 110–12.

125 *The Times*, 24 September 1983.

126 Hamilton, Interview.

127 SMM, NUMSA, Minute of Special Conference of Delegates, 11 October 1983.

128 The *Scotsman*, 12 October 1983.

129 Amos, Interview.

130 The *Scotsman*, 17 October 1983.

131 The *Scotsman*, 14 October 1983.

132 The *Scotsman*, 18 October 1983.

133 SMM, NUMSA, Minute of Special Conference of Delegates, 3 November 1983.

134 NAS, CB 363/17/8, Monktonhall Colliery, Minute of Meeting held between Management and NUM, 7 November 1983.

135 SMM, NUMSA, EC, 26 September 1983; *Glasgow Herald*, 24 September 1983.

136 *Glasgow Herald*, 29 September 1983 and the *Scotsman*, 13 October 1983.

137 John McCormack, 'Polmaise on the Boil', *Scottish Miner*, December 1983.

138 The *Scotsman*, 1 December 1983.

139 Winterton and Winterton, *Coal, Crisis and Conflict*, pp. 60–3.

140 *Courier & Advertiser*, 22 February 1984.

141 Amos, Interview.

142 The *Scotsman*, 1 December 1983.

143 NAS, CB 221/3/4, Barony CCC, 29 November 1983.

144 The *Scotsman*, 2 December 1983.

145 The *Scotsman*, 5 December 1983.

146 *Glasgow Herald*, 14 May 1983.

147 The *Scotsman*, 14 and 21 January 1984.

148 *Courier & Advertiser* and the *Scotsman*, both 27 January 1984.

149 NAS, CB 382/14/1, D.G. Brandrick, secretary, NCB, to Lawrence Daly, [outgoing] General Secretary, NUM, 6 February 1984.

150 NAS, CB 398/3/2, Seafield CCC, 6 December 1983, 17 January 1984 and 4 June 1985.

151 Neilson, Interview with Thompson.

152 Kirkcaldy Art Gallery and Museum (hereafter KAGM), Iain Chalmers, Strike Diary, 14, 17, 18, 23 and 27 February and 5 March 1984; *Courier & Advertiser*, 24 January 1984; *Glasgow Herald*, 16 and 27 February 1984, and the *Scotsman*, 10 March 1984.

153 NAS, CB 328/3/4, Killoch CCC, 6 March 1984.

154 The *Scotsman*, 28 January 1984, and *Courier & Advertiser*, 31 January and 1 February 1984.

155 *Courier & Advertiser*, 7 February 1984.

156 SMM, NUMSA, EC, and Minute of Special Conference of Delegates, both 13 February 1984; *Glasgow Herald*, 14 February 1984.

157 SMM, NUMSA, EC and Minute of Special Conference of Delegates, both 20 February 1984. See also *Glasgow Herald*, 14, 16, 21 and 27 February 1984; the *Scotsman*, 7 March 1984; *The Times*, 7 March 1984.

158 Moffat, Interview with Thompson.

159 *The Times*, 2 October 1984.

160 Many thanks to David Howell for his summary of this; Clarke, 'Mineworkers' Strike', pp. 142–4; NAS, SEP 4/6029/1, Sit Rep, 25 September 1984.

161 Richards, *Miners on Strike*, pp. 100–10; Winterton and Winterton, *Coal, Crisis and Conflict*, pp. 64–72.

162 TNA, COAL 74/4783, Coal Industry National Consultative Council Minutes, 6 March 1984.

163 Taylor, *NUM and British Politics. Volume 2*, pp. 186–7; David Peace, *GB84* (London, 2004), p. 6.

164 Eric Clarke, Interview.

165 Aitken, *Bairns O' Adam*, pp. 274–9; Stewart, 'A Tragic "Fiasco"?', 44–6.

166 Brotherstone and Pirani, 'Were There Alternatives?', 106–14.

167 SMM, NUMSA, EC, 6 March 1984.

168 The *Scotsman*, 10 March 1984.

169 The *Scotsman*, 10 and 12 March 1984.

170 NAS, SOE 12/571, Hamill, SHHD, 'Miners' Strike: Picketing at Bilston Glen Colliery, Midlothian', 13 March 1984, and J.F. Laing, IDS, Note for Ministers Meeting at 2 p.m., 13 March 1984; The *Scotsman*, 13 March 1984.

II
The strike

3

The Scottish industrial politics of the strike

Coal production ceased on 12 March in Scotland, but solidarity across the coalfield was still being consolidated one week later, when the NUMSA and SCEBTA strike committee met for the first time. Picketing was still required at Barony, where some miners were appealing for a national ballot, and at Bilston Glen.[1] These partial divisions were acknowledged in a press statement issued by Eric Clarke for NUMSA on 15 March, which referred in low-key terms to the 'growing sense of unity' among Scotland's miners. Clarke's statement also drew attention to a core issue that would come to dominate the opening months of the strike in Scotland: the coal supply to the major BSC plant at Ravenscraig in Motherwell. Clarke observed that NUMSA did not seek to 'damage' the plant, and was monitoring the availability and transportation of its fuel.[2] In private discussion the NUMSA and SCEBTA strike committee agreed two weeks later that the plant be supplied not for 'normal working', which the steel workers were seeking, but just so it could be kept 'ticking over', its furnaces burning.[3]

The industrial, political and historical importance of Ravenscraig, emphasised in Chapter 1, should not be underestimated. It was one of the key legacies of Tory regional policy in the late 1950s and early 1960s, designed to ameliorate Scotland's above-UK-average level of unemployment, and slower economic growth. Its establishment in 1958 was forced by Harold Macmillan's Conservative government on its owner, Colvilles, against the better judgement of its chairman and directors, who were convinced that it would be a 'financial disaster'. The government prevailed, considering that losses incurred at Ravenscraig would be offset by savings in unemployment maintenance, and the intended multiplier benefits for lighter industry, which could develop with a supply of strip metal previously unavailable in Scotland.[4] By 1984 many of the other regional policy projects that followed Ravenscraig, notably the car plant at Linwood and the aluminium smelter at Invergordon, were gone, exposed to unforgiving competitive pressures. These were exacerbated after 1979 by the withdrawal of government subsidies and macro-economic and fiscal policies – including a tight control of inflation, increased borrowing costs and an escalating pound in global currency markets – that stiffly accentuated a broad trend in

UK economic management to the privileging of financial over manufacturing interests.[5] Ravenscraig, however, part of the nationalised BSC since 1967, was still alive. This was largely a political issue. While the Tories substantially increased their House of Commons majority in the 1983 General Election, in Scotland they made no headway, losing one constituency – to Charles Kennedy of the Social Democratic Party, in Ross and Cromarty – and gaining no others. Thatcher's government was bolstered, therefore, by 21 Scottish Tory MPs, but popular distaste for the continuing loss thereafter of stable industrial employment resulted in significant damage to her party in the District Council elections of 3 May 1984. This coincided more or less exactly with the climax of the miners' siege of Ravenscraig. Control of the City of Edinburgh District Council was lost by the Tories to Labour, which now led 25 of the 33 District Councils in Scotland that were subject to political contest. The leader of Dundee's victorious Labour group, Ken Fagan, told reporters that local authorities would 'help people who have been battered to death by the present government'.[6] This was a major development in Scotland's political trajectory, accentuating radically the anti-Conservative trend evident in the 1960s and 1970s, and which would assume fuller form in subsequent General Elections and local authority polls.[7] The political and ideological 'distance' between Thatcherism and the Scots, the subject of a recent agonised analysis by David Torrance,[8] contributed to the complexity of the miners' strike in Scotland. It certainly had a particular bearing on developments at Ravenscraig. The government could not easily evade its responsibility for this publicly owned establishment, as it had divested itself of blame for the private sector losses at Linwood and elsewhere. Ravenscraig's longevity duly owed much to the reluctance of ministers to incur further political losses in Scotland, particularly as senior BSC managers viewed it from the early 1980s onwards as the most marginal of their five integrated operating plants.[9]

The plant's life was threatened in 1984, with striking miners attempting to inhibit the flow of coal and other materials – including iron ore – that enabled BSC to maintain the blast furnaces, coke ovens and production. This has been portrayed as selfish and foolish, unnecessarily straining Scottish labour's solidarity. Keith Aitken articulates this conventional interpretation in his history of the STUC, adding that the NUM ignored the real and highly understandable anxieties of steel workers. Only the assiduous work of STUC officials prevented a major fissure.[10] David Stewart's analysis of the campaign to save Ravenscraig explicitly criticises the NUM for picketing the plant.[11] This he characterises as one of the NUM leadership's three central errors, along with the decision not to ballot its members nationally before the strike, and the inability to secure an early settlement in talks with the NCB, either in June and July or September 1984.[12]

This chapter explores the highly distinctive Scottish industrial politics of the strike, with a chronological focus from March to October 1984, when support for the strike was pretty solid across the coalfield in Scotland, and adopts a different perspective on Ravenscraig. Here it is argued that the plant was

targeted precisely because of the 'campaign' to protect it, which had an important cross-party character, incorporating Scottish Nationalists, Liberals, Social
Democrats and even some Tory figures as well as its Labour Party and trade
union core. In this cross-party connection it is worth noting that the first
Parliamentary strike-related question about Ravenscraig, on 2 April, was asked
by James Wallace, Liberal MP for Orkney and Shetland.[13] Wallace and others
were reminding the Tories about the political costs – to the government – of
Ravenscraig closing, and it was this pressure that NUMSA was seeking to
maximise. In these terms the strikers were very far from having embarked on a
fratricidal course of action. It was risky, and perhaps not clearly presented to the
workers of Ravenscraig, who resisted it and whose union officials – as Scottish
Office papers indicate – routinely leaked details of inter-union talks to BSC
management and hence to the government. But in attempting to push the
government back, in highlighting further the political importance of employment and production at Ravenscraig, and in the absence of any other strong
levers, given the strike's limited impact on power generation and supply,
NUMSA's broad approach was in fact highly pragmatic and logical. Ravenscraig
and other industrial units would only be saved, NUMSA maintained, if the
miners won the strike. 'Don't just support us,' Eric Clarke recalls saying to the
steel workers' union leaders, 'join us.'[14] Subsequent events suggest that this
analysis was correct: employment at the strip mill was preserved for only seven
years beyond the end of the strike.

The dangers of 'rank-and-filism' in the writing of labour history, concentrating on workplace relations and activism at the expense of analysing the vital
organisational and institutional dimensions of working-class experience, were
highlighted in the 1980s by Jonathan Zeitlin,[15] and have recently been reasserted
by Alastair Reid, in his account of trade unionism in the shipbuilding industry.[16] The analysis developed in this book so far, particularly in Chapter 2, has
rightly privileged the importance of workplace experience. This chapter focuses
more on the type of organisational and institutional elements that Zeitlin and
Reid see – along with social relations – as central to labour history. The inter-
union and inter-industry developments associated with the Ravenscraig struggle
clearly demonstrate the importance of trade union leadership, with McGahey
and his officials responding to the pressures from below that brought the strike
into existence. In exploring this dimension of coalfield politics the chapter
places in broader context the factors of colliery and community, which were
explored in the first part of the book, and which re-emerge in Chapters 4 and 5.
The Ravenscraig episode illustrates too the range of politicised allies that the
government was utilising to defeat the miners: the highly partial management of
the nationalised industries, with a prime role occupied by Bob Haslam, BSC
chairman; a politicised or at least highly malleable police force, that in
Strathclyde responded to Haslam's entreaty to prevent miners from travelling to
BSC premises at Ravenscraig and Hunterston, the Ayrshire coastal terminal
which imported coal and other materials passed through; and the private sector
road haulage firms, notably Yuill and Dodds of Strathaven in South

Lanarkshire, which helped BSC, the police and the government to break the miners' blockade by carrying materials from Hunterston to the steel mill.

The chapter proceeds with a discussion of Scottish industrial politics, including inter-union relations, and Ravenscraig. The analysis then proceeds to the strikers' attempted blockade of Ravenscraig, focusing especially on the first ten days of May. Further inter-union and inter-industry developments in the summer, including two major dock strikes provoked by the BSC's handling of imports, are then examined. The government's approach to the strike – and the resources expended on policing the miners' pickets at Ravenscraig and Hunterston – is emphasised at different points throughout. The chapter concludes by summarising the position at Ravenscraig at the end of the summer, as the 'Back to Work' campaign – organised by the NCB with the support of the government – began to attain some momentum in the coalfields.

Scottish industrial politics and Ravenscraig

'High political' accounts of the strike, including those that broadly sympathise with its aims, often dwell on differences between individuals within the NUM's leadership. These are usually explained in terms of personality rather than economic or political structures. Scargill is generally portrayed as volatile, vain, inflexible and 'impossibilist' or unrealistic, while McGahey usually appears as stable, pragmatic – 'despite' his Communism – and principled.[17] During the strike a range of observers privately expressed the view that the miners would have been better led had McGahey rather than Scargill succeeded Joe Gormley as NUM President in 1982. These encompassed trade union and political leaders, and other supporters of the strikers, including Jock Stein, then Scottish national football team manager, who knew McGahey from his earlier life as a Lanarkshire miner.[18] Subsequent literature has developed this theme, articulating a counter-factual lament that the strike could have had a different outcome with McGahey as NUM President.[19] Scargill eventually accepted, or chose not to resist, a return to work without a settlement, and no guarantees of future job and colliery security; McGahey, on the other hand, with his ostensibly greater intellect and more flexible approach to negotiation, would apparently have secured an agreement that prolonged significantly the life of a large portion of the industry.[20] In further illustration, perhaps, of the 'cultural circuit' of coalfield political memory, this position is reflected in the testimonies of some strike participants. David Hamilton, NUM delegate at Monktonhall and a member of the NUMSA executive, recalls that 'Mick would have found a mechanism' for ending the strike 'honourably', with pits and jobs preserved by agreement. Pressed to detail what that 'mechanism' might have been, Hamilton – with a self-deprecating laugh – emphasises McGahey's formidable intelligence and cunning: 'I don't know, but Mick would have found a way through it.'[21] Similar observations are offered by Willie Clarke and Iain Chalmers, both of Seafield, and Eric Clarke.[22]

The ending of the strike, with the improbability that McGahey would have found the type of settlement that eluded Scargill, is examined in Chapter 5. In terms of how the strike was pursued, however, the contrast between Scargill and McGahey merits greater elaboration at this juncture. Personality questions were important: Scargill's charisma and rhetorical talents as instruments in consolidating the solidarity of the strike – in Scotland as elsewhere – are often underestimated.[23] But they were accompanied by more significant political differences that were shaped by the contrasting regional, social and industrial environments of Yorkshire and central Scotland. The strike in Scotland was shaped by the distinctive politics of the NUMSA leadership. The strong Communist Party strain in Scotland's coalfields was not, of course, unique, with similar traditions in South Wales, parts of Yorkshire and Kent.[24] But there was a pronounced and separate Scottish component, emphasising distinctive national economic, social and industrial characteristics, which required devolved political arrangements in Scotland. It is no coincidence, as Chapter 1 noted, that McGahey and NUMSA more broadly were early trade union advocates of Home Rule for Scotland, and shaped the STUC's lasting commitments in this area from the late 1960s onwards. With these twin influences – Communism and devolution – the industrial politics of the Scottish coalfield resembled those of South Wales, perhaps, more than any other area of the British coalfield.[25]

The analogy with South Wales helps to elaborate further the impact on NUMSA's politics of Scotland's distinctive economic, industrial and social characteristics. Here it is worth reflecting on the sensitive comparison by Leighton S. James of coalfield identities and politics in South Wales with those in the German Ruhr from the 1890s to the 1920s. The German coalfield was industrially, religiously and ethnically diverse, inhibiting absolute labour solidarity, and encouraging instead mutually antipathetic Social Democratic and Communist traditions. In South Wales the greater industrial, religious and ethnic homogeneity produced roughly opposite traditions: relative solidarity, greater moderation and closer cooperation until the 1920s between Labour and Communist forces.[26] In the Scottish coalfield the restructuring of the 1950s and 1960s, examined in Chapter 1, contributed to escalating industrial militancy and politically consolidated the pre-existing Communist tradition. Like the Ruhr of the 1890s–1920s, however, although with different effects, coalfield politics in Scotland were imbued with a wide range of economic, industrial and ethno-religious ingredients. As a strong but minority force in the Scottish labour movement, and in a prolonged period of economic and industrial retrenchment from the 1950s onwards, McGahey and other NUMSA officials worked with a diverse body of trade unionists and across the political frontier between the Communist Party and the Labour left, seeking in most junctures to construct the broadest degree of working-class unanimity.[27] This was pursued from the 1981 coalfield crisis and onwards through the Triple Alliance of miners, railway and steel workers, and more broadly within the STUC and its multiple constituents: engineers and others engaged in industrial manufacturing, transport workers, local government, health service, and other public sector employees. In the great crisis of 1984–85 the NUM in Scotland was able to construct an even wider political alliance against pit closures and job losses, encompassing sympathetic church leaders, who supported the strike in communities and in their sometimes very public lobbying and criticism of the NCB and the government.[28] There was a flavour here of the old 'Popular Front', where Communist Party members in the latter 1930s and then in the Second World War, after the Nazi invasion of the Soviet Union in June 1941, sought common action with all anti-fascist 'progressive' forces, irrespective of their party political or social identities. So McGahey's Scottish industrial locale was wider, arguably, than Scargill's comparatively narrow – and perhaps politically isolating – Yorkshire industrial locale, in which coal predominated, with only perhaps steel as an alternative significant political presence. McGahey and his Scottish colleagues routinely encountered and developed a keener sense of industrial and political pluralism, involving dialogue and the balancing of competing forces.[29] This may explain the greater apparent tendency – exhibited by McGahey and the NUMSA leadership more broadly – to collegiality in trade union affairs than that exhibited by Scargill, particularly during the strike.[30]

So NUMSA's politics and approach to the strike were distinct from those of the NUM in Yorkshire. Yet differences of strategy were smaller. Despite their greater commitment to pluralism and persuasion NUMSA officials – as much as Scargill and other non-Scottish NUM officials – were convinced that the strike provided an opportunity to exert leadership in the broader trade union movement. This required other trade unionists, including the steel workers, to accept that their interests were served by supporting the strike. McGahey made this claim explicit at the STUC conference in Aberdeen on 17 April: 'Maggie Thatcher can have her septuagenarian American,' he said, referring to Ian MacGregor, 'but I have got young boys! They are fighting for their livelihood. They are fighting for their future and not only their own future, but the future of young engineers, young electricians, young steel workers. They are fighting for the youth of this country, and they are telling this Government: "We will not be bought off! Keep your filthy money, and we will keep our jobs and work with dignity".'[31]

The miners' assertion of wider labour movement leadership was further encouraged by the low regard that McGahey and other miners' leaders held towards the officials of the steel workers' union, the ISTC, both nationally and at Ravenscraig.[32] From time to time McGahey reminded the press about the NUM's support for the steel workers in their dispute with management and the government in 1980–81, hinting that this was not being reciprocated in the miners' strike.[33] Privately he was more critical, telling Tony Benn, Labour MP for Chesterfield, and a group of left trade union leaders in central London on 22 May, that the ISTC was a "sweetheart" union, a company union', and identifying the reluctance of the steel workers to cooperate with the miners at Ravenscraig as one of the NUM's main problems in the strike.[34] Abe Moffat, SCEBTA President, was equally critical, telling Willie Thompson in 1986 that ISTC officials in Scotland were politically and industrially 'sectarian', not only incapable of recognising the common interests of steel and coal workers, but blindly insisting that Ravenscraig men 'compete' against their fellows in other BSC establishments.[35] Oral history testimony reinforces this narrative. Iain Chalmers and Rab Amos recall supporting the steel workers in 1980–81 by encouraging others at Seafield and Monktonhall to 'black' new supplies of metal, even although these were needed underground. So they were dismayed in 1984 when Ravenscraig men maintained production with supplies of coal that the NUM had sought to blockade.[36] Willie Clarke remembers his irritation with Tommy Brennan, ISTC convenor at Ravenscraig, who on shared public meeting platforms with the NUM would speak nostalgically, emotionally even, about his long-deceased grandfather, a coal miner. The strike was not about the grandfathers of the workers and trade unionists of 1984, Clarke recalls thinking, and telling Brennan, but about their grandchildren. Protecting the interests of younger and future generations required the type of industrial and political action – including if necessary the cessation of production at Ravenscraig – that Brennan actively opposed, through passing intelligence of NUM strategy, gathered in Triple Alliance meetings, to BSC managers and therefore to the government.[37]

Tensions between NUMSA and ISTC officials were clear from the final week of March. One-third of the normal weekly supply of coking coal at Ravenscraig, some 8,000 tonnes, came from Polkemmet,[38] and the rest from imports stockpiled at Hunterston. K.W. McKay of the Scottish Office's Industry Department advised government ministers and other officials that without Polkemmet coal normal operations – based on imports still coming into the plant by rail – could be sustained for five to six weeks, according to Jim Dunbar, BSC's director at Ravenscraig.[39] But NUMSA and SCEBTA officials, perhaps alive to BSC management's opportunistic attempt to increase imports under the guise of 'normal' operations, intimated their dissatisfaction at a Triple Alliance meeting in Edinburgh on 27 March. George Bolton, NUMSA Vice President, told journalists that pickets would be mounted to reduce supplies to Ravenscraig, to cut its capacity to between 20 and 30 per cent.[40] Details of this 'stormy' encounter were relayed by ISTC officials to BSC managers, who passed them to the government.[41]

Further talks between ISTC and NUM officials followed on Thursday 29 March, where the steel men requested that coal movements be maintained so that Ravenscraig keep pace, in production terms, with its closest rival in the struggle for survival, the BSC plant at Llanwern in South Wales.[42] The miners considered this proposal for a few days before privately reaffirming on 2 April an earlier decision that Ravenscraig should only receive enough coal to keep its furnaces burning.[43] McGahey observed that the plant had enough coal for a week of full production and so there was no 'emergency'.[44] In private talks with ISTC officials he went slightly further, indicating that NUMSA could not guarantee continued support for any rail transfers from Hunterston to Ravenscraig. This was again conveyed to the government via BSC management by ISTC officials, Clive Lewis, Scottish Divisional Officer, and Tommy Brennan.[45]

The insecurities of Ravenscraig workers and union officials have been emphasised in the literature, notably by Keith Aitken and David Stewart.[46] They were
to an extent demoralised by the outcome of the 1980–81 dispute, noted in
Chapter 1, with jobs in the industry roughly halved since 1979 to 71,000,[47] and
their troubles are acknowledged in the oral testimonies of some of the strike
participants. Nicky Wilson and David Hamilton – regulars on the Ravenscraig
and Hunterston picket lines – argue that NUMSA's approach to the ISTC and
its actions at BSC premises were regrettable. The steel workers were 'our people',
who supported the miners, morally and materially, with substantial financial
collections at Ravenscraig for strike funds throughout 1984 and into 1985,
despite the picketing and tensions in the early months of the strike.[48] Wilson
and Hamilton, it might be noted, retained mainstream labour movement positions at the time of their interviews for this book in 2009, as elected head of the
Scottish miners and Labour MP for Midlothian. Their enduring emphasis on
the common humanity, dignity and solidarity of Scottish labour might therefore
usefully be contrasted with the testimony of Eric Clarke, Hamilton's retired
parliamentary predecessor, who, like Rab Amos and Iain Chalmers, both
Communist Party members in 1984–85, and Willie Clarke, a Communist
Councillor in Fife, emphasises the political and intellectual weaknesses of steel
industry union representatives, and the clear practical sense of the strikers'
approach to Ravenscraig.[49]

Uppermost in the thinking of the ISTC officials, of course, was the possibility
that Ravenscraig, if shut down by the miners, would never reopen. Ian
MacGregor, former chairman of BSC, and still on the corporation's directorate,
articulated this prospect in pungent terms over the weekend of 31 March and 1
April.[50] This was discussed by the STUC General Council on 4 April, with
George Bolton and Clive Lewis present, the latter expressing the fear that BSC
management would use a cessation of production as a 'convenient' pretext to
close Ravenscraig.[51] In any event the intelligence on the strikers' strategy and
tactics relayed by ISTC officials allowed BSC management to make important
contingency planning. Dunbar advised McKay of the Scottish Office on 4 April
that he had already contacted a non-unionised haulage firm, with a view to
supplying Ravenscraig from Hunterston by road, and spoken to Strathclyde
Police about controlling and breaching the likely NUMSA and SCEBTA picket
which would result.[52] Ministers luxuriated in these internal labour movement
anxieties. Peter Walker, Secretary of State for Energy, responded to questioning
on the subject by asserting that the threat to Ravenscraig was entirely the
creation of the strikers.[53] At Ravenscraig on 5 April ISTC officials offered a
crucial concession to management, intimating a willingness to breach their
agreements with the mining and rail unions by working with road hauliers to
protect production and employment.[54] This private undertaking to break the
strike is important, contrasting with Clive Lewis's public insistence several
weeks later, on 30 April, that the ISTC could not 'entertain the idea' of lorries
bringing coal through NUM and SCEBTA pickets. 'My members,' he told
reporters, 'will not be seen as strike-breakers.'[55]

In the intervening period an agreement between the NUM, the ISTC and the railwaymen, established on 9 April, had been in place, allowing two daily trains, amounting to a weekly supply of 16,000 tonnes.[56] This was roughly two-thirds of the volume required for full production, and came under pressure from two sources: the NUM's approach in England and Wales, involving a total ban on rail movement of coal, which NUMSA was being pressed to accept, and Ravenscraig management's insistence that supply be increased to secure optimum production, particularly as its South Wales rivals, Llanwern and Port Talbot, were operating at near full capacity.[57] The position was complicated by the impending arrival at Hunterston of a Norwegian cargo vessel, the *Obo King*, laden with 65,000 tonnes of coal. On 24 April the NUMSA and SCEBTA strike committee restated the objective of halting production while preserving the plant,[58] and on 27 April a Triple Alliance meeting in Edinburgh resolved to cut daily supply to a single train. This was opposed by Brennan and Lewis, whose account of the meeting reached McKay at the Scottish Office on the following Monday, 30 April. At a further Triple Alliance meeting that same Monday Lewis reprised the steel workers' worries that the crisis would result in the closure of Ravenscraig.[59] This meeting was described by BSC officials, when they heard news of its contents, as 'unproductive'. At this point – McKay reported on 1 May – Dunbar, the plant's director, decided to 'accelerate' the plan to bring coal to Ravenscraig by road.[60]

It is likely that BSC management and workers were exaggerating the physical dangers to Ravenscraig. NUMSA and SCEBTA officials certainly thought so, privately regarding ISTC officials as being 'less than frank' about the true situation.[61] On 2 May, during further inter-union talks in Edinburgh, just before the final decision to load lorries that left Hunterston at 2 p.m., McGahey duly 'extracted' an admission from the steel men that the plant was still running at 70 per cent capacity.[62] This indicated a marginal increase in production since the end of March, when Dunbar reported to the Scottish Office that the plant could run at 50–60 per cent capacity with existing supplies. So bringing materials in by road was really designed to raise production rather than maintain survival, which was not threatened so long as the Triple Alliance agreement – a daily train – held. This is important, given that the literature criticises the miners' unions for jeopardising Ravenscraig, fracturing labour solidarity and selfishly privileging their strike over the jobs of steel workers.[63] In this connection it is also worth reflecting on an analysis of the strike position more generally, published in the *Scotsman* on 3 May, by Andrew Marr. This established the strike's limited impact on electricity generation and supply, and concluded that the miners' leaders were therefore acting 'with impeccable logic' in targeting the politically important steel plant.[64]

The electricity supply certainly counted against the strikers. The South of Scotland Electricity Board (SSEB) and the North of Scotland Hydro-Electric Board between them were capable of producing 5,400 megawatts without burning any coal at all, Marr wrote, which, by coincidence, almost matched peak, mid-winter Scottish demand of 5,452 megawatts. Since the power cuts and short-time working of the 1972 and 1974 miners' strikes there had been a growth in non-coal electricity generation in Scotland. Key developments were the nuclear power station at Hunterston B, providing 1,040 megawatts of electricity generation, and the natural gas power station at Peterhead, with a further 1,300 megawatts. Pressure on the power grid had been further eased by falling industrial demand, with the recession of the early 1980s, accentuated by the closure of one of Scotland's largest single electricity users, the Invergordon aluminium smelter. In addition, the SSEB's coal-burning power stations – notably Longannet, capable of producing 2,304 megawatts – were stocked with fuel sufficient to ensure normal operations for six months.[65] The six months of stocks tally had been in the public domain on the eve of the strike, trumpeted by the NCB and the SSEB,[66] and was consistent with internal Scottish Office estimates. Collated at the Scottish Office by Muir Russell, early in April, these indicated that coal stocks amounted to an 'endurance' period of 26 weeks of normal generation and supply.[67] Russell's regular reports remained broadly confident in tone. In late June, reflecting on the capacity of non-coal power generation summarised by Marr, and explored in further detail in the *Scotsman* by Frank Frazer, emphasising that overall 'coal burn' in Scotland had fallen from 8 million tonnes in 1980 to 4.5 million tonnes in 1983,[68] Russell advised colleagues that 'endurance' was now in excess of 26 weeks, and could be envisaged to February 1985.[69] In these circumstances, as Marr concluded in May, with the CBI in Scotland reporting no commercial hardship arising from the strike, and not a single business in the country said to be entirely reliant on coal, it would have been futile for the strikers to base their strategy on restricting power generation. Wider political forces had to be mobilised. In this connection the propinquity and outcome of the District Council elections on 3 May 1984 – with the comprehensive losses experienced by the Tories – is worth re-emphasising. So for the striking miners, returning to the Marr analysis, blocking the road to Ravenscraig, while admittedly dangerous, was worth pursuing, given the mounting political pressure on the Tories in Scotland.[70]

The blockade of Ravenscraig

Production was maintained at Ravenscraig by the dramatic introduction of road haulage on the afternoon of Wednesday 2 May. Three firms were initially used: Brogan's of Motherwell, Malcolm's of Paisley, and the principal carrier, Yuill and Dodds, of Strathaven in Lanarkshire.[71] James Yuill, owner-director of the last named, was unapologetic about his self-interest in breaking the miners' strike.[72] His politics, critical of trade unionism, and supportive of the government, were discussed within the Scottish Office later in the dispute. Ministers and civil servants were discussing complaints from residents in towns which Yuill's lorries passed through twice a day, often noisily during the night, and sometimes allegedly dangerously, on the one hundred-mile return run between Hunterston and Ravenscraig. These complaints, pursued by Norman Buchan, Labour MP for Paisley South, were greatly resented by Yuill, who felt he was being persecuted for supporting the government. In the Scottish Office McKay advised Michael Ancram, the Parliamentary Under-Secretary of State, that Yuill was 'a very determined man who believes strongly that the NUM action must not be allowed to succeed'.[73]

The strikers struggled to respond to this new situation. The manner in which strike organisation was constructed and operated is detailed in the following chapter, but here it should be noted that in Scotland there were six area centres for mobilisation, and transmitting intelligence to and from NUMSA's Edinburgh headquarters: Dysart in East Fife, Fishcross in Clackmannan, Dalkeith in Midlothian, Whitburn in West Lothian, Cardowan in Lanarkshire, and Ayr. On 2 May Whitburn strikers reported to Edinburgh headquarters that police officers were diverting all public traffic away from Ravenscraig, and there were hundreds of police present too at Hunterston, according to Ayrshire strikers. At 6.55 p.m. Michael McGahey phoned NUMSA headquarters himself, 'to impress upon this office the need to mount as large as possible a picket' at Ravenscraig the following morning. Strike centres were immediately informed, and all the while Yuill and Dodds kept supplies moving, with a continued 'heavy' police presence making it impossible for miners to block the road. Those who did were arrested, according to David Hamilton, whose call from Ravenscraig was logged by NUMSA headquarters at 9.50 p.m., eight hours after the first coal had arrived.[74] Roughly one hundred pickets were outside Hunterston the following morning, 3 May, with three hundred at Ravenscraig, including from 7 a.m. Michael McGahey and Eric Clarke, outnumbered by around four hundred police officers. Several strikers were arrested, among them McGahey's driver.[75] Later in the day pickets were more heavily outnumbered by police: six to one, according to Bob Graham of Lochgelly, reporting to Dysart, which had despatched two coaches to Ravenscraig. 'Boys' were 'being beat up' by police officers, he said, and arrested for swearing.[76] Martin Gostwick, editor of *Scottish Miner*, the NUMSA and SCEBTA monthly newspaper, was at Ravenscraig too on 3 May, and also emphasised police heavy-handedness, with pickets punched and their hair pulled by officers.[77]

The road haulage initiative, while stretching picketing resources, also placed great strains on the solidarity of Scottish labour. The lorries, including those belonging to Yuill and Dodds, were driven by Transport and General Workers' Union (TGWU) members. Hugh Wyper, the TGWU official responsible for road haulage in Scotland, who sat on the STUC General Council and was a Communist Party member, was urged by NUMSA officials to compel his union members to observe the miners' picket lines. Wyper detailed a Glasgow regional official to meet the Yuill and Dodds shop stewards, who intimated that the firm's drivers could not meet this request. At Ravenscraig on Friday 4 May Hamilton managed to speak to drivers before they entered the plant. Some non-coal hauliers turned back, but those with coal went in.[78] Relations between the strikers and the steel workers, inevitably, were further damaged. Brennan emerged and spoke to NUM pickets on 2 May, claiming that BSC's move to road haulage initiative had 'nothing to do with him'.[79] McGahey said this was not credible: ISTC members had accepted supplies in breach of an inter-union agreement – the daily trainload – and through a picket line.[80]

The NUM, supported by rail unions, suspended the daily train from Hunterston to Ravenscraig,[81] and prepared a much larger picket force – a 'blitz', Eric Clarke's word – for Monday 7 May.[82] At 5.30 a.m. Dysart despatched three full coaches: one from the centre itself, passing through Glenrothes and Lochore; a second from Cardenden, picking up through central Fife; and a third from Denbeath Miners' Welfare Institute in Leven, collecting from Sauchenbush in Kirkcaldy.[83] There were a thousand pickets at Ravenscraig that morning, and another hefty police presence. By mid-afternoon 35 pickets had been arrested and taken to Motherwell police station. At Hunterson 600 pickets faced 1,000 police officers, according to Neil Valentine of Ayr, reporting to NUMSA headquarters, with 21 arrested and taken to Kilmarnock police station. One of those arrested at Ravenscraig was Nicky Wilson. The bureaucratic NUMSA and SCEBTA record baldly states that he was held overnight until 8 May.[84] His memory of the event is understandably more colourful. Marshalling pickets outside the plant, he was 'huckled' by police officers, who claimed he had been throwing bottles in their direction. These had actually been propelled, Wilson says, by 'ultra-left' political activists, standing behind the miners as they pushed against the police to try and obstruct the road. Charged with Breach of the Peace, Wilson was found Not Guilty in Hamilton Sheriff Court, after NUMSA's solicitor, Manus McGuire, of Thompson's, secured legal aid for his defence. Wilson had been apprehended in the middle of the day on 7 May but briefly escaped, climbing a six-foot hedge and running through gardens of adjacent houses. He was caught and put into a police van. With no court sitting he spent the rest of the day and the night that followed with two others in a cell in Motherwell police station. They were initially euphoric, singing 'We Shall Not Be Moved', but grew tired as the hours passed, and hungry, thirsty and cold. After midnight the cell door was opened and an officer threw in cold fish and black pudding suppers, which were heavily salted. In hunger the prisoners ate nevertheless, and then, inevitably, with nothing to drink, became extremely thirsty.[85]

Wilson's experience reflected the robust and partial approach being taken by the police to the pickets and the picketing more broadly, in an increasingly violent and confrontational atmosphere, encapsulated by Yuill and Dodds fitting protective metal grilles to lorry windscreens. On Tuesday 8 May, with the *Obo King* and its 68,000 tonnes of coal due to land, according to NUMSA intelligence,[86] there were 1,500 pickets at Hunterston, and 1,500 more at Ravenscraig, with roughly equivalent numbers of police officers at each site. Major disturbances were recorded, especially at Hunterston when the lorries returned at lunchtime to collect a second load. The police claimed to have been attacked with stones and bottles; press photographs and television news footage depicted mounted police officers riding over prostrate pickets. McGahey was furious with the police's use of physical force to squeeze the lorries through.[87] There were 62 arrests: 28 from Midlothian, including David Hamilton, who was trying to negotiate with police officers,[88] thirteen from Ayr, nine from Fife, six from West Lothian, four from Stirling and two from Lanarkshire.[89] Police stopped and threatened to arrest East Fife miners at Harthill on the M8. Their morale was described as being 'very low', but they resolved, despite this 'police brutality', to undertake the same journey – back to Hunterston – the next day.[90]

The strikers were tightening the pressure on Ravenscraig and, indirectly, on the government, through this vigorous picketing and with the assistance of some TGWU members on the roads and in the docks. The TGWU's Paisley branch initiated the idea of blockading fuel to the BSC-enlisted haulage firms. Malcolm's of Paisley withdrew from the BSC operation on 7 May, and Grangemouth TGWU members operating from the BP refinery's fuel depots blacked deliveries to Yuill and Dodds on 8 May. Dockers at Hunterston then intimated that they would not handle the *Obo King*, a change of policy from the previous week, on the basis that the road haulage operation had altered the situation entirely. Tugboat men indicated that they too would black the vessel, meaning that it could only land at Hunterston if unusually benign weather prevailed.[91] The *Scotsman* reported the 'growing realisation that the sporadic lorry deliveries to Ravenscraig cannot keep the plant alive for any length of time',[92] and Gordon Murray, the Scottish Office's 'liaison' man in London, described the position as 'finely balanced'. There was a distinct possibility that the pickets would succeed in halting deliveries, in which case production at Ravenscraig would cease within three days.[93]

With the strikers close to an important victory, Bob Haslam, BSC chairman, made a crucial intervention. On 8 May he advised Department of Energy officials that Ravenscraig was not attracting sufficient police protection, likening its impending closure to the mass blockade of the Saltley coke depot during the 1972 miners' strike, noted in Chapter 1. This was a telling reference to a central episode in the Thatcherite narrative of unacceptable union 'violence' and power.[94] Haslam's careful and highly political approach then included a question: were police officers acting to stop pickets from gathering at Ravenscraig?[95] McGahey claimed some miners had been stopped in exactly this manner on 4 May. The Fife men were halted at Harthill on the day of Haslam's intervention, as were three busloads of pickets close to Ravenscraig, with 42 men taken to Motherwell police station and charged with Breach of the Peace. But until this point there had been no reported systematic halting of pickets at a distance from either of the BSC sites.[96] Haslam was perhaps aware of this, his careful approach geared to altering the position without attracting any potential charge of directly intervening in police operational matters. Department of Energy officials communicated his thinking to the Scottish Office.[97] It cannot be verified that it was also conveyed to Strathclyde Police, but it was surely no coincidence that Haslam's intervention was followed within 48 hours by a change of policy. At 9 a.m. on Thursday 10 May eight coaches from Fishcross, carrying 290 miners from West Fife, Clackmannan and Stirlingshire, were halted on the A80 at Stepps, en route to Hunterston. This removed 'large numbers of trouble-making pickets' from Ravenscraig and Hunterston, in the words of the Scottish

Office daily situation report, and immediately improved supply to the plant.[98] Roderick Nicholson, Strathclyde's Assistant Chief Constable, claimed that he alone was responsible for initiating this action, to prevent 'large numbers bent on disorder' from mustering at the BSC sites.[99] Haslam, maintaining a discreet distance, nevertheless wrote within a fortnight to Sir Patrick Hamill, Chief Constable of Strathclyde, offering thanks for the force's successful efforts in dispersing pickets and relieving the pressure on Ravenscraig.[100]

The Fishcross men were roughly treated on 10 May. They sat on the road in protest, and were arrested and photographed by police: 'treated like criminals', in the illuminating words of Iain McCaig of Solsgirth, speaking to Willie Thompson in 1986.[101] The men were held for several hours at different Glasgow police stations without food or drink, according to John McCormack, NUM delegate at Polmaise, who was present and relayed events to union headquarters.[102] McCormack's highly colourful account appears in Guthrie Hutton's collection of strike memories: 'I was in the first bus and this old geyser with the braid and that on his cap says to the bus driver "turn back".' In deadpan manner McCormack told the police that the men were travelling to a picnic, pointing out a stock of pies and sandwiches in the boot. But 'before you could say Jake Robertson there was motors coming from everywhere, boom, boom across the road, and the men were saying "What are we going to do?", and I says "Get out in the middle of the road, they cannae lift the lot of us" – and they lifted every one us – 295 men!' [103] The same episode was recalled with some bitterness too by several Cowie strikers,[104] these recollections consistent with Jean Stead's 1987 account. This presented the episode as an important peaceful protest, and a significant counterpoint to the dominant discourse of violent struggle and confrontational picketing that was articulated by the police – 'large numbers bent on disorder' – as well as the government and its many media supporters.[105]

The new position, with BSC's determined road haulage effort and the more zealous policing, denuded the picketing of effectiveness, and made it dangerous too. This was recognised by Tam Coulter, a member of the NUMSA executive in 1984. Interviewed by Willie Thompson in 1986, he likened the exchanges at Ravenscraig to fighting tanks with cavalry, as the mighty lorries thundered through the pickets at high speed.[106] NUMSA suspended its opposition to rail movement of coal on 11 May, and a Triple Alliance meeting that day produced a new inter-union supply deal.[107] Road haulage was duly suspended on 31 May, with Ravenscraig receiving 18,000 tonnes per week and operating once more at 70 per cent of capacity.[108] Meanwhile the *Obo King* docked on a calm sea without needing the tugboat men, and unloaded half its cargo before being blacked by the ISTC as part of the new inter-union deal on rail supplies. The new deal, brokered in part by Jimmy Milne, STUC General Secretary, and Alex Kitson, TGWU Deputy General Secretary,[109] lasted a month, before NUMSA, under pressure from the NUM national executive, resumed the blockade of Ravenscraig.[110] This was in the context of the brutal culmination on 18 June of the NUM's action at BSC's Orgreave coke works near Sheffield, which included large-scale picketing and very heavy policing to maintain outward flow of materials to the steel works at Scunthorpe. Many Scots were present. Their eye-witness accounts, whether articulated at the time or twenty years later, emphasised an extremely frightening encounter with state power. Pickets faced paramilitary-uniformed officers bearing riot shields and long batons, supported by horse-mounted officers, dogs and snatch squads.[111] There were serious injuries but no mortal casualties at Orgreave, although one Scottish striker was killed elsewhere on picketing duty that week: Joseph Green, from Blairhall in West Fife, a miner at the 'Big K', Kellingley in North Yorkshire. He was involved in a fatal accident on 15 June at Ferrybridge Power Station in West Yorkshire. On 21 June members of the Scottish Area strike committee discussed Green's death and arrangements for his funeral, the following day at Pontefract,[112] which, a Sheffield reminiscence website relates, was attended by 8,000 people.[113]

At Ravenscraig the strikers resumed their attempted squeeze on the government. This was undermined, once again, by inter-union intelligence filtered by steel union officials back to BSC management, the government and the police. Over the weekend of 16–17 June ISTC officials told Jim Dunbar that train supplies would be suspended at midnight on 18 June. Dunbar duly planned the resumption of road deliveries, which took effect on Wednesday 20 June. Yuill and Dodds was back in business, the firm's fifty lorries, supported by a renewed policing operation, on the way to clocking up 4.5 million miles between Hunterston and Ravenscraig by the end of the strike.[114] On 3 July Scottish Office officials noted that 67,000 tonnes of coal and coke had been delivered to Ravenscraig by road during the previous week, massively exceeding the weekly tonnage of 18,000 permitted under the inter-union rail agreement.[115] The revised road arrangements allowed Dunbar to satisfy his ambition of holding the plant above 80–85 per cent capacity, with continuous steel production more than allowing the blast furnaces to remain intact.[116] McGahey privately excoriated what he saw as the folly of the ISTC officials, who refused to 'recognise that their destiny' – the very preservation of Ravenscraig – 'lay with the miners and the winning of the present dispute'.[117]

The strikers had been held back by the combination of road haulage and heavy police intervention. The legality and broader monetary and social costs of this police action attracted considerable political disquiet. John Maxton, Labour MP for Glasgow Cathcart, procured from Michael Ancram the significant information that policing costs at Ravenscraig and Hunterston in the first week of May, encompassing additional overtime only, amounted to £577,000.[118] This bears emphasis. In October 1985 the government – again by parliamentary answer – indicated that the total policing costs incurred in Scotland during the strike, excluding basic salary costs, were £5,052,000.[119] So 11.4 per cent of the total additional police costs in Scotland in the year-long dispute were incurred at Hunterston and Ravenscraig in this single week in May, in what appears to have been the definitive incident of the Scottish strike. Ravenscraig was kept open and in production, but only just, on the basis of a huge police effort.

Broader issues were articulated in two meetings involving Labour MPs, primarily from mining constituencies, and led by Donald Dewar, Shadow

Secretary of State for Scotland, first with Sir Patrick Hamill, Strathclyde Chief Constable, on Monday 21 May, and then with George Younger, Secretary of State for Scotland, on Wednesday 23 May. Here Hamill and Younger both rationalised the action by referring to the 1967 Police (Scotland) Act, Section 17 of which enabled officers to 'guard, patrol and watch so as to prevent the commission of offences', and 'to present order, and to protect life and property'. Younger was briefed to insist that the police had delayed their intervention 'until after mass picketing and violent scenes had taken place'.[120] This might be taken as an inflated reference, perhaps, to the events at Ravenscraig on 3 May, when a handful of arrests were made, or the picketing at Hunterston and Ravenscraig on 7 and 8 May, when there were numerous arrests, but no reports of serious injury.[121] Younger's officials also advised him to reject any suggestion that police 'snatch squads' targeted particular individuals, despite the arrests of well-known NUMSA and SCEBTA officials, including David Hamilton and Nicky Wilson.[122]

Hamill judged that his meeting had gone fairly well, advising the Scottish Office of the Labour MPs' 'reasonable' approach, typified in their decision to avoid publicising the encounter. Younger's officials impressed on him the need to avoid commenting on particular 'alleged' incidents and to emphasise the police's 'operational independence'.[123] The Labour MPs had no knowledge, of course, of Haslam's intervention of 8 May, but they nevertheless picked a substantial hole in the government's claim of non-involvement by exploring a statement made by the Lord Advocate at roughly the same point. This focused on Section 17 of the 1967 police legislation, and the police's obligation to control or curtail the activities of persons travelling to a place where it was likely that a Breach of the Peace would occur. On 23 May Dick Douglas, MP for Dunfermline West, told Younger that two days earlier Hamill had referred to the Lord Advocate's advice when explaining the policy of stopping pickets on the open road.[124] The wider implications of the police's actions – on relations with the community, and the picture in the UK more widely – are considered in Chapter 5. Here, however, it is worth emphasising one further aspect of the policing at Hunterston and Ravenscraig. Officers were potentially armed with new legislation, introduced by the Conservative government since 1979, setting clear restrictions on the collective conduct of industrial disputes. But the government's strategy during the strike was to keep these new laws – unpopular with the broad body of trade unionists – out of the strike, with the intention of minimising political controversy. Peter Walker, Secretary of State for Energy, feared that solidarity between striking miners and other unionised workers would be strengthened if these laws were deployed, and ministers discouraged the NCB and BSC from using them to restrain picketing.[125] The police ignored the new laws too, prohibiting the movement and regulating the behaviour of striking miners by using older common law implements in England and Wales, and in Scotland, as has been seen, by deploying the 1967 Police (Scotland) Act.[126]

Stepping Stones: industrial politics and the government

The strikers' defeat at Ravenscraig illuminated the character and scale of the forces opposing them, marshalled by the Conservative government. Outwith Scotland this was made dramatically visible also at Orgreave on 18 June. 'They [the pickets] took a tanking that day,' recalls Cath Cunningham, an activist in Fife, 'and it made you reflect quite a lot about where we were going with this strike, and realise what we were up against in terms of the force, the resources and finance that the government was prepared to put in to ensure that the outcome would be in their favour.'[127] The government's position – hardening into an ambition to inflict complete defeat on the strikers – was further illustrated in the months that followed, especially during dock strikes at Hunterston and other ports in support of the miners.

While its ambitions gradually grew as the strike progressed, the government's approach remained consistent throughout, shaped by the cautious but determined 'Stepping Stones' anti-trade union strategy. This required isolating the striking miners from other groups of unionised workers. The approach was plainly observable in the opening weeks of the strike, when ministers talked up its dangerous implications for the jobs of steel workers. The approach became clearer still during the blockade of Ravenscraig, and then during the summer, as ministers and officials, including those in the Scottish Office, worked carefully to keep the strikers' potential allies out of the dispute, particularly in the ports. Dock workers, including men at Hunterston, were antagonised more than once by incursions on their working customs arising from over-hasty efforts, chiefly by BSC management, to speed the passage of coal imports to steel plants. Waterfront strikes resulted, early in July and then in August, which the government settled as quickly as possible, by persuading some groups of port workers that there were no plans to abolish the National Dock Labour Scheme, which guaranteed their employment security and privileges, and provided some joint industrial regulation. Dock workers had been anxious about threats to the Scheme since the 1960s, with the revolution in containerised shipping, which transformed the labour process and shifted traffic and jobs to rapidly expanding non-Scheme ports, notably Felixstowe and Harwich.[128]

BSC management advised the Scottish Office in late June that further imports of coke – to maintain the operational target of running Ravenscraig at 80–85 per cent capacity – would be required by late August, when Hunterston's stocks would be near exhaustion.[129] This was complicated by a national dock strike that commenced on 10 July, after BSC employees handled materials in the Humber port of Immingham that should, under Dock Labour Scheme regulations, have been left to registered dock workers, who were TGWU members. This was a major issue of principle, to the TGWU and registered dock workers. The 'indefinite strike' declared across Britain, which brought Scotland's ports to a 'standstill' by 11 July,[130] worried the government. An emergency ministerial committee, chaired by the Secretary of State for Transport, Nicholas Ridley, emphasised that 'industry', while relatively unconcerned about the impact or duration of the miners' strike itself, was nevertheless 'very anxious' that the related stoppage in the ports be brought to a rapid end.[131] Keen to obtain an early settlement, and maintain the relative isolation of the striking miners, Ridley told the House of Commons that BSC's transgression of work practices in Immingham would not be repeated, and that the government had 'no plans to change or abolish the Dock Labour Scheme'.[132] He also sought to put pressure on the TGWU and striking dock workers by asking officials to gather reports of industrial 'lay-offs' – including in Scotland – arising from the suspension of imports and exports. These were to be presented as 'hardships' caused by the strike, with Ridley keen to hear about 'concrete examples' of redundancies among union members.[133]

John Prescott, the Labour Party's Transport Spokesman, pushed Ridley to harden the government's commitment so that there would be no legislative changes to the Dock Labour Scheme before the next General Election. Ridley refused to do so,[134] but after lengthy talks between union and employer representatives at the Advisory, Conciliation and Arbitration Service (ACAS), on the future use of non-registered labour in Scheme ports, dockers resumed work on Monday 23 July.[135] Further difficulty was already being anticipated at Hunterston, however, with the expected arrival early in August of the Liberian-registered *Ostia*, with 95,000 tonnes of Australian coking coal for Ravenscraig.[136] The 24 TGWU dock workers at Hunterston, Clyde Port Authority (CPA) employees, would be reluctant to handle this cargo because road haulage to Ravenscraig had broken the Triple Alliance inter-union agreement on railway supply. If BSC employees at Hunterston unloaded the cargo without TGWU dock workers then the terms of the Dock Labour Scheme would also be breached. This could precipitate labour protests in other Scheme ports, on a par with the strike in July.[137]

The potential for wider conflict shaped a lengthy delay in the *Ostia*'s arrival at Hunterston. Norman Tebbit, Secretary of State for Trade and Industry, advised Peter Walker that caution was essential, to prevent another damaging UK-wide strike. Tebbit is usually depicted as one of the Thatcher government's strongest advocates of labour market and trade union 'reforms', to weaken the collective rights and privileges of workers.[138] His call for a patient approach to the unloading of the *Ostia* further illustrates the character of the 'Stepping Stones' anti-union strategy, with the government engaging its labour 'enemies' one at a time. The broader goal of isolating the striking miners was given priority over BSC's needs at Hunterston and Ravenscraig, despite pressure from Younger as well as Haslam for the *Ostia* to be berthed immediately and unloaded by BSC employees. The intervention of Younger, generally an emollient figure who faced the Tories' declining position in Scotland by distancing himself from the frankest expressions of Thatcherism,[139] is therefore significant, involving a direct appeal to the Prime Minister for a more confrontational approach, which she refused.[140] The distinct politics of Scotland and Ravenscraig were once more in evidence, with Younger anxious that the steel plant might be shut down – at substantial cost to the reputation of the government and the Conservative Party in Scotland – without the rapid transmission of the *Ostia*'s supplies. Thatcher ignored this, and blandly commanded that Scottish public opinion, which she presumed to support BSC's attempt to maintain Ravenscraig at optimum production, be 'mobilised' against the TGWU.[141]

The Prime Minister's limited grasp of Scottish politics and public opinion is conceded even by those who continue to praise her,[142] but her support for Tebbit's position – based on the same tactical reading of the 'Stepping Stones' strategy – was perhaps emboldened by intelligence that national TGWU officials wanted to avoid another strike. John Connolly, the union's national docks officer, was said to favour a 'Scottish context' solution to the *Ostia* impasse. Local talks involving representatives of the various parties involved – BSC, CPA and TWGU – were unsuccessful,[143] but Tebbit still delayed, wanting further evidence, perhaps, that dock workers across the UK would not support a stoppage at Hunterston. This, his office reported to the Prime Minister's office on 15 August, involved awaiting a ruling from the National Dock Labour Board, to which the Clyde Dock Labour Board had referred the question of whether the *Ostia* could be discharged without registered dock workers.[144] On 22 August the National Board concluded that this was not possible. Tebbit's office now accepted that the Ravenscraig position was 'urgent': without more coal the ovens would be banked up on 28 August, ending production shortly afterwards.[145] This was close to the outcome sought by NUMSA and SCEBTA since the start of the strike. So at this point, with further talks involving the CPA and the TGWU still not producing an agreement, the government supported immediate BSC action. The *Ostia*, anchored off Belfast Lough for two weeks, came into Hunterston on 23 August, and BSC employees discharged 90 per cent of its cargo. This was an attempt to work within the letter of the Dock Labour Scheme, which preserved a tenth of BSC unloading at Hunterston for dock workers, while clearly evading its spirit, which required inter-union cooperation.[146]

Registered dock workers across Scotland – in Greenock, Glasgow, Ardrossan, Ayr, Troon, Leith, Burntisland, Kirkcaldy, Dundee and Aberdeen – came out on strike in protest within 24 hours.[147] There was less solidarity elsewhere in the UK, as perhaps Tebbit and his officials had predicted. John Connolly contacted his members, advising them that 'outside labour' had been used without TGWU approval at Hunterston, and so the Dock Labour Scheme had clearly been breached, necessitating further strike action.[148] Support for a strike followed in some English ports, notably in London and on the Humber, where the July strike had originated. There were reservations elsewhere, however, notably at the large container port of Tilbury on the Thames, where some workers criticised the 'violent minority' allegedly leading the miners' strike, and demanded a national ballot of TGWU dock members on whether to support the Hunterston stoppage.[149]

In conversation with Fred Lindop in the early 1980s, before the events examined here, Joe Bloomberg, an activist in the London docks, characterised Tilbury workers as politically unsophisticated 'carrot crunchers' who often failed to recognise what he and others saw as the necessity of industrial action on other parts of the river.[150] Yet on this occasion the Tilbury men appeared to speak for others in at least some port areas who went against TGWU officials by working normally. These men were worried perhaps about over-extending their hand against the Conservative government, despite the apparent victory that had been secured in the July strike. Ministers were pleased by this. In the Scottish Office Michael Ancram circulated an anti-strike broadsheet produced by the Tilbury workers, which he obtained at a ministerial meeting on 29 August, as evidence that the strike might be short-lived.[151]

The dock strike in Scotland caused minor difficulties, with action at Aberdeen delaying transport to the mainland of livestock from Orkney and Shetland, where there would be no grazing after October,[152] and in Dundee, where supplies of raw jute were held up. But across the UK there was no major economic disruption,[153] and the Association of British Chambers of Commerce reported on 12 September that the strike's impact was smaller than that in July, with 65 per cent of imports and exports unaffected.[154] At Hunterston a further major cargo vessel, the *Argos*, docked on 6 September and BSC employees unloaded coal for Ravenscraig, in the same way that the *Ostia* had been unloaded two weeks earlier.[155] Moved perhaps by this limited impact, and with the dock strike reported to be nearing collapse by 7 September, John Prescott attempted to broker an agreement in Glasgow between ISTC and TGWU officials. This revolved around a weekly volume of 18,000 tonnes of coal to Ravenscraig by rail, matching the Triple Alliance agreement that operated in June, although Prescott intimated that incremental increases could be possible, to 20,000 and then 22,500 tonnes.[156] This was 'sabotaged', according to Jeremy Bray, the Labour MP whose Motherwell constituency contained Ravenscraig, by Haslam and Tebbit, who on the day of the Prescott talks urged the plant's director, Jim Dunbar, to take a 'firm line' against the proposed settlement.[157] Bray told reporters that this version of events had been confirmed to him by Haslam's office, and complained to George Younger about the 'macho attitude' of Tebbit and BSC management.[158]

The dock strike ended several days later after a TGWU delegate conference in London.[159] Some activists, part of the minority that favoured extending the strike, argued that no assurances regarding BSC cargo handling at Hunterston had been obtained. This could expose dockers elsewhere to further incursions on their working arrangements, with the possibility that the Dock Labour Scheme would be abolished. The *Financial Times* observed that employers were pursuing this outcome, which was now on the government's agenda.[160] Tebbit and his colleagues, so keen to play a cautious hand in August, and emboldened by the relatively low impact of this second strike, were indeed contemplating an attack on organised labour in the ports. This would be pursued, in classic Thatcherite 'Stepping Stones' manner, following the defeat of the striking miners, with the abolition of the Scheme in 1989.[161]

At Ravenscraig, beyond the Hunterston-related supply worries, there were few disturbances in the mid-summer and early autumn of 1984, certainly nothing to compare with the vigorous picketing that nearly closed the plant in May. This was partly a question of the resources available to NUMSA and SCEBTA, with pickets required from mid-August to prevent strike-breaking at Barony, Killoch, Seafield, Frances, the Longannet complex, Polkemmet and Monktonhall as well as Bilston Glen.[162] On the last day of July BSC management and the police were, however, surprised by 'guerrilla' pickets at Hunterston and Ravenscraig. There were 200 at the port and 50 at the plant, putting pressure on supplies temporarily.[163] In mid-October a much larger NUM presence mustered at Ravenscraig, some 650–700 pickets gathering but then dispersing in foul weather.[164] This was amid the NUM's renewed hopes for victory, unexpectedly raised by the projected strike across the coalfields of NACODS members, the deputies and safety men without whom pits could not remain open. In McGahey's absence George Bolton told the NUMSA and SCEBTA strike committee that a NACODS strike would bring power cuts and the realisation of the miners' strike aims.[165] At the Scottish Office there was an expectation that NACODS members in Scotland would take a 'tough and militant' line in the event of a strike, exercising the maximum of 'brinksmanship' on the question of safety.[166] For the miners, of course, this hope was fleeting. Within a week the NACODS executive had been persuaded to call off the strike before it began, moved by a government-approved and ACAS-brokered new formula for discussing and agreeing the closure of pits. McGahey advised the NUMSA and SCEBTA strike committee that this left open the danger of pit closures on economic grounds.[167] At Seafield and Bilston Glen there were strong verbal exchanges between NUM and NACODS members, and at each pit the latter briefly observed what was in effect an unofficial strike, although safety cover remained in place.[168] The prevailing trend was now decidedly against the strikers, in Scotland as elsewhere in the coalfields.

Conclusion

The industrial politics of the strike in its first six months had a distinctive Scottish dimension which this chapter has examined. The strikers' strategy involved halting steel production at Ravenscraig. This was criticised at the time, by some supporters as well as opponents of the strike, for threatening the security of the plant, and therefore the jobs of those who worked there. This view of events at Ravenscraig, along with an emphasis on the mistaken absence of a pre-strike ballot, and the opportunities supposedly missed by the NUM leadership to effect a pragmatic settlement to the dispute, features prominently in the literature on 1984–85. The argument here has stressed an alternative interpretation. The electricity supply position was extremely unfavourable for the strikers: there was no realistic prospect of power cuts before the end of the 1984–85 winter. So the NUMSA leadership had to find other ways of exerting pressure on the government. Given the particular industrial and electoral politics of Scotland, Ravenscraig was in fact an obvious and compelling target, as the government's efforts to keep the plant open and producing steel make demonstrably clear. Ministers keenly realised that the already precarious position of the government and the Conservative Party in Scotland would have been damaged even further had Ravenscraig closed.

So the NUMSA leadership's strategy was logical, and it was also very nearly successful. Only extremely heavy police intervention in the second week of May, encouraged by the head of BSC, Bob Haslam, who was apparently working in concert with government ministers and officials in Whitehall and Edinburgh, secured the freedom of the highways for the road haulage of coal. This was decisive, enabling Ravenscraig to continue operating, and saving the government from a strategically important political defeat. This action was legally dubious, involving a direct erosion of the civil liberties of the miners who were stopped in transit, and reflected the government's determination to win at Ravenscraig, and in the strike more broadly. Circumstances ensured that BSC managers, including Jim Dunbar, director at Ravenscraig, operated as the government's partners in breaking the miners' strike. The steel workers' union representatives in Scotland, notably Tommy Brennan, Ravenscraig shop stewards' convenor, were also co-opted as government confederates against the miners. They fed intelligence of NUMSA strategy and tactics from Triple Alliance inter-union meetings to their managers at Ravenscraig. Brennan and his fellows must have known that this information would be passed to the Scottish Office and Strathclyde Police, and used to weaken the impact of the miners' strike.

This was a tactical expression of the general Thatcherite 'Stepping Stones' anti-union approach, dividing potential from actual labour opposition, and isolating the striking miners. This was evident also in the government's handling of events in the ports, when Norman Tebbit, Secretary of State for Trade and Industry, over-ruled Scottish Office attempts to accelerate imports of coal for Ravenscraig. This might have resulted in a second major dock strike, damaging economic prospects and business fortunes, and greatly strengthening the striking miners' position. Tebbit only authorised the unloading of the imports once it had become clear that a substantial number of dock workers in England would not support their Scottish brothers. 'Don't just support us,' were Eric Clarke's words, it will be remembered, to Brennan and other steel industry trade unionists: 'join us'. But the steel workers at Ravenscraig, and the dock workers in some major ports in England, although not in Scotland, felt that their already precarious jobs and collective rights would be further imperilled if they stood alongside the striking miners. By political tradition the Ravenscraig men and some English dock workers – notably in Tilbury – were in any case unlikely to support what they saw as illegitimate industrial action. In the communities that they sought to preserve, along with their collieries and jobs, the striking miners nevertheless struggled on.

Notes

1 SMM, NUMSA, Box 13, NUMSA Strike Committee Minutes, 19 March 1984.
2 NAS, SOE 12/571, NUM, Scottish Area, Press Statement, 15 March 1984.
3 SMM, NUMSA, Box 13, NUMSA Strike Committee Minutes, 29 March 1984.
4 Payne, *Colvilles*, pp. 374–83; Foster, 'Twentieth Century', pp. 468–9.
5 Nichols, *British Worker Question*, pp. 138–9, 174–9.
6 The *Scotsman*, 5 May 1984.
7 James Mitchell, *Conservatives and the Union. A Study of Conservative Party Attitudes to the Union* (Edinburgh, 1990), pp. 102–23.
8 David Torrance, *'We in Scotland'. Thatcherism in a Cold Climate* (Edinburgh, 2009).
9 Peter L. Payne, 'The End of Steelmaking in Scotland', *Scottish Economic and Social History*, 15 (1995), 66–84.
10 Aitken, *Bairns O' Adam*, pp. 274–9.
11 David Stewart, 'Fighting for Survival: The 1980s Campaign to Save Ravenscraig Steelworks', *Journal of Scottish Historical Studies*, 25 (2005), 40–57.
12 Stewart, 'A Tragic "Fiasco"?', 44–7.
13 *Parliamentary Debates, Sixth Series, Commons*, 57, 647–51, 2 April 1984.
14 Eric Clarke, Interview.
15 Jonathan Zeitlin, 'From Labour History to the History of Industrial Relations', *Economic History Review*, 60 (1987), 159–84, and '"Rank and Filism" in British Labour History: A Critique', *International Review of Social History*, 34 (1989), 42–61.
16 Alastair J. Reid, *The Tide of Democracy. Shipyard Workers and Social Relations in Britain, 1870–1950* (Manchester, 2010).
17 Routledge, *Scargill, passim*; Beckett and Hencke, *Marching to the Fault Line, passim*.
18 Archie Macpherson, *Jock Stein: The Definitive Biography* (Newbury, 2004), p. 27.
19 Adeney and Lloyd, *Miners' Strike*, pp. 49–52, Stewart, 'A Tragic "Fiasco"?', 42–6.
20 Beckett and Hencke, *Marching to the Fault Line*, pp. 163–5, 180–2.
21 Hamilton, Interview.
22 Willie Clarke, Interview; Chalmers, Interview; Eric Clarke, Interview.
23 Saville, 'An Open Conspiracy', 316.
24 Taylor, *NUM and British Politics. Volume 2*, pp. 24–6; Pitt, *The World on our Backs*.
25 Francis, *History On Our Side, passim*.
26 Leighton S. James, *The Politics of Identity and Civil Society in Britain and Germany: Miners in the Ruhr and South Wales, 1890–1926* (Manchester, 2008).
27 McIlroy and Campbell, 'McGahey', p. 245.
28 Amos, Interview; Eric Clarke, Interview; Maxwell, *Chicago Tumbles*, pp. 44–5.
29 Angela Tuckett, *The Scottish Trades Union Congress. The First Eighty Years, 1897–1977* (Edinburgh, 1986), pp. 357, 376, 383, 410, 419.
30 Routledge, *Scargill*, pp. 138–85.
31 STUC, *87th Annual Report, Aberdeen, 1984* (Glasgow, 1984), pp. 475–82.
32 Bolton, Interview with Thompson; NAS, SOE 12/571, David Connelly, Scottish Office Industry Department (IDS), to various officials, 29 March 1984, and SEP 4/6028, Sit Rep, 3 April 1984.
33 The *Times*, 7 April 1984.
34 Tony Benn, *The End of an Era. Diaries, 1980–1990*, edited by Ruth Winstone (London, 1992), pp. 353–4.
35 Moffat, Interview with Thompson.
36 Amos, Interview; Chalmers, Interview.

37 Willie Clarke, Interview.

38 The *Scotsman*, 8 March 1984.

39 NAS, SOE 12/571, K.W. McKay, IDS, Coal Dispute: Effect on Ravenscraig, 26 March 1984.

40 The *Scotsman*, 28 March 1984.

41 NAS, SEP 4/6028, David Connelly, IDS, to various officials, 29 March 1984.

42 The *Scotsman*, 30 March 1984.

43 SMM, NUMSA, Box 13, NUMSA Strike Committee Minutes, 29 March and 2 April 1984.

44 The *Scotsman*, 3 April 1984.

45 NAS, SOE 12/571, Sit Rep, 5 April 1984.

46 Aitken, *Bairns O' Adam*, pp. 274–9; Stewart, 'Fighting for Survival', *passim*.

47 Beckett and Hencke, *Marching to the Fault Line*, pp. 30–2.

48 Wilson, Interview; Hamilton, Interview.

49 Amos, Interview; Chalmers, Interview; Eric Clarke, Interview; Willie Clarke, Interview.

50 The *Scotsman*, 2 April 1984.

51 Glasgow Caledonian University Archives (hereafter GCUA), STUC General Council Minutes, 4 April 1984.

52 NAS, SOE 12/571, K.W. McKay, IDS, Coal Dispute: Effect on Ravenscraig, 26 March 1984.

53 *Parliamentary Debates, Sixth Series, Commons*, 57, 647–51, 2 April 1984.

54 NAS, SOE 12/571, Sit Rep, 5 April 1984.

55 The *Scotsman*, 1 May 1984.

56 NAS, SOE 12/571, Sit Rep, 9 April 1984.

57 The *Scotsman*, 1 May 1984.

58 SMM, NUMSA, Box 13, NUMSA Strike Committee Minutes, 24 April 1984.

59 The *Scotsman*, 1 May 1984.

60 NAS, SEP 4/6028, K.W. McKay, IDS, Coal Dispute: Effect on Ravenscraig, 24 and 30 April and 1 May 1984.

61 Bolton, Interview with Thompson.

62 The *Scotsman*, 3 May 1984; Moffat, Interview with Thompson.

63 Aitken, *Bairns O' Adam*, pp. 274–9; Stewart, 'Fighting for Survival'.

64 The *Scotsman*, 3 May 1984.

65 The *Scotsman*, 3 May 1984.

66 The *Scotsman*, 10 March 1984.

67 NAS, SEP 4/6048, A.M. Russell to Private Secretary, Secretary of State, 3 April 1984.

68 The *Scotsman*, 22 June 1984.

69 NAS, SEP 4/6048, A.M. Russell, 'Note for the Record', 25 June 1984.

70 The *Scotsman*, 3 May 1984.

71 The *Scotsman*, 2 May 1984.

72 'James Yuill, 1934–2006', *Transport News Network*, 4 September 2006, www.tnn.co.uk /UKNews/plonearticle.2006-09-04.7892083892, accessed 19 October 2010.

73 NAS, SEP 4/6029/1, K.W. McKay, Assistant Secretary, Police Division, to the Private Secretary of Michael Ancram, 15 October 1984.

74 SMM, NUMSA, Box 10, Area Coordinating Committee, Reports, Wednesday 2 May 1984.

75 NAS, SEP 4/6028, Sit Rep, 4 May 1984; *The Times*, 4 May 1984.

76 KAGM, 75.3/1/1, NUM Dysart Strike Centre, Report, 3 May 1984.

77 'It's Blue Murder – Almost', *Scottish Miner*, June 1984.

78 SMM, NUMSA, Box 10, Area Coordinating Committee, Reports, Wednesday 2 May and Friday 4 May 1984.

79 SMM, NUMSA, Box 10, Area Coordinating Committee, Reports, Wednesday 2 May 1984.

80 SMM, NUMSA, Box 13, NUMSA Strike Committee Minutes, 8 May 1984.

81 The *Scotsman*, 5 May 1984.

82 SMM, NUMSA, Box 10, Area Coordinating Committee, Reports, Friday 4 May 1984.

83 KAGM, 75.3/1/1, NUM Dysart Strike Centre, Report, 6 May 1984.

84 SMM, NUMSA, Box 10, Area Coordinating Committee, Reports, Tuesday 8 May 1984.

85 Wilson, Interview.

86 SMM, NUMSA, Box 10, Area Coordinating Committee, Reports, Friday 4 May 1984.

87 The *Scotsman*, 8 and 9 May 1984.

88 *Scottish Miner*, June 1984.

89 SMM, NUMSA, Box 10, Area Coordinating Committee, Reports, Friday 4 May 1984.

90 KAGM, 75.3/1/1, NUM Dysart Strike Centre, Report, 8 May 1984.

91 The *Scotsman*, 4, 7 and 9 May 1984.

92 The *Scotsman*, 8 May 1984.

93 NAS, SEP 4/6028, Sit Rep, 8 May 1984; *The Times*, 8 and 9 May 1984.

94 Phillips, 'The 1972 Miners' Strike', 194–5.

95 NAS, SEP 4/6028, W. Baird, SHHD, to David Connelly, IDS, and Gordon Murray, Dover House, regarding intelligence from R. Priddle, Department of Energy, 8 May 1984.

96 NAS, SEP 4/6048, Sit Reps, 4 and 9 May 1984.

97 NAS, SEP 4/6028, W. Baird, SHHD, to David Connelly, IDS, and Gordon Murray, Dover House, regarding intelligence from R. Priddle, Department of Energy, 8 May 1984.

98 NAS, SEP 4/6028, Sit Rep, 10 May 1984.

99 The *Scotsman*, 11 May 1984.

100 NAS, SEP 4/6048, David Connelly, IDS, note to ministers and officials, 22 May 1984.

101 McCaig, Interview with Thompson.

102 SMM, NUMSA, Box 10, Area Coordinating Committee, Reports, Thursday 10 May 1984.

103 Hutton, *Coal not Dole*, p. 30.

104 Steve McGrail and Vicky Patterson, *'For as Long as it Takes!' Cowie Miners in the Strike, 1984–5* (Cowie, 1985), p. 28.

105 Stead, *Never the Same Again*, pp. 56–61.

106 Coulter, Interview with Thompson.

107 GCUA, STUC General Purposes Committee Minutes, 16 May 1984.

108 NAS, SEP 4/6048, Sit Rep, 14 May 1984 and McKay to A.M. Russell, 31 May 1984.

109 The *Scotsman*, 12 May 1984.

110 SMM, NUMSA, Box 13, NUMSA Strike Committee Minutes, 15 June 1984.

111 Tam Mylchreest, NUM Delegate, Castlehill and Harry Ellis, Steelend Strike Centre, in *Scottish Miner*, July 1984; Harry Cunningham, 'Miners' Strike – 20 Years On', *The Citizen*: www.thecitizen.org.uk/articles/vol3/article26f.htm, accessed 8 December 2008; Hutton, *Coal Not Dole*, pp. 26–8.

112 SMM, NUMSA, Box 13, NUMSA Strike Committee Minutes, 21 June 1984.

113 Sheffield Forum: www.sheffieldforum.co.uk/archive/index.php/t-290104.html,

accessed 1 December 2010.

114 'James Yuill', *Transport News Network*.

115 NAS, SEP 4/6027, Sit Reps, 3 and 4 July 1984.

116 NAS, SOE 12/572, K.W. McKay, IDS, notes, 13 and 18 June 1984, and Sit Rep, 21 June 1984; SEP 4/6028, K.W. McKay, IDS, note, 20 June 1984.

117 SMM, NUMSA, Box 13, NUMSA Strike Committee Minutes, 21 June 1984.

118 *Parliamentary Debates, Sixth Series, Commons*, 60, 44, 14 May 1984.

119 Sarah McCabe and Peter Wallington with John Alderson, Larry Gostin and Christopher Mason, *The Police, Public Order, and Civil Liberties. Legacies of the Miners' Strike* (London, 1988), pp. 167–8.

120 NAS, SOE 12/571, 'Note for meeting on Wednesday 23 May, 10 a.m.'

121 NAS, SEP 4/6048, Sit Reps, 3 and 8 May 1984.

122 NAS, SOE 12/571, 'Note for meeting on Wednesday 23 May'.

123 NAS, SOE 12/571, 'Note for meeting on Wednesday 23 May'.

124 NAS, SOE 12/571, Policing of the Miners' Dispute: Secretary of State's Meeting with a deputation of Labour MPs led by Mr Donald Dewar on 23 May 1984, Dover House.

125 Adeney and Lloyd, *Miners' Strike*, pp. 157–60.

126 John McIlroy, 'Police and Pickets: The Law Against the Miners', in Beynon, *Digging Deeper*, pp. 101–22.

127 Hutton, *Coal Not Dole*, p. 28.

128 Fred Lindop, 'The Dockers and the 1971 Industrial Relations Act, Part 1: Shop Stewards and Containerization', *Historical Studies in Industrial Relations*, 5 (1998), 33–72.

129 NAS, SOE 12/572, K.W. McKay note, 18 June 1984.

130 NAS, SEP 4/6027, Sit Rep, 11 July 1984.

131 NAS, SOE 12/571, R. Scott, Liaison Division, Dover House, note of meeting on dock strike, 18 July 1984.

132 *Parliamentary Debates, Sixth Series, Commons*, 64, 33, 16 July 1984.

133 NAS, SOE 12/571, R. Scott, note of meeting on dock strike, 17 July 1984.

134 *Parliamentary Debates, Sixth Series, Commons*, 64, 40–1, 16 July 1984.

135 *The Times*, 23 July 1984.

136 NAS, SEP 4/6027, K.W. McKay, note, 19 July 1984.

137 NAS, SEP 4/6027, clippings from *Glasgow Herald*, 21 August 1984, and the *Scotsman*, 28 August 1984.

138 Beckett and Hencke, *Marching To the Fault Line*, pp. 34, 37–8.

139 David Stewart, *Path to Devolution and Change, passim*.

140 NAS, SEP 4/6027, Tebbit to Walker, 6 August 1984, and K.W. McKay, draft letter, Younger to Tebbit, and Confidential Note to MISC 101, both 16 August 1984.

141 NAS, SEP 4/6027, K.W. McKay, note of 13 August 1984.

142 David Torrance, *'We in Scotland', passim*.

143 NAS, SEP 4/6027, K.W. McKay, IDS, notes of 10 and 13 August 1984.

144 NAS, SEP 4/6027, Ruth Thompson, Private Secretary to Tebbit, to David Barclay, Private Secretary to Thatcher, 15 August 1984.

145 NAS, SEP 4/6027, Ruth Thompson to David Barclay, 17 August 1984.

146 NAS, SEP 4/6027, David Connolly, IDS, Note on Dock Strike, 23 August 1984.

147 NAS, SEP 4/6027, David Connolly, IDS, Note on Dock Strike, 24 August 1984.

148 NAS, SEP 4/6027, Statement issued by John Connolly of the TGWU, 29 August 1984.

149 NAS, SEP 4/6027, Tilbury Dockers' Broadsheet, no date, but presumably circulated on Monday 27 August 1984.

150 Modern Records Centre, University of Warwick, MSS 371/QD7/Docks 2/3, Transcript of interview between Fred Lindop and Joe Bloomberg, p. 15.

151 NAS, SEP 4/6027, Raymond Wilson, PS to Michael Ancram, to various Scottish Office Ministers and Industry Department of Scotland officials, 29 August 1984.

152 NAS, SOE 12/571, Geoffrey Robson, Scottish Development Department (SDD), to Parliamentary Secretary, Secretary of State, 'Dock Strike: Orkney and Shetland', 30 August 1984.

153 NAS, SOE 12/571, Notes on Dundee, R.J.W. Clark, SDD, 3 September 1984 and D.K.C. Jeffrey, SDD, 4 September 1984.

154 NAS, SEP 4/6029/1, Sit Rep, 12 September 1984.

155 NAS, SEP 4/6029/1, Sit Rep, 6 September 1984.

156 NAS, SEP 4/6029/1, clippings from *Financial Times*, 7 and 14 September 1984.

157 *Glasgow Herald*, 14 September 1984.

158 NAS, SEP 4/6029/1, Copy of Press Statement by Jeremy Bray, MP, with letter from Bray to George Younger, 14 September 1984.

159 NAS, SEP 4/6029/1, Sit Rep, 19 September 1984.

160 NAS, SEP 4/6029/1, *Financial Times*, 18 and 19 September 1984.

161 Department of Employment, *Employment in the Ports: The Dock Labour Scheme*, Cm. 664 (HMSO, 1989); Peter Turnbull, Charles Woolfson and John Kelly, *Dock Strike. Conflict and Restructuring in Britain's Ports* (Aldershot, 1992).

162 SMM, Box 13, NUMSA Strike Committee Minutes, 13 and 20 August 1984.

163 NAS, SEP 4/6027, Sit Rep, 31 July 1984.

164 NAS, SEP 4/6029/1, Sit Rep, 19 October 1984.

165 SMM, Box 13, NUMSA Strike Committee Minutes, 22 October 1984.

166 NAS, SEP 4/6029/1, Sit Rep, 19 October 1984.

167 SMM, Box 13, NUMSA Strike Committee Minutes, 29 October 1984.

168 NAS, SEP 4/6029/1, Sit Reps, 25 and 29 October 1984.

4

Communities and commitment

'HERE WE STAND', wrote Michael McGahey, in April 1984 in the *Scottish Miner*: 'We are strong because justice is on our side; our women folk are speaking up for us on television; we are protecting the people's coal. They are weak because they are nothing but industrial vandals and bully boys.'[1] Here was the moral economy of the coalfields which 'they', the 'vandals' of the NCB and the Conservative government, had transgressed: the economic security of stable and unionised employment had been violated, and community resources – pits, jobs, 'the people's coal' – had been attacked. It is significant too that McGahey, from the beginning of the strike, was talking proudly about the central role of women. The strike was in defence of collieries, but it was also, as McGahey and many others emphasised repeatedly, about protecting the communities and all of the people – men, women and children – that relied on the industry.

The relationship between community and industry in the Scottish coalfields was, however, far from straightforward. It had been loosened by the restructuring outlined in Chapter 1, with pre-Second World War village pits gradually closed and superseded in the industry by 'cosmopolitan' collieries, a process all but complete by the 1970s, so that most miners travelled some miles each day to work. The very nature of 'community' was also contested: mining communities were far from cohesive, in Scotland as elsewhere, comprising an array of sometimes competing economic, social and political interests.[2] This chapter probes this problematic relationship by examining pit-level differences in strike commitment in Scotland in 1984–85. It establishes that this was largely a question of community-based organisation, and socially embedded material and moral resources. These shaped endurance by reducing the economic cost of striking, and heightening the social cost of strike-breaking. The chapter builds on an earlier analysis of pit-level strike commitment, which focused mainly on the economic variables,[3] and consists of three parts. The first relates the 'rationality' of striking and strike-breaking to the character of community-based collective organisation in the Scottish coalfields in 1984–85. A number of community-based factors that indirectly reduced the economic cost of striking are examined. The second part moves the analysis to material resources that more directly reduced the economic cost of striking. These were not present in equal quantities in all coalfield communities, and this helps to explain the distinctive pit-level strike histories of 1984–85. Two in particular are highlighted: the wages of married women in employment, and council housing density, the latter significant because Labour-controlled local authorities effectively deferred rents and rates from striking miners for the duration of the dispute.[4] These resources, married women's wages and local authority housing, with deferred rents, were unavailable in significant quantities to miners in the great disputes of the 1920s,[5] and participants in 1984–85 aver that without them their strike would have been impossible.[6] These two 'cost-saving' material resources are used to construct an innovative conceptual model for understanding Potential Strike Endurance (PSE) in 1984–85. This ranks pits in their predicted capacity for endurance. Chapter 2 emphasised the important origins of the strike in workplace politics. So the PSE model contains a third variable, a 'Militancy Index', capturing the quality of pre-strike, pit-level industrial relations, and deployed as a proxy for likely willingness to strike. The PSE pit-level rankings are then measured against Actual Strike Endurance (ASE) rankings, based on back to work figures compiled by the NCB and captured in Scottish Office daily situation reports. A third set of pit-level rankings is also established, to explore the possible impact of pre-strike economic performance (EP) on strike endurance. With some qualifications, standard interpretations of the relationship between pre-strike performance and strike endurance suggest the likelihood of a negative correlation: miners at more 'profitable' pits were more likely to have behaved in an economically 'rational' way by breaking the strike, particularly in Nottinghamshire.[7] In Scotland the correlation appears to have been largely positive: the strike was intensely solid at the most 'viable' Longannet complex pits. Scottish miners, it will be emphasised, were moved at least in part by economic arguments, seeing their pits as vigorous industrial resources with a long-term future, and worth defending through strike action when they were threatened by the NCB and the government.

Women in Nottinghamshire and other parts of the English coalfields reinforced strike-breaking, urging their men to join others who worked. Community resources could therefore be used against the strike, to strengthen the resolve of those who wished to work when facing pressure to strike from outwith the community, often from travelling pickets.[8] In Scotland, however, women played a vital and diametrically opposite role, supporting and in some ways leading the strike. Their vital contribution in elevating the social costs of strike-breaking is explored in the third part of the chapter. This focuses essentially on moral and political resources which, like material resources, were unevenly distributed across the Scottish coalfields. Women in Fife and to an extent in Midlothian participated actively in the strike. They were, as McGahey wrote in April 1984, highly effective political advocates of the strike, in the media and at rallies and other public gatherings. Women bolstered endurance in several ways, especially in their moral economy analysis of coalfield pits and jobs, which they defended as collective resources to be preserved for the future

benefit of their communities. Women helped to stigmatise the miners who jeopardised this future through strike-breaking, or directly 'selling' their jobs, by
accepting redundancy or transfer. The 'scabs', it is observed, were abused in
highly gendered terms, raising significantly the social cost of their actions. In
Ayrshire, however, the role of women was less developed, reduced – some
women recalled shortly after the strike – to relatively passive support for the
men. This they found personally and collectively unsatisfying. Worse, it lowered
the social cost of strike-breaking, and was a factor in the eventual weakening of
the strike at Killoch and Barony, where male endurance was not buttressed by
the type of moral leadership exhibited by women in Fife especially.

In her study of women in Durham in the 1926 lockout Hester Barron emphasised that the dominant tendency was for miners' wives to strengthen resistance
against the employers. Women had more to lose from lower wages than men,
given the gendered social organisation of domestic labour and the household
budget in the coalfields. As defeat seemed to come closer it was the women,
having borne the substantial portion of the sacrifice, who were the more
entrenched in their determination to keep fighting.[9] So it was in some parts of
Scotland in 1984–85, most notably in West Fife, where women played the decisive role in resisting the end of the strike in its closing months.[10]

Strike 'rationality', communities and organisation

Economic 'rationality' and striking are not often linked together. It is, indeed,
usually the actions of strike-breakers that are understood in economically
rational terms. This is derived from Mancur Olson's 1965 rational choice analysis, dwelling on the 'free rider' who profits from the collective action of other
economic actors without sharing their costs. A 'rational worker', he estimated,
could undermine action in pursuit of collective benefits, especially in strikes,
when 'all the economic incentives affecting individuals are on the side of the
workers who do not respect picket lines', their wages going up while strikers
receive nothing.[11] Economically rational motives have duly been attributed to
the actions of those in the 1984–85 strike who continued working, or returned
to the pits early, particularly in an English context. Miners at economically
'profitable' pits, notably in Nottinghamshire, are depicted as having little to win
from the strike: their jobs were not threatened, and they would only have lost
earnings by striking to defend miners elsewhere.[12] In Scotland, however, the
economically rational model, if it applies, seems to have operated more in the
opposite direction. This chapter will show that miners with the strongest sense
of job security – or lowest insecurity – were those who exhibited the greatest
strike commitment.

The Scottish experience in 1984–85 duly demonstrates that the 'choice'
between striking and strike-breaking was not a straightforward calculation of
individual monetary incentives. Communal attitudes to the economics of coal-
getting were important; and the social values of the moral economy more
broadly were also vital. This reinforces the 'social context' criticism of rational

choice analysis. In this tradition Gilbert, for example, observes that Olson adopted too narrow a view of rationality, with actions assessed in terms of a monetary cost-benefit schema that overlooked social factors.[13] The community, in short, can exert substantial social pressure on 'free riding' individuals who, operating only on economic motives, might resist participation in collective action. Hence Neville Kirk's sustained criticism of rational choice as a means of understanding collective behaviour, which he pursues in explaining the intense solidarity of slate quarry workers in Edwardian-era Ballachullish. Kirk links his analysis to social choice theory, the principal exponent of which is Amartya Sen, where socially embedded individuals weigh their interests in broader terms than the immediate economic future.[14] Social and cultural customs, and shared material experiences, along with powerful localised values and networks, were decisive in conditioning collective behaviour in Ballachullish.[15]

A similarly broad rationale was offered in Scotland in 1984–85 by striking miners. They accepted the loss of immediate income as the price of defending their longer future, and mobilised the customs and values of the coalfield's moral economy to raise the social cost of strike-breaking. Until January or February 1985 only a small minority of miners were prepared to meet this cost. The behaviour of these strike-breakers might be understood as an expression of short-term economic rationality. Immediate monetary rewards were balanced, however, by the substantial social penalties incurred by working miners, which they continued to experience after 1984–85, through acquiring the strike-breaker's stigma. In this connection the concept of 'hyperbolic discounting' is highly germane. It is used by Avner Offer to describe forms of human behaviour which trade short-term gratification against long-term disutility: the future is 'discounted' to pay for the present. The most extreme expression of such discounting is suicide. More frequently, it assumes the form of physically unhealthy but often psychologically satisfying social habits, such as smoking tobacco or drinking alcohol 'excessively'.[16]

The trade-off between the present and the future was occasionally emphasised by protagonists in the miners' strike. In the first week of November 1984 Allan Stewart, the Minister for Industry and Education at the Scottish Office, praised the 'courageous miners' who had broken the strike. By returning to work they were defending the future of the industry in Scotland, he claimed, which the strikers were jeopardising.[17] Subsequent developments suggest the opposite interpretation: it was the strike-breakers who were economically irrational and discounted the future. They helped to defeat the strike, leading to the long-term loss of employment – and hence earning potential – in deep coal mining. They earned wages during the strike, of course, and so gained in immediate monetary terms, but their longer-term earning potential was greatly narrowed by the accelerated closure of pits, although some emerged with enhanced redundancy payments, a factor examined in the final part of this chapter. All who returned in the summer and early autumn also lost substantial social assets, however, some of which were intangible, such as abandoned friendships, and others more tangible, like the frequently reported tendency of working miners to move house, away from a community that rejected, ostracised and perhaps physically attacked them because of their actions.[18] Some strike-breakers, however, were older, nearer retirement, and attached limited importance to the future. Their actions cannot quite be characterised as future discounting, or even substantially irrational, for many returned to work to earn wages for a short while before taking redundancy with enhanced monetary terms.[19]

Coalfield community enmity was directed more strongly against younger than older strike-breakers, and especially against those who returned to work early, in the summer of 1984. This is important, because union activists, officials and committed strikers generally differentiate in their narratives between early strike-breakers – sometimes characterised as the 'super scabs' – and those who resumed work in the final three months, especially after Christmas. There is generally sympathy or at least empathy with the actions of the latter, rationalised in terms of the inevitability of defeat by January or February, and the immense financial sacrifices made by all who endured the first eight or nine months of the strike.[20] These men were 'fallen soldiers', says Rab Amos, a phrase he attributes to Ron Todd, TGWU General Secretary during the strike. At Monktonhall, where Amos was SCEBTA delegate, hardly any workers, it might be recalled from Chapter 2, received a full week's wage between August 1983 and March 1985, with the pit-level strike in September–November 1983 followed by the national overtime ban and then the national strike from March 1984. One Monktonhall man who broke the national strike near the end typified the constraints of many. Having sold his possessions more or less entirely, his only remaining item of furniture was 'a Portybelly beach chair'.[21]

For the early strike-breakers, on the other hand, there remains only contempt. Nicky Wilson talks briefly about 'Conroy', the Cardowan 'super scab' who tried to mobilise working miners at the Longannet complex; David Hamilton does not name the 'professional footballer' who broke the strike early at Monktonhall, remembered by Amos as John Martin, who kept goal part-time for Airdrie, only after prompting; Iain Chalmers likewise did not name the 'toe rag' who taunted pickets at Seafield from the safety of a bus speeding through police lines into the colliery, either brandishing a wad of money, or baring his bum; Eric Clarke shakes his head recalling Harry Fettes of Bilston Glen, who flirted with Communist Party membership at one point, before breaking the strike from June onwards, standing for election to Lothian Regional Council as a Conservative Party candidate, and unsuccessfully suing the NUMSA leadership in the High Court in Edinburgh, claiming the strike was illegal.[22]

These early strike-breakers were rare figures, however, in Scotland. The vast majority of miners remained solidly out, largely because communities were able to reduce the economic cost of striking and raise the social cost of strike-breaking. Communities were drawn together in 1984–85, to mobilise these capabilities, through a pattern of territorial organisation established at the start of the strike. There were six area-based strike centres, each with an organising committee: Dysart in East Fife, covering Frances and Seafield, as well as the NCB workshops in Cowdenbeath; Fishcross in Clackmannan, near the border with West Fife, and covering Comrie as well as the Longannet pits and Polmaise; Dalkeith in Midlothian, covering Bilston Glen, Monktonhall and the NCB workshops at Newtongrange; Whitburn in West Lothian, for Polkemmet; Cardowan in Lanarkshire, where no pits remained but hundreds of miners – mainly employed at the Longannet pits – remained resident; and Ayr, for Barony and Killoch.[23] The Fishcross committee was chaired by Tam Mylchreest, NUM delegate at Castlehill, with 32 members drawn from fifteen local centres in the villages of West Fife, Clackmannan and Stirlingshire. This was the general pattern across Scotland, with area centres coordinating the efforts of dozens of local centres, established generally in miners' welfare clubs. The Cowdenbeath local centre was formed in the Miners' Welfare Club on Broad Street on the first day of the strike, and sent two members, Harry Cunningham from the NCB workshops and Iain Chalmers from Seafield, to the Dysart area centre.[24] Most locals were in daily contact with area centres, which met two or three times per week and sent delegates each Monday to Edinburgh for a Scottish Area meeting.[25]

Strikers tended to identify with a 'local' centre by place of residence as much as place of employment. Iain Chalmers, when he wasn't on the road picketing, spent much of the strike at 'home', in the welfare clubs around Cowdenbeath.[26] This is worth emphasising, remembering that the industrial restructuring of the 1960s and 1970s, examined in Chapter 1, had loosened the connection between community and pit in the Scottish coalfields. A common theme of participant testimony, indeed, is that the strike 'returned' miners to their communities.[27] For Nicky Wilson, who worked at Cardowan from 1967 and was the SCEBTA delegate when it closed in 1983, this was the central feature of 1984–85, with the strikers defending an industry that 'looked after its communities'. Wilson helped organise miners in the numerous settlements adjoining Glasgow: Auchenairn, Bishopbriggs, Croy, Glenboig, Kilsyth, Kirkintilloch, Lennoxtown, Moodiesburn and Muirhead, among others. The 'soup kitchens' were based in these villages, where a 'sense of community' had remained, despite the closure of local pits in the 1960s and 1970s. Partly this was the consequence of the 'cosmopolitan' colliery travelling culture which in Lanarkshire survived the closure of Cardowan in the summer of 1983. Some 400 or so of its 'red bus' and 'blue bus' men were still travelling together in the winter and early spring preceding the strike, to the Longannet pits. They went on strike together, and stayed on strike together.[28]

Within this activist narrative emphasis on the solidarity of coalfield communities there may be an element of what oral historians term 'composure': how interview subjects construct memories on the basis of experience subsequent to the events being recalled, and within changing economic, social, political and cultural parameters.[29] There is certainly a discernable narrative in coalfield memories of social decline arising from the disappearance of the industry,[30] so it might be thought unsurprising that strike participants – speaking after the dissolution of the mining industry and the crumbling of its ancillary features, notably stable unionised employment – would highlight the relative cohesion of coalfield communities in the mid-1980s. In this connection, however, it is significant that the activist-generated ephemeral literature of 1984–85 also privileged the solidifying role of communities during the strike.[31] Residential and community-based organisation was also characterised as being important by some of those who spoke to Willie Thompson in 1986, cementing solidarity in moral as well as material terms. Those who lived furthest away from the centres, and were less engaged in the communities, especially younger, single men, were regarded as the most 'vulnerable' to NCB entreaties to return to work.[32]

The daily routine work of the area and local centres was vital to strike endurance. The area centres marshalled picketing, fund-raising and political work, and distributed food and other resources to the local centres, which were a point of contact, for news and support. The biography of one of the area centres, Dysart, can be traced through daily log books detailing phone calls, other messages and a range of organisational, political and practical activities.[33] Seafield and Frances were the most northerly collieries in Scotland, so Dysart was responsible for fund-raising in Dundee and Aberdeen, and attempting to prevent imported coal from landing at the many North Sea coast harbours. This was a particular preoccupation during the Ravenscraig siege in May and June, and placed a great strain on Dysart's limited resources, with pickets frequently despatched for days on end to Inverness and Peterhead. Help was occasionally received from friendly port transport contacts in Dundee, including HM Customs staff as well as dock workers, who contacted the centre on several occasions with news that a coal ship was passing up the Tay to Perth.[34]

It proved impossible to halt the flow of strike-breaking coal to power stations, and the analysis of the electricity supply position in Chapter 3 showed that in any case the strikers had little prospect of exerting meaningful pressure in this area. But in other ways the activism of the area and local centres was highly important. A daily hot meal and weekly shopping bag were vital, especially to single miners, and it was in the dozens of local centres, the 'soup kitchens' in welfare clubs, that women consolidated the strike, blending material and moral substance.[35] 'Food on the table,' says Rab Amos, was a 'political statement', more important, arguably, than anything else in sustaining the strikers' morale and solidarity.[36] In school holidays this provision was bolstered when area centres secured local authority provision of daily lunches for children. In Lanarkshire and Ayrshire this came through Strathclyde Regional Council's Social Work department.[37] In East Fife the Dysart centre collected food, crockery and cutlery from Fife Region's School Meals Services Stores in Glenrothes and distributed them to local centres.[38] Maintaining a dignified family life remained difficult, and was particularly acute at Christmas, but in some communities this potential ordeal was transformed into an exciting and rewarding experience, chiefly due to the imagination and organisational endeavours of women. In Midlothian pantomime tickets were obtained after lengthy lobbying of theatres by women, who also negotiated special discount gift vouchers with British Home Stores on Princes Street in Edinburgh.[39] Elsewhere Christmas was 'rescued' by material support from the STUC and other trade unions in Scotland, the UK and across Europe, with toys, food and other groceries from France, the German Democratic Republic and the Soviet Union. The large task of distributing the toys, gifts from the French CGT trade union, was marshalled from Edinburgh's McDonald Road Library by Helen Hunter, chair of the Lothian women's groups, assisted by Rab Amos.[40]

Fund-raising was organised through the six areas, but collected centrally by the Scottish Area strike leadership. In this way money from larger urban areas, where employees in industry and public services, plus trade unionists and others likely to support the strike were concentrated, was distributed equitably across the coalfields. So funds raised in Glasgow by the Cardowan centre, or in Dundee by Dysart, were indirectly shared with strikers outwith Lanarkshire or East Fife. A fraction of Dundee resources did go directly to Dysart, with groups of workers in the city – encouraged by a local women's group – 'adopting' more than 70 East Fife coalfield babies born during the strike, paying for bedding, clothing and other infant essentials.[41] The centralised fund-raising was transparent and legitimate, but there may have been occasional instances of covert, localised 'rent seeking', with some strikers retaining a modest quantity of money for immediate use in their own communities.[42] The NUMSA leadership also suspected that some financial support was syphoned off by 'alien forces', as Michael McGahey called them, members of 'far left' groups and parties who partly funded their own activities with money collected 'for the miners'.[43]

The official fund-raising effort gathered roughly £60,000 a month for NUMSA, including an approximate total of £300,000 raised in Fife over the course of the strike.[44] The *Scottish Miner* published a 'Roll of Honour', acknowledging the strike's principal financial supporters. In June 1984 this included £8,960 from workers at the Kestrel Marine shipyard in Dundee, where workers were facing redundancy after completing a North Sea Oil rig sea-bed template,[45] and £500 from the writer and artist Alasdair Gray, won as a literary prize, as well as £1,400 from the ISTC members at Ravenscraig,[46] partial amends, perhaps, from men who had been working with strike-breaking coal. Broader support came from others in the labour movement, especially the print workers' union, SOGAT 82, and the STUC mobilised significant fund-raising efforts, including a Christmas appeal that yielded £34,000.[47]

These funds were welcome, but a strike of 14,000 men could not have been maintained for long on £60,000 a month. Let it be assumed that the £300,000 gathered by the Dysart centre was disbursed entirely in East Fife, although it is known that a portion was in fact transferred to strikers elsewhere. Divided equally among the 3,000 or so strikers at Frances, Seafield and the Cowdenbeath workshops, this would have amounted to just under £2 a week per man. Hence the much greater importance of the social and material resources already embedded in communities, and mobilised during the strike. These resources included the vital social influence exerted by communities generally, and women in particular, over local businesses. This helped to reduce the economic cost of striking. The communities adjacent to the Fishcross area centre exerted 'pressure' on coal contractors and hauliers, telling those continuing to carry coal that they would not have their contracts with NUM members and supporters renewed after the strike, and that their safe passage through mining villages could not be guaranteed.[48]

This type of community constraint on small business rational economic choice was evident in other parts of Scotland. In Midlothian a women's support group was established at Dalkeith in May. One of its members, Margot Russell, in memories of the strike that were published in 2001, articulates mixed perspectives on the relationships between strike families and traders, especially shopkeepers and grocers. Credit and other privileged terms were offered partly on grounds of political or social sympathy, as in the case of Fred Ayres, a former miner, whose coach company provided pickets and support groups with favourable rates for demonstrations and recreational trips. But something akin to rational social choice was also apparent: traders recognised that their long-term prospects were dependent on maintaining stable relationships with customers in the communities where they were situated.[49] This was evident too in Fife.[50]

Interaction between shoppers and shopkeepers is a reminder that in their social composition mining 'communities' were not homogeneously working class. There was only one pit village remaining in Scotland, Fallin in Stirlingshire, home to Polmaise. Elsewhere coal miners constituted varying proportions of the communities they inhabited. The wide spatial spread of the Longannet complex workforce, reaching Lanarkshire as well as Stirling, Alloa and Clackmannan, and West and Central Fife, has been emphasised. These areas encompassed villages in North Lanarkshire, the Hillfoots of Clackmannan and West Fife where miners were a significant local presence, but also larger towns – notably Dunfermline – where they were a smaller population fragment. This may have had some implications for strike endurance. Coulter and McCaig, speaking separately to Willie Thompson, commonly emphasised the enclosed solidarity of the West Fife and Clackmannan villages.[51] This is consistent with analyses of inter-war coalfield politics, Campbell and Gilbert separately observing that mobilising smaller communities could be more straightforward than a larger collective of individuals or workers, particularly where the former were ranged against a hostile exogenous force, such as a big employer based outside the locality.[52]

This, more or less, was the position in 1984–85. Iain Chalmers and Willie Clarke likewise suggest that endurance in 1984–85 was stronger among Central Fife miners, clustered in the small towns and villages around Cowdenbeath, than among miners in the larger towns further east, especially Glenrothes.[53] Alex Nicholson, an East Fifer, concedes that strike solidarity was probably stronger among miners in West and Central Fife. This owed something, he thinks, to the prime importance of coal industry employment further west. This produced 'larger characters', like the Leishmans of Lochgelly and Lumphinnans, whose number included Jim, the loquacious footballing bard of Dunfermline Athletic, whose support for the strike in 1984–85 encompassed a goal-scoring appearance in a fund-raising match in Cowdenbeath.[54] These men were 'mair forward' than their eastern fellows, and 'stronger talkers', with a deeper commitment to preserving their core economic resource. Hence 'the union boys' at Seafield, Willie Clarke and Jocky Neilson, were from Ballingry and Lochgelly, near Cowdenbeath.[55] Political tradition was surely also important: six of the Cowdenbeath strike committee's fourteen members were Communists.[56] In East Fife there was greater economic diversity and the Communist tradition was slightly less pronounced, but the differences should not be exaggerated. Solidarity may gradually have softened in Glenrothes and the Methil conurbation, but, reinforcing the sense that localised communities are easier to mobilise, in the Wemyss villages, clustered around the site of Michael Colliery, which closed after the disastrous fire in 1967, it remained intense. 'If one man got kicked' in these villages, Nicholson says, 'everybody was limpin'.[57]

In Ayrshire and Midlothian – both served by two relatively large pits – the miners were commonly dispersed across a variety of localities, in size and type, from fairly large mixed occupational towns, such as Kilmarnock and Dalkeith, to relatively homogeneous large villages, notably Drongan and Gorebridge. David Hamilton acknowledges the greater occupational and social diversity of Midlothian as a factor in potentially diminishing the cohesion of the strike at Monktonhall and especially Bilston Glen. But 'there was still a big feeling about community because miners still dominated' in the various settlements, whether 'people who had worked in the pit in days gone by, or people who were still in the pit', plus their relatives'.[58] The presence in mining communities of retired miners and mine union activists was indeed an additional strike-building resource in 1984–85. Iain Chalmers remembers the example and venerable counsel of coalfield elders, with their experiences of the great lockouts of 1921 and 1926, although memories of these earlier struggles could be unsettling as well as inspiring. On Cowdenbeath High Street he received a donation from an elderly man one Saturday morning. Another elderly man, seeing this from across the road, shouted, 'Is that conscience money, ya bastard?' The second man crossed the road to tell Iain that the first had been 'a scab' in 1926.[59]

Material resources: reducing the economic cost of striking

The community basis of strike organisation outlined above, with the gathering and distribution of food and other essentials, buttressed by the general solidarity of the area and local centres, reduced the economic costs of striking. These costs were lowered further by material resources located within the coalfields. Two are identified and explored here: the supply of income to households with male members on strike through the wages of Married Women in Employment (MWE); and household expenditure saved by local authority housing tenants as Labour-led District Councils deferred housing rents and rates for the duration of the strike,[60] examined here as Council Housing Density (CHD). These resources were not widely available to miners in the great disputes of the

1920s,[61] having been developed in the 'modernisation' of Scotland's economic, industrial and social capacities after the Second World War. This process reduced and restructured employment in the coal industry, with the move from village pits to cosmopolitan collieries examined in Chapter 1, and altered greatly the gender composition of the paid workforce in coal communities, with new opportunities for women in services and consumer goods manufacturing. Much housing inherited from the pre-1947 coalfields was unfit for habitation by the 1950s and 1960s. Local authorities made good this private sector failing, which was a more general Scottish phenomenon.[62] The disappearance of Glencraig in Central Fife and the movement of its people in the 1950s to the local authority housing of Ballingry, a few hundred metres north, illustrates this. In 1981 CHD in Ballingry was 94 per cent.[63]

In one other respect the strikers of 1984–85 were less well off than the locked out of 1926. In the earlier crisis miners' dependants in a number of local authorities received enhanced relief payments,[64] although these were contested by some rate-payers on anti-union and class grounds.[65] In 1984–85, by contrast, the Department of Health and Social Security downgraded benefits available to the dependants of strikers, on the false assumption that the NUM was providing weekly strike pay. There was no strike pay, although pickets occasionally received £1 or £2 per day in expenses, a useful incentive, especially for single men without working partners.[66]

Relative pit-level access to the two strike-building resources in 1984–85, MWE and CHD, which are calculated on the basis of data from the 1981 Population Census, is shown in Table 4.1. Bilston Glen had a rate of Married Women in Employment of 53.7 per cent, the highest in the coalfields, and so it is ranked 1 for MWE; Polkemmet had the highest Council Housing Density and so it is ranked 1 for CHD.

Establishing pit-level MWE and CHD values is methodologically complex, because of the partial separation of collieries from communities. The data was constructed on the reasonable expectation that miners at particular collieries lived in historic mining settlements in the district council areas, or in some cases in the immediately neighbouring district council areas, within which their pits were situated. The method is shown in Box 4.1.

The MWE rankings are subject to three important qualifications. First, it is probable that the Census under-reports female economic activity, especially in the informal economy.[67] Second, they are not based on evidence from identified coalfield households, but are drawn from aggregate data, so they include many women who were not directly connected to mining households. Third, they aggregate part-time and full-time work, and so do not capture the relatively small scale of a proportion of women's earnings. They are nevertheless highly illuminating, establishing the variable range of economic opportunities open to women across the coalfields, and consequently the contrasting availability of a vital economic resource to strikers at different pits. Female earnings were arguably a modest addition to household income in normal circumstances, but in the immense crisis of the strike – with male income forfeited completely –

Table 4.1 Married women in employment (part-time and full-time) and council housing density by colliery in Scotland, 1981

Colliery	MWE (per cent)	MWE rank	CHD (per cent)	CHD rank
Bilston Glen	53.7	1	63.0	11
Monktonhall	50.5	2	72.1	7
Polkemmet	48.7	3	84.3	1
Seafield	45.1	5	82.3	2
Frances	45.1	5	82.3	2
Killoch	39.4	11	82.2	2
Barony	39.4	11	82.2	2
Solsgirth	45.1	5	67.0	8
Castlehill	45.1	5	67.0	8
Bogside	45.1	5	67.0	8
Comrie	44.6	10	55.3	12
Polmaise	46.3	4	80.2	6
Scottish Coalfields	46.8		74.0	
Scotland	45.2		54.6	

Sources: Census 1981 Scotland. Scottish Summary, Volume 1; Report for Central Region, Volume 1 and Volume 4; Report for Fife Region, Volume 1 and Volume 4; Report for Lothian Region, Volume 1 and Volume 4; Report for Strathclyde Region, Volume 1 and Volume 4.

Box 4.1 Establishing MWE and CHD values for Scottish collieries in 1984

Seafield and Frances: CHD to encompass mining settlements in Kirkcaldy District Council plus those in Dunfermline District Council settlements to the east of the M90, with Cowdenbeath at the western fringe; MWE from average of Kirkcaldy District and Dunfermline District Councils.

Bogside, Castlehill and Solsgirth: CHD to comprise Clackmannan and Dunfermline District Council settlements to west of M90; MWE from average of Dunfermline District and Clackmannan District Councils.

Comrie: CHD and MWE on basis of Dunfermline District Council.

Polmaise: CHD comprising average of Bannockburn and Carseland in Stirlingshire District Council; MWE on basis of Stirlingshire District Council.

Bilston Glen: CHD to encompass Bilston, Bonnyrigg, Loanhead, Penicuik, Dalkeith, Gorebridge, and Mayfield in Midlothian District Council; MWE on basis of Midlothian District Council.

Monktonhall: CHD based on Dalkeith, Danderhall, Gorebridge, and Mayfield in Midlothian District Council and East Lothian District Council settlements; MWE an average of Midlothian and East Lothian District Councils.

Polkemmet: CHD based on Whitburn and Armadale in West Lothian District Council; MWE on basis of West Lothian District Council.

Ayrshire pits: CHD and MWE based on Cumnock and Doon Valley District Council.

they provided a basic means of economic stability. Men who participated in the strike say that spouses working full-time continued to do so and those with one part-time job took a second and sometimes even a third part-time job. Women working part-time may also have been better able to help the strike politically and morally than women who were occupied full-time.[68] The strike as a whole in Scotland, it should be added, benefited from this resource: local authority areas in which coalfield settlements were located encompassed higher rates of economic activity than the Scottish average. The volume and range of available paid work, including manufacturing plus public and private sector service employment, is emphasised as a factor in building endurance by female strike supporters, especially in the Lothians and Fife.[69] There was, however, one highly important exception: Ayrshire, where the narrower span of material sustenance raised the relative economic cost of the strike. This was perhaps reflected in the weakening and then dissolution of commitment at Barony and Killoch in the strike's closing months. The CHD rankings also include many non-mining households. The Bilston Glen rank, for instance, is derived from 17,700 households, roughly ten times the number of employees at the pit. They are valuable nevertheless, demonstrating that in coalfield settlements CHD was significantly higher than the overall Scottish value, providing a further major strike-enabling resource in 1984–85.

A third variable in establishing potential strike commitment is constructed in Table 4.2, a Militancy Index (MI), which captures the character of pit-level industrial relations going into the national dispute in March 1984. This, along with the MWE and CHD, forms the basis of the Potential Strike Endurance (PSE) rankings that are shown in Table 4.3.

It is important to remember that each of these variables – MWE, CHD and MI – are rankings. They show the relative rather than absolute Potential Strike Endurance of each pit. The MI component is vital in this respect, capturing pit-level varieties of strike willingness, a key contributor to Potential Strike Endurance. It combines two pit-level sub-variables that were examined in Chapter 2: support for industrial action against pit closures and an NCB pay offer, in a national union ballot in October 1982; and the workplace disputes of 1983–84, arising from managerial incursions on union rights and working practices, amid threatened closures and job losses.

The sub-variables of ballot vote and pre-strike dispute are ranked in Table 4.2, producing values in the third and fifth columns that are added in the sixth column to produce the overall MI rankings. Polmaise is ranked 1 for MI. In the 1982 ballot 99.3 per cent of the pit's union members voted for a strike; it experienced a four-week lockout in the summer of 1983, and after its closure was announced in January 1984 the workforce agitated for a national strike. Bilston Glen is 12 in the MI rankings, recording the lowest vote in Scotland for industrial action in 1982, although this still exceeded the average across the British coalfields of 39 per cent, and there was no significant pre-strike dispute at the pit in 1983–84.

In Table 4.3 the MWE, CHD and MI rankings are added to produce a sum in

Table 4.2 Pre-strike pit-level industrial relations and militancy index (MI) rankings

Colliery	Pit-level 'Yes' vote, 1982 NUM ballot[a]	Ballot rank value	Pit-level dispute, 1983–84? 1983–4?	Pit-level dispute rank value	Sum rank values	MI rank
Bilston Glen	56.5	12	None	9	21	12
Monktonhall	74.2	2	7-week lockout/strike	2	4	2
Polkemmet	69.0	8	Brief lockout	8	16	7
Seafield	72.5	3	4-week lockout and strike, continuing 12 March 1984	3	6	3
Frances	71.1	6	1 week lockout, continuing 12 March 1984	5	11	5
Killoch	60.4	10	Brief lockouts	6	16	7
Barony	58.5	11	Brief lockouts	6	17	10
Solsgirth	68.3	9	None	9	18	11
Castlehill	71.4	5	None	9	14	6
Bogside	72.5	3	Lockouts and closure threatened	4	7	4
Comrie	70	7	None	9	16	7
Polmaise	99.3	1	Lockouts and closure announced	1	2	1
Scottish average	68.4					

Source: Scottish Miner, December 1982, pp. 1–4. [a] Percentage of votes for industrial action, including strike action, against job closures and NCB pay offer.

Table 4.3 Pit-level potential strike endurance (PSE) rankings in the Scottish coalfields, 1984

Colliery	MWE rank[a]	CHD rank[a]	MI rank[b]	Sum rank values	PSE Rank
Seafield	5	2	3	10	1
Polmaise	4	6	1	11	2
Monktonhall	2	7	2	11	2
Frances	5	2	5	12	5
Polkemmet	3	1	7	11	2
Bogside	5	8	4	17	6
Solsgirth	5	8	11	24	10
Barony	11	2	10	23	9
Killoch	11	2	7	20	8
Castlehill	5	8	6	19	7
Bilston Glen	1	11	12	24	10
Comrie	10	12	7	29	12

Sources: [a] As Table 4.1; [b] As Table 4.2.

the fifth column, from which the PSE rankings are established. In CHD terms Polmaise was ranked 6, and in MWE terms ranked 4. So the sum of its rankings was 11, the second equal lowest of the twelve pits, alongside Monktonhall, which ranks highly in MI and MWE terms, and Polkemmet, which ranks highly in CHD and MWE terms. Seafield is ranked 1 in PSE terms, a combined ranking total of 10 resulting from an MI rank of 3, a CHD rank of 2 and an MWE rank of 5. The lowest in the overall PSE rankings is Comrie, due to low MWE and CHD rankings.

The pre-strike disputes, it will be remembered, reflected the economic difficulties arising from the 1980 Coal Industry Act, which set the target of subsidy-free financial independence by 1984, and falling demand for coal, with the recession and reduced scale of energy-intensive forms of manufacturing, alongside the increasing relative growth in electricity generation of oil, gas and nuclear power. The consequent vulnerability of the industry in Scotland, compounded by the reliance for custom on a small number of power generators, themselves under pressure to reduce costs, is detailed in Table 4.4. This ranks the pit-level economic performance (EP) of collieries using NCB data from the Monopolies and Mergers Commission's 1983 report. EP rankings are the sum of four ranked factors: output, output per manshift, costs per tonne of production, and losses per tonne of production.[70]

Table 4.4 Performance measures from NCB Scottish collieries, 1981–82, and pit-level economic performance (EP) rankings

Colliery	Output (000s tonnes)	Output rank	OMS[c] (tonnes)	OMS rank	Costs (£ per tonne)	Costs rank	Loss (£ per tonne)	Loss rank	Sum ranks	EP Ranking
Bilston Glen	892	1	2.06	5	42.70	5	4.60	4	15	5
Monktonhall	895	1	2.31	4	38.30	4	8.20	5	14	4
Polkemmet	390	8	1.39	11	54.50	11	9.00	7	37	10
Seafield	848	3	1.98	6	44.10	6	8.70	6	21	6
Frances	254	10	1.85	8	53.10	10	17.80	11	39	11
Killoch	698	4	1.58	10	49.0	8	16.70	10	32	7
Barony	227	11	2.00	6	50.20	9	13.80	8	34	8
Solsgirth[a]		5		1		1		1	8	1
Castlehill[a]	1955	5	3.19	1	31.20	1	1.50	1	8	1
Bogside[a]		5		1		1		1	8	1
Comrie	374	9	1.61	9	48.30	7	16.60	9	34	8
Polmaise[b]	N/A		N/A		N/A		N/A			
NCB average			2.4		39.48					

Source: National Coal Board, Volume Two, Appendix 3.5 (a), NCB Deep Mines. Operating Results 1981–82 – Scottish Area. [a] Figures for Solsgirth, Castlehill and Bogside are composite for Longannet complex; [b] Polmaise was classed as a Development Pit in 1981–82, not producing coal; [c] Output per manshift.

Pre-strike economic performance and strike commitment, to reiterate, are usually linked inversely. 'Good' performance in Nottinghamshire, for instance, broadly reduced 'rational' economic support for the strike, and those working throughout probably outnumbered the strikers by a ratio of 10:1.[71] The strike was 'strongest' in Yorkshire, where performance was varied, and in the 'peripheral' areas of the British coalfield – Kent, South Wales, Durham, Northumberland and Scotland – where production costs generally speaking were highest, pits less 'profitable' or more 'unprofitable', and closures and job losses most pronounced before 1984.[72] The data produced here, however, suggest a modified interpretation. Within Scotland there was, in fact, a positive correlation between relatively good pre-strike economic performance and strike endurance. This is evident, with minor qualifications, in the data summarised in Table 4.5, which includes a third set of pit-level rankings, Actual Strike Endurance (ASE). These are based on back to work figures collated by the NCB and passed to the Scottish Office, where they were captured in daily situation reports.

The back to work data is not straightforward. The NUMSA strike committee also collected back to work figures, which suggest a lower rate of attendance. The variations between NCB and NUMSA/SCEBTA data are relayed in Table 4.6. The NCB clearly had an interest in exaggerating the back to work numbers, which NUMSA and SCEBTA obviously sought to downgrade. Each was probably recording different data. NUMSA and SCEBTA counted only those who broke the strike by reporting for work, not including members who by agreement with the NCB were undertaking 'safety' tasks, maintaining pumps and other equipment that preserved the collieries for future, post-strike operations. The NCB, on the other hand, may sometimes have counted these men, along with members of NACODS and the colliery managers' union, BACM, who were not, of course, on strike, but assisting strike-breakers to produce coal. More dubiously still, the NCB is thought to have further boosted the number of 'working' miners by counting men who were not there at all: absentees. In Chapter 2 the case of Seafield illuminated the extent of daily absenteeism. Across all NCB holdings in 1982–83, it will be remembered, some 10.3 per cent of employees were absent. In 1984–85 the NCB apparently added the entire assumed volume of daily absentees to the proportion of those regarded as not striking and therefore 'working'.[73]

Even allowing for NCB exaggeration of the back to work figures, Tables 4.5 and 4.6 still record a notable record of solidarity across the Scottish coalfields. Only at Bilston Glen were significant numbers of men working before the late autumn, and just more than 50 per cent of the miners across Scotland were still on strike in March 1985. The relative pit-level experiences captured in the NCB data are, more importantly, broadly confirmed in the NUMSA/SCEBTA data: strike endurance was weaker at Bilston Glen and the Ayrshire pits of Barony and Killoch than elsewhere. Among the 10,050 or so miners at the other pits there was a remarkable degree of solidarity. By 5 November, on the possibly exaggerated NCB figures, just 185 of these men, or 0.02 per cent of the combined non-Bilston Glen/Ayrshire workforce, had broken the strike. This climbed to 10.6 per cent by 3 December, 12.7 per cent by 7 January and only scaled 20 per cent on 4 February. More than two-thirds of the non-Bilston Glen/Ayrshire miners were *still* on strike on 5 March. This does not quite match the hyper-intensity of solidarity in South Wales, where only 6 or 7 per cent of the area's entire body of 20,000 miners broke the strike,[74] but it is remarkable nevertheless. The NCB and NUMSA/SCEBTA records also confirm the existence of particularly intense pockets of solidarity, notably in West Fife, Clackmannan and Stirlingshire. The first five in the ASE rankings – Comrie and Polmaise plus the Longannet pits – were all attached to the Fishcross centre, where between 800 and 900 miners, roughly one in five of those employed in the area before the strike, and perhaps double the general average across the Scottish coalfields, regularly reported for picketing duty.[75]

Table 4.5 Pre-strike employment, working miners and actual strike endurance (ASE) rankings at Scottish collieries, selected dates, June 1984 to March 1985

Colliery	Pre-strike Employees, March 1984[a]	Working miners						Average % working, on selected dates	ASE rank
		3/9	5/11	3/12	7/1	4/2	5/3		
Bilston Glen	1,800	145	214	919	1000	1096	1244	42.8	12
Monktonhall	1,700	7	16	252	352	439	632	16.6	8
Polkemmet	1,100	6	4	150	170	430	704	22.2	9
Seafield	1,600	4	8	58	66	88	507	7.6	6
Frances	800	6	17	21	20	33	330	8.8	7
Killoch	1,350	3	1	158	287	881	1316	32.7	11
Barony	800	0	1	101	116	332	656	25.1	10
Solsgirth	1,100	0	3	4	4	7	27	0.7	3
Castlehill	1,300	2	1	17	17	19	44	1.3	5
Bogside	850	1	1	1	6	8	22	0.8	3
Comrie	800	1	0	0	1	1	8	0.3	1
Polmaise	450	0	0	0	0	0	0	0.0	1
Scottish coalfield[b]	14,000	205	401	2242	2676	4355	6797	19.4	

Sources: NAS, SEP 4/6027, SEP 4/6028 and SEP 4/6029, Scottish Office Sit Reps, March 1984 to March 1985. [a] Approximate Figures, based on Oglethorpe, Scottish Collieries, and Scottish Office Sit Reps. [b] Scottish coalfield total includes data from other NCB units, including workshops.

The pit-level ASE rankings in Table 4.5 are calculated by averaging the percentages of miners working in the first week of September, November and December 1984 and then January, February and March 1985. Bilston Glen is ranked 12. Coal was being produced there by the end of June,[76] with the position already 'very serious', according to NUMSA officials in Midlothian. The colliery duly absorbed much of the strike's picketing resources throughout the summer, with miners travelling there daily from East Fife in July,[77] and 'outside help' brought in from Northumberland and Durham.[78] It remained the centre of strike-breaking in Scotland until early February 1985, when a majority were working also at Barony and Killoch. In the spring and early summer strikers at

Table 4.6 Competing NUMSA/SCEBTA and NCB back to work figures, December 1984

Colliery	NCB figure, 22 November 1984	NUMSA/SCEBTA figure, 23 November 1984	NCB figure, 11 December 1984	NUMSA/SCEBTA figure, 21 December 1984
Bilston Glen	785	500	970	505
Monktonhall	169	174	273	200
Polkemmet	68	66	138	60
Seafield	40	32	59	32
Frances	17	19	21	18
Killoch	101	71	162	162
Barony	56	55	103	102
Solsgirth	4	4	4	2
Castlehill	16	13	16	16
Bogside	1	Nil	4	Nil
Comrie	Nil	Nil	1	3
Polmaise	Nil	Nil	Nil	Nil
Total	1600	1016	2355	1232

Sources: SMM, NUMSA, Box 11, Area Coordinating Committee, Reports; NAS, SEP 4/6029, Sit Reps, 22 November and 11 December 1984. NCB totals include employees at workshops and other non-colliery units.

Monktonhall had found it unnecessary to picket their own pit, able to concentrate on bolstering the stoppage at Bilston Glen.[79] But from October the strike showed signs of weakening there too, possibly owing to the apparent harassment of local union officials. David Hamilton was arrested at both Ravenscraig and Hunterston in May. He was arrested again at the end of October, this time in Midlothian, and imprisoned before trial on strike-related public order charges in December. Financial inducements were offered by the NCB to all strikers to return in November, which stimulated a moderate increase in work resumption generally, but especially in Ayrshire and at Monktonhall. Yet Monktonhall is 8 in ASE rankings, for strike-breaking was stemmed there in January and February 1985, perhaps partly because Hamilton was cleared of all charges at Edinburgh Sheriff Court.[80] Table 4.1 showed that Longannet's pits had access to lower than coalfield average resources, in terms of MWE and CHD. But numbers working there before February, and at Comrie, nearby in West Fife, were in single fingers, 'disappointing', in Scottish Office terminology,[81] and the strike remained solid in East Fife until February. The endurance at Seafield, where by this point – remembering the pit-level dispute that preceded the national stoppage – miners had been on strike continuously for twelve months, is particularly noteworthy.

Table 4.7 summarises the relationships between the three sets of pit-level rankings. These indicate a strong predictive element to the PSE, when measured against the ASE. First, three pits are in both the PSE and ASE 'top' six: Seafield, Bogside and Polmaise. Second, while Comrie moves eleven places from one set to the other, and Polkemmet and Solsgirth move by seven places, there are seven

Table 4.7 PSE, ASE and EP rankings in the Scottish coalfields, 1982–85

Colliery	PSE	ASE	EP
Seafield	1	6	6
Frances	5	7	11
Bogside	6	3	1
Comrie	12	1	8
Castlehill	7	5	1
Solsgirth	10	3	1
Polmaise	2	1	–
Monktonhall	2	8	4
Bilston Glen	10	12	5
Polkemmet	2	9	10
Killoch	8	11	7
Barony	9	10	8

Sources: see Tables 4.3, 4.4 and 4.5.

pits that move by only three ranks or less. Third, and perhaps most strikingly, Bilston Glen, Barony and Killoch occupy three of the 'bottom' five positions in each set. There is also a fairly consistent positive correlation between the ASE and EP. Four pits appear in the 'top' six of each set, and four more appear in each 'bottom' six. Aside, again, from Comrie, only Bilston Glen moves – downward – more than four places from the EP to the ASE rankings. This second correlation is highly significant, demonstrating that in Scotland pre-strike performance was generally a positive factor in building strike endurance. This is contrary to standard assumptions, reflected in the literature especially on Nottinghamshire, about good performance undermining pit-level commitment.

The Bilston Glen case is worth elaboration here. Its loss-making problems are acknowledged by Andrew Taylor, who adds, however, the common observation that it nevertheless 'was perceived to have a future', and so its workers 'resisted striking'.[82] Bilston Glen's relatively strong pre-strike performance is emphasised elsewhere in the literature, where it appears as Scotland's 'super pit', its 'rational' economic miners breaking the strike because they were digging up 'profitable coal', unworried about their prospects.[83] The analysis in Chapter 2 showed that senior NCB officials, including Ian MacGregor, publicly exaggerated the achievements at Bilston Glen, the 'jewel in the crown', to divide its miners from those at 'Second Division' Monktonhall. While there were no major pre-strike disputes at Bilston Glen, the position was in fact highly precarious in 1982 and 1983, with managers recurrently bemoaning the allegedly poor nature of production, and offering dire predictions about future prospects, with the likelihood of closure or at least the substantial loss of employment.[84] Similar themes were evident at Barony, and at Killoch too, where, it will be remembered from Chapter 2, management told Wheeler in September 1983 that workforce morale was low because of the expectation that the pit was 'next for closure'.[85] Relatively weak performance, in other words, or even, in the case of Bilston

Glen, management and workforce perceptions of relatively weak performance, may have reduced strike endurance in 1984–85.

'Good performance' in Scotland was, of course, relative, as the NCB average output per manshift and operating costs and losses per tonne in Table 4.4 indicates, although the Aberystwyth and Andrew Glyn critiques of NCB financial methods, outlined in Chapter 1, should be remembered. All Scottish pits were operating at a loss, and all were closed by the NCB and its successor, British Coal, within five or six years of the end of the strike. Yet it is nevertheless important to note the particularly strong correlation between the high EP and ASE rankings at the Longannet complex pits, where output per manshift in 1982 exceeded the average for *all* NCB holdings, not just those in Scotland, and where production was boosted by the miles of underground conveyors that brought coal directly into the power station.[86] The relatively positive economic position of the Longannet pits appears to have been a valuable resource around which strikers could organise, protecting economically and socially valuable assets, with perceived long-term potential.

The cases of Comrie and Polmaise, joint 1 in ASE rankings, qualify the emphasis here on the correlation between performance and endurance. Comrie, 12 in the PSE rankings, owing to low MWE and CHD rankings, and joint 8 in the EP rankings, may be an outlier, although its MI ranking was 7. It may also be that the relatively weak pre-strike production position there actively – against the general Scottish trend – strengthened strike commitment, reducing the incentive to return. The same may be so of Polmaise, following its closure announcement in January in 1984.[87] Yet at both pits the factor of production – or at least of potential production – possibly influenced strike commitment in positive terms, with workforce representatives talking about the need to develop large coal reserves that could be viably worked and marketed. Comrie had a large customer, the South of Scotland Electricity Board, which purchased 75 per cent of its output in 1983, despite pressures on the generator to lower costs. This gave the men some confidence in the future.[88] At Polmaise, it will be remembered from Chapter 2, the NCB said that severe faulting made further mining uneconomic. The workforce, through their union officials, retorted that beyond the faulting lay twenty or thirty years of coal. This could be extracted as easily as 'sticking a knife into a dumpling'.[89]

Moral resources: raising the social cost of strike-breaking

Economic variables explain in large part the pit-level varieties of strike endurance in 1984–85. But they do not do so entirely. Moral economy factors, outlined in this section, were also important, raising the social cost of strike-breaking more at some pits than others, and illuminate especially perhaps the different strike histories of the Midlothian pits, Monktonhall and Bilston Glen, which were broadly comparable in MWE, CHD and EP rankings. These moral economy and social cost considerations may also help to explain the eventual dissolution of the strike in Ayrshire, despite its higher than coalfield average

CHD value, and the solidity of the strike at the Longannet pits, reinforcing their performance-related strike potential and compensating for their below coalfield average CHD and MWE values. Moral economy factors were particularly strong at Comrie, shaped by the 'militant' industrial and political traditions of West and Central Fife,[90] and structured the intense solidarity of the strike in Cowdenbeath, where 95 per cent of the men stayed out for the duration,[91] and Polmaise, where there was not a single strike-breaker.

The only surviving 'traditional' village pit, Polmaise was to an extent distinct in Scotland. Its union officials and representatives were not connected to the Communist Party,[92] itself unusual in Scotland, and the workforce's broader social loyalties were of a slightly different hue. Polmaise encompassed men and women of Irish Catholic origin, mainly from Cowie, Fallin's neighbouring village,[93] but there are suggestions too of powerful Protestantism and even Orangeism at the pit.[94] NUMSA and SCEBTA officials, delegates and activists from elsewhere in the coalfield certainly regarded Polmaise men and women as different: unpredictable and uncompromising.[95] Yet when moved to act they did so with total commitment: they 'don't play funny', Iain McCaig told Willie Thompson, but 'for keeps'.[96] They had, as Chapter 2 demonstrated, been central in establishing support for the strike in Scotland in January and February 1984, and enforcing it on 12 March by picketing out Bilston Glen. Polmaise folk were clearly moved by moral economic factors. They articulated a profound sense of injustice when 'their' pit, the community's prime economic resource, was threatened.[97] This was the NUMSA and SCEBTA position more broadly, with the decision by NCB officials and government ministers during and immediately after the strike to abandon large reserves and established workings seen as economically irrational, morally repugnant and likened to criminal sabotage.[98]

Two further moral economy strands, elevating the social cost of strike-breaking, were evident in the Scottish coalfields: crowd action, against working miners and NCB officials; and the characterisation of jobs as collective assets. Albert Wheeler, it will be remembered, had encountered a vigorous crowd at Fallin himself, with women a voluble force, when announcing in July 1983 a lockout at Polmaise after miners had blocked the NCB's attempted transfer of several Cardowan men.[99] Children were present at Fallin, and the agency exerted by younger people was also a feature of the strike. At Ballingry on 7 June one hundred or so pupils left classes in the village junior secondary school to block a main road, deterring lorry drivers from accessing the nearby Nellie open cast mine.[100] This was reported in the *Scottish Miner*, and recalled proudly 25 years later by Willie Clarke, local resident and Councillor as well as union official at Seafield.[101]

Crowd action during the strike was often concentrated outside pits, abusing working miners, or near their homes. This was particularly robust in the first six months of the strike, and in coalfield memory miners who returned to work before the late autumn and especially before the end of the summer continue to attract substantial moral opprobrium. These, remember, were the 'super scabs', who wrote off massive future losses – to their communities but also sometimes to themselves – against the immediate material gain of NCB wages for working.

From this 1984–85 community action the echoes of the 'rough music' of inter-war and earlier industrial crowd protest – generated primarily by women – can be loudly heard,[102] with threatened and actual violence. In late July forty pickets besieged the home in Tranent, East Lothian, of a Bilston Glen strike-breaker, a coal-cutting machinery operator. The man's telephone line was cut off by the crowd, according to Scottish Office intelligence, preventing him from dialling a centralised NCB help number for strike-breakers. His wife used a neighbour's telephone; a large police force arrived, and all forty pickets, including men from Durham, Fife and Glasgow as well as the Lothians, were arrested and charged under the 1875 Conspiracy and Protection of Property Act.[103] Similar treatment was encountered by a surface worker from the Longannet complex who broke the strike in June, Jim Pearson. His Culross home was intermittently encircled over several days by dozens of men and women, and the windscreen of his van, which he used to drive to work, was smashed on several occasions. Sixty police officers were detailed to protect Pearson whenever he reported for work, to the private annoyance of Fife's Chief Constable, William Moodie, himself a former miner,[104] who regarded this as a misallocation of resources. Pearson was praised by Scottish Office ministers, notably Michael Ancram,[105] but ridiculed by strikers. Unlike the Tranent strike-breaker, who cut coal at Bilston Glen, he was a 'JCB driver' and not a 'proper' miner.[106]

These strike-breakers offended the coalfield moral economy attitudes to male work that were captured in Daniel Wight's ethnographic study of 'Cauldmoss', a working-class community in central Scotland in the mid-1980s. Wight noted that male manual work was valued in economic terms, with high earners attracting particular prestige, but it was valued in social terms too, with esteem attached to those demonstrating dexterity, physical endeavour and consistent commitment. The man whose work was of indifferent quality, or who shirked a share of the graft, was a 'waster' who burdened his community and shamed his family.[107] These attitudes, venerating work, raised the social cost of strike-breaking. Paradoxically perhaps, but understandably, in the wider context of coalfield morality, those who worked now – against the solidarity and perceived interests of their community – became 'wasters'. The repugnance was highly gendered. Women raised the social cost of strike-breaking by questioning the masculinity of men who crossed picket lines. There were strong reminders here of the gender politics in the 1926 lockout, when, in Barron's words, the 'common portrayal of blacklegs as effeminate was reinforced by the taunts of women'.[108] Women picketing outside Monktonhall in January and February 1985 told reporters that the 'real men' were still on strike. The strike-breakers, by contrast, were 'weak', capitulating to bullying managers, and 'wasters' with a major personality flaw: hopeless drinkers, perhaps, or gamblers with personal debts that they were crossing the picket line to pay off. More than one, it was said, had been close to dismissal before the strike – for drunkenness, absenteeism or poor work performance – but had been saved by the intervention of other workers and union representatives. This gravely compounded their alleged act of betrayal.[109]

In the same discursive vein Rab Amos impishly recalls Ian MacGregor's insulting characterisation of Monktonhall miners by referring to the 'Third Division' quality of work undertaken by strike-breakers, which he witnessed while undertaking safety cover and inspections in 1984–85.[110] Iain McCaig spoke to Willie Thompson in similar disparaging terms about the 'real scabs', like the 'infamous Mr Pearson', who were 'the worst kind' of men. Some had indeed been dismissed for being 'lazy swines, falling asleep down the pit', reinstated only after union intervention. In normal times the NCB would have been seeking to release these men. Indeed, in the weeks immediately preceding and following the end of the strike many of these men were paid off. With a 'golden handshake', 'hyperbolically discounting' the future, they left the industry and sometimes their community altogether.[111] This narrative strand punctuates the memories of strike activists, who remain vexed by the characterisation of strike-breakers – by NCB officials and government ministers – as 'saviours' of the industry. This was opportunistic and cynical, says Nicky Wilson: many strike-breakers were well known to managers before the strike precisely because of their poor disciplinary records, and this made them vulnerable to pressure to return to work. These men were not 'heroes' or even competent workers: they were 'weak individuals'.[112]

The gendered hounding of strike-breakers points to the partial reconstruction of gender relations in the coalfields. To some extent it reinforced the pattern of conventional relations evident to some observers,[113] by equating strike solidarity with masculinity, and women had played an important role in earlier coalfield disturbances, before the First World War, and during the 1920s, in which time there was no lasting alteration of gender roles or adulteration of male sexist attitudes.[114] Nor were these much changed by the impact of the Second World War, or nationalisation, as the authors of *Coal Is Our Life*, the sociological study of a Yorkshire mining community, emphasised in the 1950s.[115] Beatrix Campbell's account of working-class life in industrial Britain, written shortly before the strike, duly recorded the enduringly sexist character of coalfield gender relations.[116] Campbell's observations were, however, drawn from a fairly distinctive geographical region, the English north-east, where economic and cultural opportunities for women were fairly narrow, and the coal industry still comprised many older village pits as well as larger cosmopolitan collieries. In Scotland the economic and industrial restructuring of the 1950s and 1960s, which stimulated the volume and range of paid employment opportunities for women detailed earlier in this chapter, was followed by a partial erosion of sexist attitudes. A measure of changing mores can perhaps be viewed in the pages of the *Scottish Miner*, which from 1967 had carried exploitative pictures of women. This objectionable practice, described by the paper in 1967 as a 'service' to its readers, was discontinued from February 1974, and during the 1984 strike women were portrayed as taking a leading role.[117]

There was substance to this activist emphasis on the positive and progressive reconstruction of gender relations, with the 1984–85 picket-line action reinforced and extended by other forms of female involvement. This included some

degree of gender role reversal, with men engaged in child care and other aspects of domestic life, and women occupied in 'public' tasks.[118] Margaret Wright's 2008 film, *Here We Go. Women Living the Strike*, featured a number of participants from Fife, Lanarkshire and the Lothians. Cath or Cathie Cunningham, Margie Givens, Anne Hunter, Anne Kirby, Lesley McGuinness, Anne Kay McNamara, Ann Robertson, Margaret Wegg and Matilda Wilson all spoke about the transformational experience of the strike in gendered as well as class terms. Cathie Cunningham lived in Cowdenbeath, and was drawn into the strike through her husband, Harry, a member of the local and Fife area committees. Cathie was a core member of the Women's Support Group established early in the strike at Cowdenbeath, according to Alex Maxwell,[119] and helped at the Dysart strike centre. In *Here We Go* she recalled the importance of female political participation, including public speaking, with the opportunity to state the miners' case to other citizens, workers and trade unionists 'from a women's perspective'. Lesley McGuinness, who lived in Oakley, said that women's involvement was highly political, an expression of their determination to defend their communities.[120]

The personally and politically liberating nature of the strike has been documented by other women. Margot Russell, who worked part-time in the Ferranti electronics factory in Dalkeith, became involved through her partner Bill, a SCEBTA member at the NCB workshops in Newtongrange. Margot joined the Women's Support Group at Dalkeith with Nancy Hamilton, a former workmate, and Jean Hamilton. Nancy's husband, Robert Hamilton, worked at Monktonhall, along with his brother, David, the pit's NUM delegate, and the husband of Jean.[121] Margot and Bill joined the Labour Party, as did Jean and David, who had been a Communist,[122] consolidating in this way the miners' influence in the Midlothian constituency. Margot, emboldened by her strike experiences as an organiser, lobbyist and speaker, enrolled at Esk Valley Further Education College, studying English Literature, and later, after redundancy from Ferranti, took a job as an optician's receptionist. When Eric Clarke became MP for Midlothian in 1992 she was employed in his parliamentary constituency office, again in Dalkeith. This work, secured on the basis of confidence and capabilities acquired through the strike, differed greatly from her pre-strike experience of manual employment.[123] She was later elected as a Labour member of Midlothian Council, for the Dalkeith ward.[124]

The engaged participation in the strike of Cunningham, McGuinness, Russell and so many other women encompassed local, regional and national campaigning, and fund- and consciousness-raising.[125] While rooted in the highly distinctive social and political contingencies of 1984–85, this involvement nevertheless brings to mind the 'gendered citizenship' that Annmarie Hughes ascribes to working-class women who were active in inter-war Scottish community, local and national politics. Whether through Cooperative Women's Guilds, for instance, or Independent Labour Party intervention on infant and maternal health, this constituted a distinct female contribution to the articulation and mobilisation of common, cross-gender, working-class interests.[126] So it was with many coalfield women in 1984–85, particularly those who sought to raise the social cost of strike-breaking, confronting in highly gendered terms those who transgressed the moral economy of the coalfields by returning to work. The extent of this female activism was varied, however. In Ayrshire it was limited, especially in and around the urban centre of New Cumnock where, Willie Thompson was told by male activists in December 1985, the strike was consequently weakened. The essential problem was male chauvinism. The New Cumnock men were 'men's men', unable to adapt to the 'modern world' and restricted by the conviction that women had no place in the strike. The 'consequences were there to be seen', in the crumbling of the strike from December 1984 onwards.[127] The correlation between restricted female participation and weakened strike commitment was also emphasised in the recollections of Mauchline women, recorded in the summer and autumn of 1985.[128]

Male chauvinism remained, of course, a substantial force elsewhere in the Scottish coalfields. Willie Clarke still regrets the sexism of some Fife miners, notably around Comrie, where, perhaps not coincidentally, the MWE ranking was also low.[129] Many women who participated in the strike directly encountered engrained sexism as a result, in their communities, and sometimes within their own homes. Their determined provision of moral leadership as well as material support was all the more remarkable, according to Ella Egan, who convened the NUMSA Women's Support Group.[130] This was rewarded by at least a limited reconfiguration of gender politics, particularly in Fife, and to some extent in Midlothian.[131] Daily reports from the NUM's strike centre at Dysart outline especially from May 1984 onwards the growing involvement of women in the direction as well as the maintenance of the strike.[132] In West Fife, Tam Mylchreest told Thompson, 'women were in front ay us, no beside us'.[133] This trend was reportedly evident at Monktonhall too, and the wide and varied character of female involvement in Midlothian was marked in an exhibition at Edinburgh City Art Centre in October 1984, *Not Just Tea and Sandwiches*. The exhibition was partly organised by Edinburgh's first-ever Labour ruling group, elected in the District Council elections in May, and its feminist interpretation of the strike was guided by the new administration's women's committee. Jean Stead hints that the confidence and ambitions of the administration in general and its women's committee in particular had been greatly elevated by the work in Midlothian of the women in the miners' support groups.[134]

These and other women arguably had a greater stake in the strike than their men. They bore the main burden of the strike's financial hardships, compounded when the Department of Health and Social Security cruelly 'turned the screw' on families by docking a notional strike pay of £15 a week from state benefits. Margot Russell recalled that this meant a benefit provision of £24.75 per week for a family with two children under the age of five years,[135] between £60 and £65 at 2011–12 values. She and so many other women knew what had been invested in pursuit of victory, and understood intimately what would be lost – stable, well-paid employment – in defeat.[136] Margaret Wegg, who had worked in the canteen at Cardowan, told Margaret Wright in 2008 that the longer the strike continued, the more determined women became. 'We weren't gonnae go back under her terms,' she said, referring, of course, to the Prime Minister.[137] Ella Egan and Tam Coulter reached the same conclusion in 1986: it was women who kept the strike going, particularly after the first three or four months. Young women, Coulter said, those with young husbands and children, were fully conscious of the limited prospects beyond the mines, and older women had sons in the pits.[138]

The close engagement of women with the strike in Fife and parts of Midlothian was related to female labour market participation, but not entirely. In Midlothian this was above the coalfield average but in Fife just marginally below. It may instead have owed something to the Communist Party tradition, especially in Fife. Communist women expected a greater involvement in public life,[139] and Communist men – more or less – accepted the desirability of this.[140] This tradition shaped NUMSA's ambition after the strike to open membership to women on the same terms as men, a clear acknowledgement of their joint role in the struggle to defend the industry and its communities. Such an initiative was blocked at a federal level in the union nationally, but in Scotland the area leadership supported it unconditionally.[141] Various strike participants in this connection recall the words of Michael McGahey, to the effect that a working-class movement without women is like a bird with one wing: 'it will never fly'.[142]

Women helped to raise the social cost of strike-breaking, it has been noted, by harrying those who returned to work. They also did so by helping to articulate a crucial element of the coalfield moral economy: the characterisation of jobs as collective resources rather than the property of the employer or the individuals who occupied them. These were to be preserved for the benefit of the community, including its future inhabitants, unless and until the workers and their collective representatives agreed otherwise in joint industrial bargaining with management. This coloured the attitude of the coalfield crowd to the related question of voluntary redundancy. Jobs could not be 'sold' by miners for redundancy payments. This had been seen before the strike, when the closure of Cardowan in 1983 ignited a series of pit-level disputes, including the Polmaise lockout, with Lanarkshire men who accepted transfers or redundancy payments, while the union was campaigning to save the pit, regarded as 'renegades'. In the same way the NUM branch secretary at Bilston Glen was successfully challenged in 1982 for his position by Jackie Aitchison, having offended many activists by saying that he would accept redundancy if it was offered.[143]

When Cardowan's closure was announced by Wheeler the average age of the 1,100 or so who worked there was 39.[144] This is important, for the moral economy view of transfers and redundancy was age-sensitive. This was partly a material rather than simply a moral question, with younger miners less given to hyperbolically discounting their future, and so carrying a stronger rational economic incentive to retain employment in the industry. At Castlehill, for instance, where the strike was highly solid, the average age was just 38.[145] Yet those younger men who left – for whatever reason – were strongly criticised by those who remained from a moral rather than a 'rational' perspective. The moral discourse can be read too in the relative absence of criticism of older miners, aged 50 and up, and especially aged 55 and up, with long service to the industry, who accepted redundancy. 'Go,' Iain Chalmers recalls thinking: 'enjoy'.[146]

Monktonhall especially, and Seafield to an extent, were pits with relatively young workforces by the end of 1983, with few older miners, and certainly hardly any aged 55 and up. Men in this age category had accepted either industry-wide or pit-level severance terms since 1980, when, according to Ned Smith, the NCB's Industrial Relations Director, the Coal Industry Act stimulated cost-reducing investment in redundancy packages.[147] Bilston Glen was different, however. David Hamilton recalls that the NCB deliberately held older miners at Bilston Glen, while offering redundancy terms to their neighbours at Monktonhall. Here rational economic or material elements again were reinforced by moral factors, with the younger men at Monktonhall more receptive to the argument that jobs and pits had to be defended for the community by striking. This argument, it will be recalled from Chapter 2, had apparently been pursued more vigorously by Monktonhall than Bilston Glen union representatives after the closure of Kinneil in 1982. The older Bilston Glen men, it would seem, were in any case less open to this argument. They broke the strike because they were near the end of their working lives and wished to remove obstacles to the collection of redundancy terms, which were linked to length of service. They returned to work early, in other words, so that they could leave the industry early, and very many did so, either before or shortly after the end of the strike.[148] The extent to which these older men, unlike younger strike-breakers, were hyperbolically discounting the future might therefore be questioned. Perhaps even the opposite case might be made, that they were trading immediate social cost or disutility – the stigma of the 'scab' – for perceived long-term benefit, the future security of enhanced or maximised redundancy payment. The stigma of strike-breaking was not, admittedly, easily shrugged off in the long run, although some participants tend to bracket the older men who returned to work in this manner with the younger men, the 'fallen soldiers', often fathers with young children, who delayed returning to work until deep into the winter. The bulk of the older returnees, of course, like these younger men, had also observed the strike for the majority of its duration.[149]

The concern that longer-serving miners would disproportionately bear the high costs of dismissal apparently also influenced the collapse of the strike in Ayrshire in January and February 1984. Here it was believed, wrongly, that the NCB could legally sack miners who had been on strike continuously for a year. Men feared dismissal in this manner, which would result in lost redundancy benefits, including financial compensation.[150] The social costs of strike-breaking were therefore reduced in Ayrshire, just as the economic costs of striking were elevated, with the relatively low MWE rankings of Barony and Killoch, although this modest level of formal economic activity might have been mitigated slightly by informal methods. The Scottish Area strike committee also heard in February 1985 that the NCB had contacted 1,200 older strikers in Fife, Stirling and Clackmannan, indicating that they would be offered highly favourable redundancy terms upon returning to work for just four weeks.[151] This perhaps contributed to the eventual weakening of the strike in East Fife, although the position at Longannet's pits and Comrie hardly altered.[152]

Conclusion

This chapter has established that relatively few miners in the Scottish coalfield were tempted to 'discount' the future 'hyperbolically' by strike-breaking. Most miners saw that any short-term economic gains derived from wages for working during the strike would be massively outweighed by long-term economic and social costs: collieries and jobs would be lost if the strike were defeated; and men who broke the strike would bear a substantial social stigma. The chapter has further established, however, that there were, ultimately, significant pit-level varieties of strike commitment. These were largely a matter of material resources and moral variables that were present in uneven quantities across the coalfields. The chapter developed a model for predicting relative pit-level Potential Strike Endurance (PSE), based on three pre-strike, pit-level variables: Married Women in Employment (MWE), Council Housing Density (CHD), and a Militancy Index (MI). The material resources of female earnings and deferred housing rents and rates lowered the economic cost of striking. Pre-strike industrial relations were also important, shaping pit-level strike willingness, and therefore the potential for differentiated pit-level endurance. There was a fairly close match between the PSE rankings and Actual Strike Endurance (ASE) pit-level rankings: seven pits moved just three places from one set to the other; Barony, Killoch and Bilston Glen were in the bottom five of each set. Pre-strike economic performance (EP) was also significant, explaining in part the eventual crumbling of the strike at Barony and Killoch, and the solid-ity of the strike at the Longannet complex. There was indeed a strong positive correlation between EP and ASE rankings, with four pits – the Longannet three plus Seafield – in the top six of each set, and four others in the bottom six of each set. This qualifies the usual assumption in the literature that the correlation between pre-strike performance and actual strike commitment was negative.

The connection between these economic variables and actual endurance was uneven, however, with significantly different strike histories, for instance, at Bilston Glen and Monktonhall, which drew upon similar pre-strike economic variables, although the character of industrial relations at the two pits was different. Hence the importance of moral economy factors, which appear to have rendered the social cost of strike-breaking higher at some pits, such as Monktonhall, than others, especially Bilston Glen. These moral economy factors drew on established customs and expectations surrounding the opera-tion of the nationalised coal industry, including approaches to pit closures, which Wheeler's pre-strike initiatives plainly transgressed, and attitudes to job losses and ownership. Miners as individuals could not in every circumstance legitimately 'sell' their job, by accepting transfer or redundancy. The job, like the pit, was a community resource, to be preserved for future, collective benefit. Men 'sold' their jobs by breaking the strike and those who did so also 'sold' their communities, at substantial personal cost. The social cost of job 'selling', through redundancy, transfer, or even strike-breaking, was, however, to some extent age-sensitive. Older men were broadly forgiven for discounting the future by accepting redundancy, and to a lesser extent their acts of strike-breaking, to preserve redundancy terms, were also, eventually, understood. Younger men, on the other hand, who accepted redundancy were 'renegades', and tended to receive in much fuller form than older men the social stigma of the 'scab' when they discounted the future by returning to work. This stigma was borne most strongly by those who returned early, in the summer or early autumn, the 'super scabs'. Their stigma, it should be emphasised, was highly gendered: they ceased to exist as 'real' men. Women played a central role in this process, ridiculing the flawed masculinity of the strike-breakers. Women did much more than this, however, in generating strike commitment, assuming moral and political leadership in their communities, and providing material sustenance. They, as much as if not more than the men, knew how much had been invested in the strike, and understood how immensely expensive defeat would prove. In the long winter especially, as men returned to work, in their tens, hundreds, and then, eventually, thousands, and with no settlement apparently imminent, the resolution of women defended the integrity of the strike.

Notes

1 *Scottish Miner*, April 1984.
2 John McIlroy, 'Look Back in Anger: Mining Communities, the Mining Novel and the Great Miners' Strike', *Historical Studies in Industrial Relations*, 18 (2004), 65–108; Wight, *Workers Not Wasters, passim*.
3 Phillips, 'Material and Moral Resources'.
4 SMM, NUMSA, Box 13, NUMSA Strike Committee Minutes, 29 June 1984.
5 Campbell, *Scottish Miners. Volume One*, pp. 213–54.
6 Eric Clarke, Interview; Willie Clarke, Interview.
7 Taylor, *NUM and British Politics, Volume 2*, pp. 188–9.
8 Griffin, '"Notts. have some very peculiar history"', 92–3.
9 Hester Barron, 'Women of the Durham Coalfield and their Reactions to the 1926 Miners' Lockout', *Historical Studies in Industrial Relations*, 22 (2006), 53–83, and especially 66.
10 McCaig, Interview with Thompson.
11 Olson, *Logic of Collective Action*, pp. 2, 71–6.
12 Richards, *Miners on Strike*, pp. 182–3.
13 Gilbert, *Class, Community and Collective Action*.
14 Amartya Sen, *Rationality and Freedom* (London, 1992).
15 Neville Kirk, *Custom and Conflict in the 'Land of the Gael': Ballachullish, 1900–1910* (London, 2007), pp. 94–9.
16 Avner Offer, *The Challenge of Affluence. Self Control and Well-Being in the United*

States and Britain since 1950 (Oxford, 2006), especially pp. 39–58.

17 NAS, SEP 4/6049, Scottish Office News Release, 'NUM Rally a "Pointless Exercise"', 6 November 1984.

18 McCaig, Interview with Thompson; Maxwell, *Chicago Tumbles*, pp. 137–48.

19 Hamilton, Interview.

20 Bolton, Interview with Thompson; Willie Clarke, Interview; Hamilton, Interview; Dave Maguire, Auchinleck, in Owens, *Miners*, p. 48.

21 Amos, Interview.

22 Wilson, Interview; Hamilton, Interview; Amos, Interview; Chalmers, Interview; Eric Clarke, Interview.

23 SMM, NUMSA, Box 13, NUMSA Strike Committee, 19 March 1984.

24 Maxwell, *Chicago Tumbles*, pp. 38–40.

25 Tam Mylchreest, Interview with Willie Thompson, undated, but presumed early 1986; McGrail and Patterson, *'For as Long as it Takes!'*, pp. 6–7.

26 Chalmers, Interview.

27 Willie Clarke, Interview.

28 Wilson, Interview.

29 Penny Summerfield, 'Culture and Composure: Creating Narratives of the Gendered Self in Oral History Interviews', *Cultural and Social History*, 1 (2004), 65–93.

30 Chalmers, Interview; Goodfellow, Interview.

31 Catriona Levy and Mauchline Miners' Wives, *'A Very Hard Year'. 1984–5 Miners' Strike In Mauchline* (Glasgow, 1985); McGrail and Patterson, *'For as Long as it Takes!'*.

32 McCaig, Interview with Thompson; Coulter, Interview with Thompson.

33 KAGM, 75.3/1/1, NUM Dysart Strike Centre, Reports, March 1984 to July 1984.

34 KAGM, 75.3/1/1, NUM Dysart Strike Centre, Reports, 12 June, 18 June, 22 June 1984.

35 Maxwell, *Chicago Tumbles*, pp. 41–2.

36 Amos, Interview.

37 SMM, NUMSA, Box 10, Area Coordinating Committee, 29 June 1984.

38 KAGM, 75.3/1/1, NUM Dysart Strike Centre, Reports, 27 March and 5 July 1984.

39 Guthrie, *Coal Not Dole*, pp. 45–7; MacDougall, *Voices From Work and Home*, pp. 143–4.

40 Amos, Interview.

41 Cath Cunningham, 'Fife', in Seddon, *Cutting Edge* pp. 224–25; Neilson, Interview with Thompson.

42 Eric Clarke, Interview; Wilson, Interview.

43 SMM, NUMSA, Box 13, NUMSA Strike Committee Minutes, 24 April 1984.

44 Maxwell, *Chicago Tumbles*, p. 68.

45 Dundee City Council, June 1984 – Bygone News: www.dundeecity.gov.uk/bygone /jun1984, accessed 22 November 2010.

46 *Scottish Miner*, July 1984.

47 GCUA, STUC General Purposes Committee Minutes, 19 December 1984, and General Council Minutes, 9 January 1985.

48 McCaig, Interview with Thompson.

49 MacDougall, *Voices From Work and Home*, pp. 141–2.

50 Maxwell, *Chicago Tumbles*, p. 62.

51 Coulter, Interview with Thompson; McCaig, Interview with Thompson.

52 Campbell, *Scottish Miners. Volume One*, pp. 159–212; Gilbert, *Class, Community and Collective Action*, pp. 33–8.

53 Chalmers, Interview; Willie Clarke, Interview.

54 Maxwell, *Chicago Tumbles*, p. 52.

55 Nicholson, Interview.

56 Maxwell, *Chicago Tumbles*, p. 39.

57 Nicholson, Interview.

58 Hamilton, Interview.

59 Chalmers, Interview.

60 Maxwell, *Chicago Tumbles*, p. 48; SMM, NUMSA, Box 13, NUMSA Strike Committee Minutes, 29 June 1984.

61 Campbell, *Scottish Miners. Volume One*, pp. 213–54.

62 Cameron, *Impaled Upon a Thistle*, pp. 220–1.

63 The Lost Village of Glencraig: www.glencraig.org.uk, accessed 11 February 2010; Willie Clarke, Interview; *Census 1981 Scotland. Report for Fife Region, Volume 4* (HMSO, 1983), Table 14, 'Private Households in Permanent Buildings by tenure'.

64 Sue Bruley, 'Women', in McIlroy, Campbell and Gildart, *Industrial Politics*, pp. 234–7.

65 Annmarie Hughes, *Gender and Political Identities in Scotland, 1919–1939* (Edinburgh, 2010), pp. 189–90.

66 Maxwell, *Chicago Tumbles*, pp. 63–4.

67 McIvor, 'Women and Work', 189.

68 Hamilton, Interview; Chalmers, Interview.

69 Suzanne Corrigan, Cath Cunningham and Margo Thorburn, 'Fife Women Stand Firm', written in collaboration with Vicky Seddon, in Seddon, *Cutting Edge*, pp. 30–49; MacDougall, *Voices From Work and Home*, pp. 141–2.

70 MMC, *National Coal Board, Volume Two*, Appendices 3.3 and 3.5(a).

71 Chris Wrigley, 'The 1984–5 Miners' strike', in Andrew Charlesworth, David Gilbert, Adrian Randall, Humphrey Southall and Chris Wrigley, *An Atlas of Industrial Unrest in Britain, 1750–1990* (London, 1996), pp. 221–2.

72 Richards, *Miners on Strike*, p. 109; Taylor, *NUM and British Politics. Volume 2*, pp. 188–9.

73 Information from Professor David Howell, University of York.

74 National Museum of Wales, *Big Pit. National Coal Museum. A Guide* (Cardiff, 2005), p. 42.

75 Mylchreest, Interview with Thompson.

76 NAS, SEP 4/6028, Sit Rep, 20 June 1984.

77 KAGM, 75.3/1/1, NUM Dysart Strike Centre, Report, 20 July 1984.

78 SMM, NUMSA, Box 10, Area Coordinating Committee, Report, 24 June 1984.

79 Hamilton, Interview.

80 NAS, SEP 4/6029/1, Sit Reps, 20 and 21 December 1984.

81 NAS, SEP 4/6029/1, Sit Rep, 19 December 1984.

82 Taylor, *NUM and British Politics. Volume 2*, p. 189.

83 Newby, 'Scottish Coal Miners', p. 593; Stewart, *Path to Devolution*, pp. 96–7.

84 NAS, CB 229/3/1, Bilston Glen CCC, 31 March, 26 May, 26 July, 11 August and 8 September 1982 and 7 September, 4 October and 2 November 1983.

85 NAS, CB 221/3/4, Barony CCC, 11 January, 5 April and 23 August 1983; CB 328/3/4, NCB, Killoch CCC, 6 September 1983.

86 Ashworth, *British Coal Industry*, p. 97.

87 The *Scotsman*, 14 January 1984

88 Oglethorpe, *Scottish Collieries*, p. 142.

89 The *Scotsman*, 21 and 27 January 1984.
90 Campbell, *Scottish Miners. Volume Two, passim.*
91 Maxwell, *Chicago Tumbles*, pp. 166–7, 181–3.
92 McCormack, in Owens, *Miners*, p. 115.
93 McGrail and Patterson, '*For as Long as it Takes'.*
94 Brotherstone and Pirani, 'Were There Alternatives?', 110–11.
95 Eric Clarke, Interview; Wilson, Interview.
96 McCaig, Interview with Thompson.
97 McCormack, 'Polmaise on the Boil'.
98 Scottish Trades Union Congress, *88th Annual Report, 1985*, pp. 209–12.
99 The *Scotsman*, 2 and 7 July 1983.
100 Maxwell, *Chicago Tumbles*, p. 77.
101 *Scottish Miner*, June 1984; Willie Clarke, Interview.
102 Hughes, *Gender and Political Identities*, pp. 185–7.
103 NAS, SEP 4/6027, Sit Reps 26 and 27 July 1984.
104 Neilson, Interview with Thompson.
105 NAS, SEP 4/6027, Sit Reps, 28 and 29 June and 6 and 18 August 1984; Note by Jane Morgan, Private Secretary to Michael Ancram, 6 July 1984 and Note by R. Patton, Police Division, SHHD (to Jane Morgan), 11 July 1984.
106 McGrail and Patterson, '*For as Long as it Takes'.*
107 Wight, *Workers Not Wasters, passim.*
108 Barron, 'Women of the Durham Coalfield', 79.
109 Stead, *Never the Same Again*, pp. 68–75.
110 Amos, Interview.
111 McCaig, Interview with Thompson.
112 Wilson, Interview; Chalmers, Interview; Hamilton, Interview.
113 W.W. Knox, *Industrial Nation: Work, Culture and Society in Scotland, 1800–present* (Edinburgh, 1999), pp. 287–8.
114 Bruley, 'Women', pp. 238–45.
115 Dennis, Henriques and Slaughter, *Coal Is Our Life*, pp. 117–70, 180–1.
116 Beatrix Campbell, *Wigan Pier Revisited: Poverty and Politics in the Eighties* (London, 1984).
117 *Scottish Miner*, October 1967, January and February 1974 and June 1984.
118 Holden, *Queen Coal*; Levy and Mauchline Miners' Wives, '*A Very Hard Year'*; McGrail and Patterson, '*For as long as it takes!'*; Stead, *Never the Same Again.*
119 Maxwell, *Chicago Tumbles*, pp. 98–100.
120 *Here We Go. Women Living the Strike*, Presented and Directed by Margaret Wright, TV2DAY, Independent Video Production, 2009.
121 MacDougall, *Voices From Work and Home*, pp. 138–9.
122 Hamilton, Interview.
123 MacDougall, *Voices From Work and Home*, pp. 146–7.
124 Midlothian Council, Councillors, Dalkeith Ward, Margot Russell: www.midlothian .gov.uk/Article.aspx?TopicId=2&ArticleId=10441, accessed 22 November 2010.
125 Maxwell, *Chicago Tumbles*, pp. 101–4.
126 Hughes, *Gender and Political Identities.*
127 Ayrshire strike leaders, Interview with Willie Thompson, 9 December 1985.
128 Levy and Mauchline Miners' Wives, '*A Very Hard Year'.*
129 Willie Clarke, Interview.
130 Egan, Interview with Thompson.

131 Corrigan, Cunningham and Thorburn, 'Fife Women Stand Firm'; *Here We Go*.
132 KAGM, 75.3/1/1, NUM Dysart Strike Centre, Reports, May to June 1984.
133 Mylchreest, Interview with Thompson.
134 Stead, *Never the Same Again*, pp. 133–4.
135 MacDougall, *Voices From Work and Home*, p. 142.
136 Jean Hamilton, 'Give us a Future, Give us our Jobs!', written in collaboration with Vicky Seddon, in Seddon, *The Cutting Edge*, pp. 211–21.
137 *Here We Go*.
138 Coulter, Interview with Thompson.
139 Neil Rafeek, *Communist Women in Scotland: Red Clydeside from the Russian Revolution to the End of the Soviet Union* (London, 2008).
140 Thompson, 'Miners' Strike'.
141 Egan, Interview with Thompson.
142 Chalmers, Interview; Willie Clarke, Interview.
143 SMM, NUMSA, EC, 12 July 1983 and Minute of Special Conference of Delegates, 12 July 1983; Jackie Aitchison, Dalkeith, in Owens, *Miners*, pp. 94–5.
144 *Glasgow Herald* and *The Times*, both 14 May 1983.
145 Mylchreest, Interview with Thompson.
146 Chalmers, Interview.
147 Smith, *Miners' Strike*, pp. 12–15.
148 Bolton, Interview with Thompson.
149 Hamilton, Interview.
150 Levy and Mauchline Miners' Wives, 'A Very Hard Year'.
151 SMM, NUM Scottish Area, Strike Committee, 18 February 1985.
152 NAS, SEP 4/6029/1, Sit Rep, 11 February 1985.

5

Ending and aftermath

The strike ended painfully in Scotland, and in stages. It collapsed unofficially in Ayrshire in the last week or so of February. A return at the other pits gradually followed an NUM delegate conference vote to end the strike, in London on Sunday 3 March, and two NUMSA and SCEBTA delegate conferences on 4 and 6 March, the second reversing the decision of the first to stay out. Deliberation was particularly difficult in West Fife and Clackmannan. The East Fife strikers were back at work on Wednesday 6 March, and the West Lothian and Midlothian strikers on Thursday 7 March, but the Longannet complex and Comrie strikers did not return until Monday 11 March. Miners at Polmaise stayed out for one more week.[1]

This chapter analyses this ending, and examines its immediate aftermath. The emphasis in this book on the primacy of community and colliery factors is restated: local contingencies, as Chapter 4 demonstrated, were important in extending the strike into 1985; and there were distinctive pit-level experiences after the strike, although there was a common tendency across the Scottish coalfields to greater managerial control. This signalled a further erosion of the moral economy of the coalfields, with its employment security and joint industrial regulation of the workplace. Such eventuality demonstrated the importance too of high politics, which have been de-emphasised slightly at other points in this book. The radical erosion of the moral economy of the coalfields was, after all, related to the government's broader economic and social objectives, such as reducing the role of public enterprise, marginalising trade unions, and redistributing workplace authority from employees to employers. The government's desire to downgrade joint regulation and diminish coalfield employment is illuminated by the manner of the strike's ending. Three factors are identified here: the fruitless pursuit of a negotiated settlement, which was sabotaged repeatedly by government intervention; the highly partial policing of pickets and strikers by Scottish constabularies; and the NCB's strike-breaking strategy in Scotland, which was wilfully provocative, involving a relatively high level of victimisation of strikers, when measured against other NCB territorial areas, and exaggerated threats that the strike was jeopardising the survival of collieries. The question of victimisation was paramount in delaying the end: 206 men were sacked by the NCB in Scotland because of acts that they were alleged to have committed in pursuit of the strike. A large number of these men had been convicted by the courts, mainly for public order offences, but a significant number had not been. The sense of injustice arising from these dismissals, which continues to burn, more than 25 years later, was a factor in the tense and unforgiving pattern of coalfield workplace and industrial politics after the strike, with renewed anti-union managerial initiatives, and highly fractious exchanges between strikers and strike-breakers.

The difficulties of reaching a settlement

There is a counter-factual literature of the strike, referred to at different points in this book, broadly focusing on the leadership and strategy of the NUM, and especially the personality of Arthur Scargill. Much of this literature arises, essentially, from understandable human and political feelings of regret: if the strike had developed differently, then there might also have been an alternative outcome. The coal industry, in other words, with its provision of stable and relatively well-paid, unionised employment, could have survived in reasonable health, into the 1990s and perhaps even the 2000s or 2010s. The counter-factual literature mourns the absence of a pre-strike ballot, the picketing of steel works and the consequent divisions between miners and other groups of unionised workers. Above all, however, it bemoans the NUM leadership's conduct of negotiations with the NCB over a possible settlement to the strike. Scargill is characterised as an unyielding, unimaginative and unskilled negotiator, and compared unfavourably with the pragmatic and shrewd McGahey.[2] This binary distinction – between Scargill and what actually happened on the one hand, and McGahey and what might have happened on the other hand – is echoed in the testimony of some of the strike participants in Scotland,[3] as the discussion of NUMSA's strike strategy in Chapter 3 indicated. David Hamilton is certain that a settlement would have been reached by the summer of 1984, at the latest, if McGahey had been in charge of negotiations, and Willie Clarke laments what he sees as the limited intellectual and imaginative properties of Scargill and his Yorkshire supporters.[4]

Scargill and McGahey were clearly different from each other intellectually, politically and temperamentally. The basis of the counter-factual alternative ending to the strike is nevertheless elusive. What, to be precise, would a settlement satisfactory to the striking miners, including those whose pits were immediately threatened, have looked like?[5] The NCB could not accept a reversal of its decisions on Polmaise, Cortonwood, Herrington, Bullcliffe Wood and Snowdon, the five pits marked for closure prior to the strike. Nor could it accept the unions' determined defence of all other pits, unless 'exhausted'. The improbability of any alternative course of events is illuminated in the minutes of a meeting of the Scottish Area strike committee on 23 July. This followed the unsuccessful conclusion of the lengthiest round of talks with the NCB during the dispute, on 18 July. McGahey reported that while the NCB had agreed to withdraw its proposals of 6 March, outlining the contraction of capacity in the longer term, the five pits immediately threatened would probably still be closed. Talks had broken down over the NCB's insistence on using 'beneficially' when defining the criteria for pit closures: a colliery could be shut when it no longer contained coal reserves that were 'workable or which could be beneficially developed'. The word 'beneficially', McGahey emphasised, had an 'economic connotation'. So 'if a colliery was not beneficial in terms of profits, it was not economically viable', and the NCB could close it. The NUM had to oppose this, 'rejecting any concept of uneconomic closures, this being the basic, fundamental and central question of the whole dispute'. The question was particularly acute, of course, in Scotland, where no pit was 'profitable' according to the NCB, and so all would be vulnerable if the 'beneficially developed' proviso was accepted. If this is understood then it is difficult to sustain the notion that McGahey – contemplating an agreement that could have sacrificed the entire Scottish coal industry – would have settled where Scargill could not. McGahey, it must also be emphasised, recurrently distanced himself from any criticism of Scargill's conduct of the strike generally, including the decision not to hold a national ballot and the conduct of negotiations with the NCB.[6] The government, he told the Scottish Area committee in July, was seeking to isolate the President, who was acting with the unanimous support of the NUM's national executive, and an extraordinary Annual Conference held two weeks or so earlier.[7] Critics of Scargill, in these terms, were also critics of the policy of the NUM, and the generality of miners who were on strike. This explains why Jimmy Reid's attacks on Scargill, noted in this book's Introduction, and published, moreover, in newspapers and magazines that supported the Conservative government and opposed the strike, angered the strikers and many others in the labour movement. McGahey, it was remembered on Reid's death, pithily characterised his former Communist comrade as 'Broken Reid'.[8]

Counter-factualism and its dangers are further illustrated by the account of the negotiations written in 1986 by Ned Smith, the NCB's Industrial Relations Director before the strike, a position which he retired from, exhausted and saddened, in January 1985. Smith disliked Scargill, whom he described as manipulative and an 'entertainer' or 'actor' rather than a serious industrial personality. McGahey, by comparison, was a 'hard man' but a 'kind man' who once rebuked Smith for making 'ribald' comments to a waitress at a dinner, asking 'if I would like anyone to speak to my daughter in that way'. McGahey was a pragmatic and effective negotiator too, according to Smith, accepting some closures to protect the larger interests of the industry. In these terms Smith provided a variant of the counter-factual view, claiming that a McGahey presidency would have altered events by preventing the strike from happening at all. But Smith also showed that, with the strike under way, the 'beneficially developed' proviso was impossible for the NUM to accept.

Smith's account illuminates too the crucial factor that counter-factual literature tends to evade: the NCB Chairman, Ian MacGregor, and the government were by the summer committed to 'the grinding defeat' of 'our employees' and 'the dreadful bitterness which that entailed'. MacGregor and the government were consequently prepared to derail any settlement that the strikers could claim as victory. This was the source of Smith's growing unhappiness and ultimate resignation. He was certain that MacGregor, operating under government instruction, was opposed to reaching an agreement on pit closures after June. Before the penultimate round of talks in London that the NUM believed to be meaningful, in September, the Chairman took a telephone call that Smith overheard. MacGregor told the caller that there would be no agreement. McGahey, it should be emphasised, advised the NUMSA strike committee that he too was convinced that MacGregor was taking instructions from the government during these and later talks.[9]

The prospects of 'peace' were further diminished by two factors, according to Smith. First, there was the instruction in early September to NCB Area Directors to accelerate the organised resumption of work, supported by armoured buses and other strike-breaking paraphernalia. Second, there was the 'verbal violence' of the government from the summer months onwards, encapsulated in the Prime Minister's characterisation of the left wing of the NUM as the 'enemy within', and the insistence by Nigel Lawson, Chancellor of the Exchequer, that the immense economic and financial costs of the strike represented a 'worthwhile investment'.[10]

The ultimate scale of this 'investment' has recently been estimated at £6 billion, roughly £20 billion at 2011–12 prices, in lost production and tax revenues, charges for replacement coal stocks and additional oil burn, diminution of related economic activity, including that related to forfeited purchasing from mining households, and the very heavy burden of policing charges.[11] By comparison, the NCB's pre-strike projected annual losses for 1984–85, it will be remembered from Chapter 2, were only £100 million.[12] Had McGahey succeeded where Scargill had not, and secured from the NCB – despite MacGregor's opposition – an agreement on pit closures that preserved the bulk of the industry, including in Scotland, then this would surely have been destabilised by the government. Increasing ministerial confidence had been evident in Scotland in September, when Tebbit sabotaged an inter-union agreement on railway carriage of coal to Ravenscraig, as detailed in Chapter 3. The unambiguous ambition of Thatcher and her ministers thereafter, with the striking miners isolated, was to secure unconditional victory over the NUM. This would bring closer their larger strategic goals of neutralising organised labour, reducing state enterprise commitments and effecting wider economic restructuring.[13]

The government pursued this strategy through its final crisis of the strike, the threatened industrial action of NACODS members in October, which was briefly examined in Chapter 3. NACODS members, to elaborate a little, were responsible for maintaining the safety of underground workings and operations in collieries. They were not involved in the strike, and had been working more or less normally since 12 March. The NUM, in Scotland and elsewhere, had also been supplying members on a routine basis to undertake their normal share of safety operations. This practice was complicated, however, and periodically interrupted, by strike-breaking, which the NUM attempted to resist by withdrawing its members' participation from safety cover. This caused frictions in Scotland, and contributed to serious problems at several pits in August, starting at Bilston Glen, where safety cover was withdrawn on or around 7 August. The Scottish Area strike committee heard evidence that this was counter-productive, stimulating further handfuls of men, worried that the pit's future was now being jeopardised, to break the strike. The strike-breakers, in effect, became numerous enough to take responsibility for safety away from the strikers. At other pits the number of strike-breakers was too small to ensure proper safety: NUM and SCEBTA strikers went in to Frances over the weekend of 18–19 August, but did not do so at Polkemmet, the serious flooding of which was announced on 28 August.[14]

NACODS members were now drawn into the dispute by a change in NCB policy. In the opening months of the strike, pit deputies who refused to cross large pickets because they felt threatened were usually still paid by the NCB for the shift that they missed. By the autumn this policy was shifting: deputies turning away from heavily picketed pits were generally not being paid.[15] Those deputies who crossed the picket lines were now also working alongside strike-breaking miners, enabling production in Scotland as elsewhere. Substantial tensions arose. Managers at Seafield, for example, were intermittently worried in October by the number of NACODS men who were 'turned' away by NUM pickets.[16] The NACODS executive responded to the misgivings of its members by agreeing to hold a ballot on strike action in opposition to the threat of pit closures. Such strike action would have brought mining to a halt across the entirety of NCB operations, placing enormous pressure on the government. The result of the subsequent ballot, with 82 per cent of those voting in favour of a strike, scheduled to begin on 25 October, was described by McGahey in discussion with NUMSA and SCEBTA comrades as a 'magnificent result'. He warned, however, that the leadership of NACODS was seeking accommodation with the NCB, and moving its negotiating focus from pit closures to the less direct question of the colliery review procedure.[17] This was a mechanism through which unions could contest, although would never, it transpired, be able to resist closure decisions taken by the NCB. Thatcher pushed MacGregor and the NCB to agree a new colliery review procedure with NACODS, in talks at ACAS on 23 and 24 October. This was a further practical illustration of the government's incremental, anti-trade union 'Stepping Stones' strategy, and the strike was averted,[18] although pit-level problems persisted for another week or so. At Seafield NACODS members still observed NUM picket lines on 26 October and on the day shift of 1 November.[19]

Reviewing these events on 29 October, the Scottish Area strike committee agreed that a new phase was beginning, with special emphasis to be placed on the financial position, encompassing a Christmas appeal, and consolidating the strike in the communities.[20] Maintaining endurance was an acute challenge, compounded when the NCB offered the substantial strike-breaking incentive of

Christmas bonuses to men who returned to work by 19 November.[21] This seems
to have accelerated the trend to work resumption at Bilston Glen, and gave some
impetus to strike-breaking at Monktonhall and in Ayrshire. Elsewhere,
however, the Scottish Area committee was able to record that no big 'surge' had
materialised, despite the NCB's 'blandishments and immoral actions in utilising
children to blackmail fathers back to work for Christmas'.[22] The strikers were
not entirely isolated, of course, continuing to draw upon moral as well as limited
material support from the wider labour movement. In late November the STUC
convened a conference on the strike at Partick Burgh Halls in Glasgow, which
emphasised the economic and social importance to Scotland of the coal industry. The STUC presented a paper that drew upon Andrew Glyn's analysis of
NCB finances, and argued the case for the long-term future of Scottish deep
mining. The immense political difficulties of the position were acknowledged,
however, given the reality of large-scale industrial restructuring, unemployment, de-unionisation, and Thatcherite power.[23] These were vividly realised in
the conference's anti-climactic outcome, with Jimmy Milne, the STUC secretary, writing in quixotic fashion to the Prime Minister, seeking a meeting where
Scottish labour and civic representatives would impress upon her the importance to Scotland of coal mining and the desirability of settling the strike
through negotiation. Thatcher's response was predictable: she could not meet a
Scottish delegation to discuss the strike, which was entirely the illegitimate
creation of the NUM. Hardships to 'miners, their families and their communities' were the consequence of the 'unreasonable' nature of the union's 'basic
demand that uneconomic pits be kept open, regardless of the cost or whether
the coal can be sold'.[24]

Willie Clarke recalls thinking at this point – after the NACODS agreement
especially – that he was now in an invidious position. He felt the strike could not
be won, but was compelled nevertheless to ask miners – along with their families and communities – to make further and ever-larger sacrifices.[25] Ned Smith
also recognised at about the same time that the strikers would not prevail but,
unlike others at the NCB, knew the strike would not collapse. Instead a dreadful 'attrition' would materialise, encouraged by the government's triumphalist
determination to humiliate the strikers and the NUM.[26] One incident illustrates
the government's hardening and vindictive anti-strike narrative attitude, and
how it permeated the Scottish Office. A fortnight after the NACODS settlement,
the NUMSA Women's Support Group requested a meeting with George
Younger, the Secretary of State. This was refused by Younger's officials.
Margaret Gray, the Women's Support Group Secretary, persisted, indicating
that the women would publicise Younger's unwillingness to meet them as
evidence of his indifference to 'the miners, their wives and families'. One of
Younger's officials, Muir Russell, drafted a response referring to the 'sinister
"bully boys" who are an affront to the democratic traditions of responsible trade
unionism. Their despicable campaign is doomed to failure.' These words were
not used in Younger's eventual response, which was nevertheless couched in the
same politicised and adversarial terms, claiming 'it would be in the best inter-

ests of all concerned if the women's support group were to divert their energies to encouraging a democratic ballot on the first-class offer which has been made to the miners'. This was a reference, presumably, to the new review procedure that had persuaded the NACODS executive to call off its proposed industrial action,[27] but which promised no defence – as McGahey and other strike leaders in Scotland knew full well – against closures on economic grounds.

Policing and the NCB Strike-breaking strategy

Strike-breaking was still a patchy and minor phenomenon in late October, as Chapter 4 explored, but its potential was encouraged by the lost prospects of a negotiated settlement and support from NACODS, and the NCB's enhanced financial incentives for men who returned. This distracted the strikers from strategic economic targets, like Ravenscraig, or ports and power stations, for picketing was now necessarily and largely concentrated at collieries, to raise the social costs of strike-breaking by exerting community pressure on those who returned.[28] A central problem for the strikers was the intervention of the police, who reduced these social costs by protecting strike-breakers. Policing of pit-gate picketing seems to have been heavier in Midlothian than elsewhere in Scotland. An early example came on 13 August, when 22 pickets were arrested at Bilston Glen by officers who provided safe passage for about 60 strike-breakers. This was conducted with 'massive brutality and harassment', according to McGahey, reporting to the Scottish Area strike committee.[29]

Police officers – in Scotland as elsewhere – arguably had a duty to provide protection to those exercising their individual 'right to work'. Yet there is nevertheless a strong sense in which they acted partially, supporting the rights of the strike-breakers, and ruthlessly – and perhaps illegitimately – contravening the rights of the strikers. There is certainly clear evidence that strikers were being closely monitored by the police: their movements logged; their telephone calls tapped and recorded. Activists at the Midlothian strike centre in Dalkeith, suspecting this type of surveillance, telephoned local centres to 'organise' a blockade of Dunbar harbour. Meanwhile 'runners' in cars spread the real news: the strikers were going to occupy the NCB Scottish Headquarters at Green Park in Edinburgh, which they did, briefly, while the police patrolled Dunbar, searching for non-existent pickets. This story is related by David Hamilton within a wider narrative: that NCB management saw Midlothian as the strategic core of the strike, which would crumble throughout Scotland if it was broken at Bilston Glen and then Monktonhall. Lothian and Borders Police officers, in Hamilton's narrative, acted as the confederates of NCB management in pursuit of this strategic objective. Every member, he says, of the Dalkeith strike committee was arrested at one time or another, and Hamilton himself was frequently apprehended on picket lines. On one occasion first his brother and then his wife, Jean, were arrested by officers and handled roughly, in order, he maintains, to provoke him. Eventually he was charged with an alleged public order offence, committed away from the picket lines.[30] Denied bail, he was held in Saughton prison from the start of November until being found not guilty at Edinburgh Sheriff Court on 21 December.[31]

Many others were targeted in the same manner. Michael McGahey, a Bilston Glen NUM branch official and son of the union's Scottish President, was monitored by police officers, picketing at his own pit. He was arrested five times during the strike and fined £100 at Dunfermline Sheriff Court, convicted for two public order offences committed at Cartmore open cast mine in Fife in June.[32] As a consequence he was sacked by the NCB before the end of the strike.[33] Another Bilston Glen activist, Robert Aitchison, told NUM officials that he was stopped by police officers at Dalkeith bus station on the afternoon of Sunday 13 May, and taken to a police station in the town. The officers knew that Aitchison did not live in Dalkeith, and warned him that he would be arrested if seen there again. Officers took him by road to the Eskbank roundabout, two miles west of the town, where he was dropped off and told to go home.[34]

The sense of being watched was not confined, it should be emphasised, to activists in Midlothian. The Ayrshire strike leaders also proved – to themselves at least – that their telephone lines were being tapped, by managing on one occasion to organise a mass picket of Hunterston by word of mouth alone. There were no police officers at the terminal when the pickets arrived. This harassment – along with the collusion between officers and the NCB – contributed to lost respect for the police in the Ayrshire mining communities. One incident in particular stood out, when the first strike-breaker was brought to Killoch on a bus from New Cumnock. Eight police officers were on board, and stopped the bus outside the colliery to admit six strikers, who wanted to dissuade the New Cumnock man from going to work. The bus drove through the picket line, with the strikers now on board. They were dropped off in the pit yard, and made their way back out, having failed to turn the strike-breaker. Three were subsequently sacked by the NCB for trespass. The structural injustice of the position was vehemently emphasised by the Ayrshire strikers: in a reversal of the normal legal convention, that a man was innocent until proven guilty, a striker charged with breach of the peace, or trespass, was guilty unless he could establish his innocence.[35]

Police harassment of strikers sometimes took a more subtle form. Tam Coulter told Willie Thompson in 1986 that, anxious about the position at Ravenscraig in May 1984, he had reconnoitred the Yuill and Dodds depot at Strathaven, wondering whether it would be possible to sabotage the lorries. Preventing them from leaving the depot would be safer and more effective than seeking to stop them on the open highway. On a second reconnaissance trip, this time with a union companion, he was stopped near the depot by men in an unmarked red Austin Metro, who said they were officers from Strathclyde Police CID. Coulter and his companion were asked to identify themselves and explain their presence in the area. Two days later, Coulter says, a story appeared in the *Daily Record* to the effect that striking miners had been intimidating residents who lived opposite the depot.[36]

The partiality of the police, exhibited in these various incidents, was resented greatly by the strikers, and this had a lasting and damaging bearing on police–community relations. Strikers in other parts of the coalfield, especially Yorkshire, often likened the police presence in their communities, and at their collieries, to an invading force. This was exemplified to many of the strikers by the increasingly prevalent practice, unprecedented hitherto, of police marshalling inside NCB property, to help strike-breakers cross picket lines.[37] 'McGregor's men', these officers were sometimes called.[38] A similar narrative emerges from Scottish participants. Many – in Fife, at least, and Midlothian – observe that the 'local' police were usually 'alright', but trouble developed when officers from another area came into their communities. This amounted to an invasion, and indeed an occupation, by an alien and hostile force.[39]

The civil liberties of strikers were certainly transgressed, notably – in the Scottish experience – where Strathclyde Police apprehended strikers travelling to Hunterston and Ravenscraig in May 1984. This, it will be remembered, was central to the breaking of the Scottish Area strike strategy, easing the flow of materials to the steel mill, and the political pressure on the government in Scotland. A meeting between the Secretary of State for Scotland and Labour MPs had followed, where Younger suggested that miners who felt wronged by the police should pursue the matter through the courts. Alex Eadie, MP for Midlothian, and chair of the mining group of MPs, responded from an overtly class-conscious perspective: his constituents did not trust in the neutrality of the legal system, and were additionally unlikely to pursue legal action against the police because the expense was prohibitive. He added an important observation about the broader social consequence of what he saw as the government's polit-ical use of the police force: 'the damage which was being done to the police relationship with the country. If this suffers we all suffer.'[40]

The anti-strike bias of the police, reinforced by the anti-trade union preju-dices of the judiciary, is an important element in activist narratives. Eric Clarke and Nicky Wilson both emphasise that individuals convicted of public order charges in Sheriff Courts in the mid-1980s normally received fines of £15 or £20, but striking miners, going through the same courts, and convicted of the same charges, were fined much larger sums. The younger Michael McGahey's £100 fine at Dunfermline Sheriff Court, or £150 even, was more typical,[41] although there were instances of significantly larger punishments still. At Dunfermline Sheriff Court on 11 September two miners were fined £750 each, convicted for public order offences, after obstructing police officers at Castlehill. The two were said to have been wearing 'spiked belts', which may have been implements of intimidation but were not uncommon clothing accessories in 1984. One was fined an additional £200 for breaking bail conditions arising from an earlier picketing offence.[42]

The actions of the police and decisions of the judiciary elevated the economic costs of the strike. These were raised further by the NCB's strike-breaking strat-egy, which consisted of three elements. First, going back to work was encouraged through increased financial inducements, with Christmas bonuses, and the type of enhanced redundancy discussed in Chapter 4, and the provision of 'safe' transport, on buses with grille-covered windows, to collieries where 'security' was strengthened.[43] Barbed wire was erected around 'Belsen' Glen, as some miners came to call it,[44] and was still in place in July 1985, months after the end of the strike.[45] Second, there was a deliberate policy of intimidating strikers, significantly more pronounced in Scotland than elsewhere in the British coalfields. This involved victimising men who had been arrested by the police on picket lines and elsewhere by dismissing them from NCB employment. NUMSA and SCEBTA representatives and activists were targeted, to reinforce Wheeler's anti-union strategy.[46] This bears emphasis. Some men were sacked for strike-related offences demonstrated via a guilty verdict in a court of law, such as Michael McGahey, who, like his grandfather and father before him, in the 1920s and 1940s respectively, lost his job as a consequence of trade union activity.[47] Others were sacked while waiting for charges against them to come before the law courts; and some were sacked even where their legal innocence had been established. Despite being found not guilty for his alleged public order offence in December 1984, Hamilton was dismissed by the NCB.[48] Another notorious individual injustice was at Bilston Glen, where Jackie Aitchison was sacked in September for allegedly encroaching on NCB property by stepping across a white line on the road during a picket.[49] At a subsequent meeting between Lothian Regional Council's Highways Subcommittee and NCB officials it was apparently established that the line had been painted at the instruction of the colliery manager, without the local authority's approval, but Aitchison's sacking stood.[50]

The ferocity of this approach was undoubtedly in large part an extension of the abrasive managerial style adopted by the NCB Scottish Area under Albert Wheeler's directorship, which had elevated workplace tensions before the strike. Wheeler had no misgivings about inflicting defeat on the strikers, to further his assault on joint regulation of the industry. 'We were in it to win,' was how he subsequently characterised his management group's approach.[51] Table 5.1 illuminates the disproportionately large incidence of victimisation, in the NCB Scottish Area generally, and at the Midlothian pits especially, where managers executed Wheeler's strategy 'with relish', according to Rab Amos, SCEBTA delegate at Monktonhall, targeting especially union representatives and activists.[52]

Table 5.1 Strikers and strike dismissals, 1984–85: selected NCB holdings

	Strikers	Strikers dismissed	Percentage of strikers dismissed
England and Wales	131,000	800	0.61
Scotland	14,000	206	1.5
Bilston Glen	1,800	36	2.0
Monktonhall	1,700	46	2.7

Source: Hamilton, Interview; Guthrie, Coal Not Dole, p. 57; Richards, Miners on Strike, pp. 87, 100.

The third strand of the NCB's strike-breaking strategy in Scotland was to emphasise the dangers to pits arising from the neglect of normal safety operations. Wheeler replicated his policy from the overtime ban that preceded the strike, prepared to sacrifice pits by insisting that power would be switched off where strikers refused to provide safety cover: pumping and other maintenance activities would cease, and coal faces would be flooded, potentially irreparably.[53] These dangers were created by Wheeler and his managers: safety cover was being provided by strikers until the NCB organised strike-breaking. Some local managers, BACM members, sought to undertake the safety operations normally undertaken by strikers, which was the practice in the English and Welsh coalfields. Wheeler was unyielding in his response.[54] 'If your members want to do the jobs of pump men and winding enginemen,' he told a leading BACM official in Scotland, 'I'll see that's what they'll do when the strike ends.'[55] These words were apparently spoken in August, during a crisis at Polkemmet, which was flooded beyond rescue after pit management switched off the fans and pumps that kept the workings operable. This, union officials recall, was outright malevolence, instigated by the pit manager, whom David Hamilton refers to as 'one of Wheeler's kids'.[56] The loss of underground public assets, at an estimated value of £300 million, including machinery as well as the coal reserves, was resented bitterly by Polkemmet's miners as managerial sabotage of major community and public assets.[57] It still represents an affront to the moral economy of the coalfields, being likened by Eric Clarke and Nicky Wilson to wanton criminal damage. They contrast the punitive treatment of miners who were convicted of picket-line and other strike-related offences with the rewards enjoyed by coal managers generally and Wheeler especially, who secured a number of promotions within the NCB and its successor, British Coal, after the strike.[58]

If the situation at Polkemmet was calamitous, albeit arguably of management's making, the safety hazards trumpeted elsewhere by the NCB were almost certainly exaggerated. The Midlothian managers, Hamilton says, were 'trying it on' from the autumn onwards,[59] and the Frances and Seafield men were harassed with the help of the Scottish Office in February 1985. First, George Younger issued a press statement asserting that the closure of Frances was imminent, with the loss of more than 500 jobs. This was the consequence of a major underground fire, caused, it was claimed, by strikers neglecting normal maintenance and safety procedures. The strike was therefore 'threatening jobs and not defending them'.[60] The Fife strikers were then attacked by Younger in an article printed the following weekend in the *Sunday Post*. This claimed that Seafield was also in danger, and was written by Muir Russell at the Scottish Office, after conversations with Wheeler and Bill Anderson, editor of the *Sunday Post*. Russell advised colleagues that Anderson was 'looking for strong meat about the harmful effects of the strike in Scotland' and 'the wrecking results of Arthur Scargill and company'. Russell reprised the essence of his hostile response to the NUMSA Women's Support Group in November, describing the strike as 'the most pointless, unpleasant and damaging industrial dispute Britain has ever seen', 'forced on miners without a ballot and extended and sustained by violence and intimidation of a kind never seen in this country'. The flooding of Polkemmet and the 'question mark' over the Fife pits were entirely the responsibility of the NUM.[61] The article was ideological hyperbole. Coal, admittedly, was never extracted from Frances again, but that was a managerial decision, economically rather than geologically determined, and the colliery remained open until 1988.[62] The claim that employment was jeopardised at Seafield was even more tenuous: 'nonsense', according to Iain Chalmers, who recalls how easily work was resumed after the strike, with coal dug almost immediately.[63] Similarly, on16 August the NCB announced the closure of three faces at Castlehill, after management had responded to the NUM's alleged non-provision of safety cover by switching off power and safety machinery in accordance with Wheeler's policy. The pit itself, along with 600 jobs, was said to be threatened,[64] but it remained open, still employing almost 700 men, until 1990.[65] Two union representatives at Castlehill, Tam Mylchreest and Sam Cowie, staged a 48–hour underground protest against the power switch-off at the pit from 28 August. They were subsequently sacked, for alleged trespass on NCB property.[66]

Going back

'We couldnae win,' says Eric Clarke: the combined opposition of the NCB, the government, private capital and business, which helped to fund the strike-breaking movement, was overwhelming, and compounded by the practical anti-strike work of the judiciary and the police.[67] NUMSA and SCEBTA leaders probably recognised the inevitability of defeat by January 1985, and began seeking a means of bringing the strike to an end. This was the 'right thing' to do, according to David Hamilton,[68] but national union officials remained wedded to the hope – or fantasy – of outright victory. Peter Heathfield, NUM General Secretary, told a meeting of the union's left in January 1985 that the NCB would soon be 'crawling back' to the negotiating table.[69] Scargill, meanwhile, damaged the credibility of the union – and the strike – by continuing to assert verifiable untruths. One example was picket-line violence, which Scargill continued to claim was the result of police actions alone. But pickets were violent, Willie Clarke says: they had to be, for they were fighting for their jobs and communities. Pretending otherwise was a mistake, and weakened the case that the miners were attempting to argue.[70]

By the middle of February the strike in Ayrshire was over: the NCB claimed that 1,051 were working at Killoch, some 71 per cent of the workforce, and 492 working at Barony, 68 per cent.[71] Endurance in Ayrshire had eventually foundered, as Chapter 4 indicated, on the relatively marginal position of women, which heightened the economic costs of striking, and lowered the social costs of strike-breaking. False rumours also abounded that the NCB could legally sack all miners who had been on strike continuously for twelve months.[72] There was, according to local strike leaders, one additional factor: further fruitless talks that were geared to achieving a negotiated settlement. Involving the

TUC and government representatives as well as the NCB and the NUM, these were sabotaged once more at Cabinet level.[73] Morale in Ayrshire plummeted. The men had been 'built up an drapped, built up an drapped', largely by the wilfully unrealistic coverage of the talks, exaggerating the prospects of an agreement, in news media that were in any case hostile to the NUM and its strike.[74] The union leadership's insistence that the fight would continue – for another year if necessary – 'finished most of the boys', according to one of those who returned in February, speaking ten years later to Joe Owens.[75]

In East Fife the strike, which had started, remember, in February 1984, was also finally crumbling. Management recorded 119 strike-breakers on Friday 8 February, and 203 on Tuesday 19 February. On Monday 25 February there were 38 'new faces' on the day shift, a further 39 on 26 February, 39 more on 27 February, and another 29 on Thursday 28 February. On Friday 1 March a total of 341 men worked the day shift.[76] Willie Clarke and Jocky Neilson were highly troubled by this. Some of the 'influential boys' at the Dysart area centre said they could only hold the men back for one more week. The NUM South Wales Area proposal for an organised return to work had already materialised, and Clarke and Neilson travelled to Glasgow to discuss this with the executive committees of NUMSA and SCEBTA on 1 March. There was, however, a major obstacle: the 206 sacked men. Unless they were reinstated by the NCB a significant body of strikers in Scotland would refuse to go back, and so the union executives voted jointly for a continuation of the strike.[77]

On Sunday 3 March an NUM Delegate Conference in London voted 98 to 91 for a return to work, but this was opposed by all twelve NUMSA and all four SCEBTA delegates present, because of the absence of an amnesty for the sacked men.[78] SCEBTA delegates then voted to accept a resumption of work,[79] but NUMSA delegates, on Monday 4 March, initially voted narrowly against, by seven votes to six. The decisive vote to prolong the strike was cast by the Bilston Glen delegate, encapsulating, perhaps, the apparent intractability of the position facing NUMSA and SCEBTA, caught between the men returning to work, and those adamant on staying out, especially because of the victimisation question. Seafield miners voted that night for a return to work.[80] McGahey was seeking to secure this end across the coalfields 'with unity and dignity', and on Wednesday 6 March, as the Seafield and Frances miners effected their mass return along with the Cowdenbeath workshops men, a reconvened delegate conference voted by ten to five for a resumption of work. There was bitterness during this meeting, and outside afterwards, where NUMSA's leading officials, McGahey, Eric Clarke and George Bolton, were verbally abused by strikers, mainly from Stirlingshire, Clackmannan and West Fife. Delegates who had supported the resolution to end the strike, including men who had been sacked, such as David Hamilton, were spat at, and called scabs, according to Jocky Neilson.[81] McGahey, terribly, was badly assaulted on the following evening near his Edinburgh home. When facing reporters on the Monday that followed, the bruises of the attack still evident, he defiantly asserted that his assailants were not striking miners.[82]

On Thursday 7 March miners returned to work at Polkemmet, Bilston Glen and Monktonhall, marching behind bands and banners, accompanied to the gates – but not beyond them – by the sacked men.[83] Meanwhile meetings were underway in Clackmannan, West Fife and Stirling, with union representatives – desperate to maintain unity – working hard to secure a resumption of work.[84] This was effected at the Longannet pits and Comrie on Monday 11 March,[85] although the men remained 'rebellious and bitter', according to Tam Coulter. They knew the costs of defeat but accepted the decision to go back. The resumption was eased by using Alexander's buses, hired at a weekly cost to the union for Castlehill alone of £20,000. The Alexander's men, TGWU members, refusing to cross picket lines, had been sacked. Park's of Hamilton, the 'arch enemy', had been brought in to bus the strike-breakers to work, and were retained by the NCB after the strike. Without the temporary expedient of using Alexander's – which lasted two or three weeks – there might have been no resumption, and possibly violence on the Park's buses, perhaps against the drivers, resulting in additional dismissals. On 11 March the men were dropped at the pit yards by the Alexander's buses, and marched in together. This was important symbolically, showing management that the workforce would not be submissive.[86] One week later, on Monday 18 March, the Polmaise men – determined to be the last to relinquish a strike which had arguably started at their pit – finally returned to work.[87]

Iain Chalmers, on strike continuously at Seafield for thirteen months, found on preparing to go back that he had put on weight: he had been eating less, but using less energy too, and his working clothes were a tight fit. On the road to catch the bus from Cowdenbeath he was applauded by an older neighbour, leaning out of her window as he passed. The atmosphere at the pit was unpleasant. Strikers were initially kept apart from the strike-breakers, working different shifts, but there was friction at shift changeovers. The 'toe rag' who had broken the strike early, waving his bum and his wages to pickets from the bus as it sped through the colliery gates, left the industry shortly afterwards. He had discounted his own future, as well as the colliery's.[88] The new situation was confronted by the first post-strike meeting of the Colliery Consultative Committee, on 4 June 1985, attended by Scottish Area NCB and NUM officials, including McGahey and Eric Clarke. A new colliery manager, J. Soutar, outlined the difficulties facing the industry in East Fife, with the combined financial losses for Seafield and Frances likely to exceed £19 million in the financial year to 1986. McGahey spoke generally about the willingness of union officials to support Seafield's future as a 'safe and efficient colliery'.[89] But morale remained low, damaged by management's focus on the colliery's 'poor' financial position. Redundancy terms were on offer, with the proviso that they were taken by the end of 1986. Around 300 men left in the remaining months of 1985, but most stayed: there were between 900 and 1,000 when the pit closed in 1987, after a lengthy fire. Many transferred to Castlehill, including Iain Chalmers, and others to Solsgirth.[90]

At these pits, within the Longannet complex, the strike had been extremely solid. Perhaps it was as a result of this that union representatives gradually regained a footing, resisting managerial incursions on joint regulation a little more effectively than elsewhere. Overtime, for instance, now determined at most pits by management fiat, was still moderated by union involvement at Castlehill and Solsgirth.[91] But there were redundancies at the complex, tending to concentrate on older and so more experienced and generally more skilled men, and the number of accidents apparently increased. More broadly within the complex there was a managerial emphasis on degrading conditions and breaking agreements, notably on shift patterns, that union representatives could only partly withstand.[92] Enhanced managerial confidence and prerogative was evident at Polmaise,[93] and even more strongly apparent in Ayrshire, in rhetoric and practice. At Barony the CCC heard at the end of April 1985 that management planned to cut the workforce from 800 to 500 over the summer through voluntary redundancy. When union representatives said that such a radical change should have been subject to extensive consultation, the colliery deputy manager replied that 'whether the union agreed or disagreed' with management proposals was now 'irrelevant': the changes would take place regardless.[94] The same sentiment was articulated at Killoch, where the colliery manager described the pre-strike consultative arrangements at the pit as now 'irrelevant'.[95]

Tensions between management and workers, and between strikers and strike-breakers, were perhaps most strongly evident in Midlothian. At Bilston Glen managers carried the practice of downgrading joint industrial regulation and consultation further than elsewhere, introducing direct 'face to face' meetings between the colliery manager and employees in the canteen. Direct management–worker dialogue is often presented as good democratic practice, but tends in fact to be an important element of anti-trade union managerialism. Managers control the agenda in direct consultative forums, and usually issue information and instructions rather than debate the organisation and execution of work with employees.[96] Bilston Glen management reinforced the erosion of joint industrial regulation in the remainder of 1985 and thereafter. Where joint consultative meetings had been held on a fortnightly basis before the strike, they were now only once every six to eight weeks. Management continued to express a preference for direct talks with the employees, without union representatives present, even where high-order strategic questions, including the increasingly precarious production position, were being examined. The deterioration of production was explained in diametrically opposing terms by management and union representatives. The former – reprising, essentially, pre-strike arguments – emphasised low worker effort and absenteeism; the latter focused on the impact on workforce morale – and hence, on productivity – of management's anti-union initiatives, particularly the continued victimisation of strikers. Some of the sacked men had been reinstated at Bilston Glen. This was the result of a concerted effort by union officials across Scotland, led by George Bolton, although the overwhelming majority of the 206 men originally sacked, including most of the union representatives and activists, were not reinstated.[97] The older reinstated men at Bilston Glen, aged 50 and up, were now being denied the chance of redundancy on the same terms as others at the colliery. This was an echo of the pre-strike redundancy question in Midlothian, with older miners tied to Bilston Glen as a deliberate attempt by the NCB to weaken the pit's strike capacity. There was now a sense in which these men, having struggled through the strike to retain their jobs, were now being addition-ally punished, forcibly 'retained', against their will.[98]

There were other frictions at Bilston Glen. A large number of men were trans-ferred from Polkemmet after the strike, many of whom greatly resented the alien and adversarial management culture, which compounded their sense of griev-ance and loss.[99] There were also serious tensions between Midlothian strikers and strike-breakers. One alleged manifestation of these was the sabotage of cars belonging to strike-breakers, with wheel nuts said by management to have been loosened on two vehicles in July 1985 and another in September 1985, which 'shuddered' on the Eskbank roundabout. In the same month, again according to management, an underground worker – presumably a former strike-breaker – found 'human excrement' in his 'piece box', or snap tin.[100] There were similar difficulties at Monktonhall, where there was a new pit manager, Willie Kerr, who had worked until 1982 in Fife, where to some he was a hero, helping to rescue two men during the fatal accident at Seafield in 1973.[101] But in Midlothian he is remembered by union representatives as a clumsy bully. On the first day of normal operations after the strike Kerr told Rab Amos that he could no longer conduct union business during working hours. This revoked long-standing pre-strike arrangements. 'Why?' Amos asked. 'You arenae runnin the pit; Ah'm runnin the pit,' Kerr replied.[102] Kerr's determined assault on trade unionism was illustrated in two other incidents. First, there was a fatal accident just two weeks after the end of the strike. The deceased was a young miner, in his early twenties, from Bonnyrigg. David Hamilton entered the colliery between shifts shortly afterwards, with two other NUM officials, seeking to settle compensation arrangements on behalf of the dead miner's family, but was marched off the premises by security staff. 'Worse than that', Hamilton recalls, pit management then initially refused to allow privately hired buses to come into the colliery, to collect the hundreds of men attending the dead miner's funeral. This terrible event, not least because of the miscalculated behaviour of pit management, closed the divisions slightly between strikers and strike-breakers, Hamilton recalls.[103]

These divisions were not closed entirely, however, as the second episode, several months later, indicates. This stemmed from an argument in Newtongrange Park between a striker, Tam Miller, and a strike-breaker, W. Dempsey, both miners at Monktonhall. Amos says that Miller was from a 'good family' in Newtongrange, with a tradition of solid work and union membership. He was a young father too. Dempsey, meanwhile, was a 'super scab', and a member of the United Democratic Mineworkers (UDM).[104] This was the rival to the NUM established among working miners during the strike, with substan-tial financial and moral assistance from business and political supporters of the Conservative government.[105] Despite encouragement from NCB managers the UDM failed to embed itself in Scottish collieries,[106] and indeed was unable to establish any substantial position outside Nottinghamshire and the English Midlands.[107] Miller had been sacked during the strike, and was reinstated just two weeks before the argument in the park, having provided managers with assurances about his future behaviour. The two men had been in a pub nearby, Miller with a friend, and Dempsey with his wife. Dempsey told NCB officials that he had been 'severely' beaten by Miller. Miller admitted to punching Dempsey, but only after Dempsey had provoked him, saying he was lucky to have been reinstated at Monktonhall. Miller was sacked again, on Dempsey's evidence. This was contested by union representatives at a meeting shortly afterwards with management at Monktonhall. Peter Hogg of the NUM outlined the highly tenuous case against Miller: there was no police involvement in the argument, which took place outwith working hours and several miles from the colliery; and there had been no witnesses to the incident other than Miller's friend and Mrs Dempsey. Kerr nevertheless confirmed the sacking. Hogg responded by referring to the NCB's prejudicial treatment of 'our men', strikers like Miller, while extending preferences to 'the likes of' Dempsey, the strikebreaker, 'and co'. The outcome, he added, would 'only harden attitudes at the colliery and will not help cement the relationships we are trying to build'.[108]

Monktonhall union officials continued to fight back afterwards, organising a one-day strike in support of Miller, but the sacking was not revoked.[109] This unilateral managerial decision vividly exemplified the NCB's aggressive transgression in Scotland of the moral economy of the coalfields, where decisions in the workplace were jointly agreed, and the economic security of the workforce was protected. A further affront to this moral economy was the continued and lasting victimisation of the men sacked during the strike. McGahey told the STUC conference in Inverness in April that he was especially angered by the treatment of young miners, who with courage and determination had sought to defend their pits and communities, and the people's energy.[110] The injustices were further articulated in the same month by a group of Scottish Labour MPs, led by Donald Dewar and Alex Eadie, in a meeting at the House of Commons with Younger and Allan Stewart, the Scottish Office Minister for Industry and Education. Dewar emphasised the disproportionate level of sackings in Scotland, and Eadie said that the men had been denied a right of appeal that was enshrined in the conciliation mechanisms established in the 1946 Coal Industry Nationalisation Act. Younger replied that the sacked men could take their cases to an Industrial Tribunal. Dewar said that this would be entirely unsatisfactory: Industrial Tribunals could find that men had been illegitimately dismissed, but not order their reinstatement.[111]

The abandonment of existing conciliation procedures in Scotland was, it should be emphasised, a matter of managerial agency rather than legal requirement. In South Wales, where as a whole the strike was even more solid than in Scotland as a whole, the NCB Area Board sacked 42 miners during the strike: all were eventually taken back, except two men convicted of killing a taxi driver who was driving a strike-breaker to work.[112] In Scotland, by contrast, only a small number were reinstated. 'It's blood they want,' said Alex McCallum, a sacked Polmaise miner in 1986, referring to NCB management in Scotland, 'and the whole Scottish coalfield shut. Thousands of boys out of a job, aye, it's blood they want.'[113] The issue remained highly divisive within collieries and also, perhaps predictably, between collieries. In May 1985 NUM members across England, Wales and Scotland were balloted on the question of a 50p weekly levy to support miners sacked during the strike. While the majority vote was against this measure, in Scotland it was in favour. Yet the sharp cleavage within Midlothian – observable in the highly distinct pit-level strike histories – remained evident: at Bilston Glen there was a slight majority against the 50p levy, while at Monktonhall the vote in favour was by a ratio of three to one.[114]

Conclusion

The manner of the ending of the strike in Scotland, and its aftermath, in some ways resembled developments elsewhere in the coalfields. The over-arching oppositional presence of the government, and its business and media support-ers, was a factor everywhere. So too was the partiality of the policing of pickets and dispensing of criminal justice against strikers, particularly union activists. In Yorkshire, Durham and Northumberland, where the strike was initially solid, and less so in Kent and South Wales, there were also back to work movements, organised by local NCB management, which grew in momentum, particularly after Christmas. Across the coalfields, after March 1985, there was a common managerial emphasis on speeding up production, intensifying work effort, and downgrading the consultative role of labour.

In at least two other respects, however, the Scottish experience was highly distinct. First, the relatively marginal economic position of collieries in Scotland, however objectionable the NCB's measures of the true costs of coal-getting might be characterised as, meant that high-level joint industrial negotiations in pursuit of a settlement were terribly fraught. Any deal that offered the possibility of closing pits other than on grounds of exhaustion was likely to privilege 'economic' consid-erations. The term 'economic' was dangerously malleable, always liable to be equated by critics of nationalised industry generally and opponents of the NUM especially with 'profitable'. Scottish pits as a whole were extremely vulnerable on these narrow financial grounds, when measured against pits in most other NCB Areas. It is essential to emphasise this, for one objectionable feature of the literature on the strike that has been challenged here is the counter-factual notion that a 'deal' on closures could have been secured had the NUM been led by Michael McGahey rather than Arthur Scargill. This could only have come at the cost of many jobs in Scotland, with Polmaise and perhaps several other collieries – Bogside, Comrie, Frances and Polkemmet to start with – closed by the end of 1984 or 1985. McGahey well knew that the generality of Scottish strikers would not easily have accepted such eventuality.

The second distinctive Scottish aspect of the ending was closely related to the difficulties of procuring an acceptable negotiated settlement. This was the disproportionately high level of victimisation in Scotland. Sackings of men for actions that were often away from pits, and alleged rather than proven in a court of law, were part of the NCB's strike-breaking and anti-union strategy in Scotland. This strategy had clear roots in the immediate pre-strike history of workplace and industrial politics in the Scottish coal industry, pre-figuring anti-union advances that were made elsewhere either only haltingly before March 1984, or after the NUM had been defeated nationally after March 1985. In Scotland the aftermath of the strike marked the further consolidation of this process, with union representatives expelled from the industry. The capacity of those who remained to exert influence in the workplace was further eroded by managerial fiat, buttressed by additional redundancies, and the threat of further closures. The moral economy of the coalfields, with its emphasis on joint industrial regulation and economic security, had been defeated along with the strike.

Notes

1 NAS, SEP 4/6028, Sit Rep, 11 March 1985; the *Scotsman*, 19 March 1985.
2 Aitken, *Bairns O' Adam*, pp. 274–9; Beckett and Hencke, *Marching to the Fault Line*, *passim*, but especially pp. 103–46, 179–200; Fraser, *History of British Trade Unionism*, pp. 239–42; Reid, *United We Stand*, pp. 402–4; Stewart, '"Tragic Fiasco?"', *passim*, but especially 44–6; Taylor, *Trade Union Question*, pp. 294–8.
3 Joe Owens (sr.), Blackburn, in Owens, *Miners*, p. 90.
4 Hamilton, Interview; Willie Clarke, Interview.
5 Hyman, 'Reflections', 337–43.
6 McIlroy and Campbell, 'McGahey', pp. 248–9; Taylor, 'McGahey'.
7 SMM, NUMSA, Box 13, NUMSA Strike Committee Minutes, 23 July 1984.
8 Obituary, Jimmy Reid, by Brian Wilson, the *Guardian*, 11 August 2010.
9 SMM, NUMSA, Box 13, NUMSA Strike Committee Minutes, 15 October 1984.
10 Smith, *Actual Account*, pp. 29–47 (MacGregor and 'our employees'), pp. 69–70 (McGahey), pp. 90–1 (Scargill), p. 111 ('beneficially developed'), p. 112 ('verbal violence' and organised strike-breaking), pp. 127–8 (MacGregor and the September talks).
11 Brotherstone and Pirani, 'Were There Alternatives?'
12 TNA, COAL 74/4783, CINCC, 6 March 1984.
13 Hutton, *The State We're In*, pp. 85–6, 89–110; Saville, 'An Open Conspiracy', 311–12.
14 SMM, NUMSA, Box 13, NUMSA Strike Committee Minutes, 7 August, 13 August and 20 August 1984.
15 Adeney and Lloyd, *Miners' Strike*, pp. 196–7.
16 NAS, CB 398/15/7, Effects of Strike, Seafield, Daily Shift Reports, 10 October, 15 October and 23 October 1984.
17 SMM, NUMSA, Box 13, NUMSA Strike Committee Minutes, 8 October 1984.
18 Hencke and Beckett, *Marching to the Fault Line*, pp. 138–45.
19 NAS, CB 398/15/7, Effects of Strike, Seafield, Daily Shift Reports, 26 October and 1 November 1984.
20 SMM, NUMSA, Box 13, NUMSA Strike Committee Minutes, 29 October 1984.
21 NAS, SEP 4/6029/1, Sit Rep, 19 November 1984.
22 SMM, NUMSA, Box 13, NUMSA Strike Committee Minutes, 19 November 1984.
23 GCU, STUC, General Council Papers, STUC paper on coal in the Scottish Economy, presented to Special STUC conference, Thursday 29 November 1984.

24 GCUA, STUC, Milne to Thatcher, General Council Minutes 5 December 1984, and General Council Papers, Thatcher to Milne, 14 December 1984.

25 Willie Clarke, Interview.

26 Smith, *Actual Account*, pp. 147–9.

27 NAS, SOE 12/573/1, Margaret Gray's letter to George Younger, 13 November 1984, and Muir Russell's various draft responses, November 1984.

28 Amos, Interview.

29 SMM, NUMSA, Box 13, NUMSA Strike Committee Minutes, 13 August 1984.

30 Hamilton, Interview.

31 NAS, SEP 4/6029/1, Scottish Office Situation Reports, 20 and 21 December 1984.

32 NAS, SEP 4/6028, Sit Rep, 19 June 1984, and SEP4/6029, Sit Rep, 20 December 1984.

33 McGahey, in Owens, *Miners*, pp. 82–3.

34 SMM, NUMSA, Box 10, Area Coordinating Committee, Report, 13 May 1984.

35 Ayrshire strike leaders, Interview with Thompson.

36 Coulter, Interview with Thompson.

37 Adeney and Lloyd, *Miners' Strike*, pp. 123–6.

38 McCabe et al., *Police, Public Order, and Civil Liberties*, pp. 69–91.

39 Neilson, Interview with Thompson; Hamilton, Interview.

40 NAS, SOE 12/571, Policing of the Miners' Dispute: Secretary of State's Meeting with a deputation of Labour MPs led by Mr Donald Dewar on 23 May 1984, Dover House.

41 Eric Clarke, Interview; Wilson, Interview.

42 NAS, SEP 4/6029, Sit Rep 11 September 1984.

43 Maxwell, *Chicago Tumbles*, pp. 142–3.

44 *Scottish Miner*, October 1984.

45 NAS, CB 229/3/1, Bilston Glen CCC, 30 July 1985.

46 Bolton, Interview with Thompson.

47 McIlroy and Campbell, 'McGahey'.

48 Hamilton, Interview.

49 *Scottish Miner*, October 1984.

50 SMM, NUMSA, Box 8, Tribunals.

51 Adeney and Lloyd, *Miners' Strike*, p. 178.

52 Amos, Interview.

53 Adeney and Lloyd, *Miners' Strike*, pp. 184–5.

54 Bolton, Interview with Thompson.

55 Perchard and Phillips, 'Transgressing the Moral Economy', 398.

56 Hamilton, Interview.

57 Andrew Leys, Whitburn, and Owens (sr.), in Owens, *Miners*, pp. 74, 89.

58 Eric Clarke, Interview; Wilson, Interview.

59 Hamilton, Interview.

60 NAS, SOE 12/573, Secretary of State for Scotland, Statement regarding Closure of Frances Colliery, 4 February 1985.

61 NAS, SOE 12/573, A.M. Russell to Private Secretary, Secretary of State for Scotland, 6 February 1985, regarding his conversation with Wheeler; C.F. Corbett to Private Secretary, Secretary of State for Scotland, regarding Russell's conversation with Bill Anderson, 8 February 1985; clipping, the *Sunday Post*, 10 February 1985.

62 Oglethorpe, *Scottish Collieries*, p. 144.

63 Chalmers, Interview.

64 NAS, SEP 4/6027, Sit Rep, 16 August 1984.

65 Oglethorpe, *Scottish Collieries*, p. 140.

66 Mylchreest, Interview with Thompson.

67 Eric Clarke, Interview.

68 Hamilton, Interview.

69 Bolton, Interview with Thompson; Willie Clarke, Interview.

70 Willie Clarke, Interview.

71 NAS, SEP 4/6029, Sit Rep, 11 February 1985.

72 Levy and Mauchline Miners' Wives, 'A Very Hard Year', pp. 4–5.

73 Adeney and Lloyd, Miners' Strike, pp. 214–15.

74 Ayrshire strike leaders, Interview with Thompson.

75 Danny Gemmel, Auchinleck, in Owens, Miners, p. 41.

76 NAS, CC 398/15/7, Effects of Strike, Seafield, Daily Shift Reports, February to March 1985.

77 Bolton, Interview with Thompson; Willie Clarke, Interview.

78 NAS, SEP 4/6029, Sit Rep, 4 March 1985.

79 Moffat, Interview with Thompson.

80 Willie Clarke, Interview.

81 Neilson, Interview with Thompson; NAS, SEP 4/6029, Sit Rep, 7 March 1985.

82 The Times, 12 March 1985.

83 Scottish Miner, March 1985.

84 McCaig, Interview with Thompson.

85 NAS, SEP 4/6029, Sit Reps, 5–7 March and 11 March 1985.

86 Coulter, Interview with Thompson.

87 The Scotsman, 19 March 1984.

88 Chalmers, Interview.

89 NAS, CB 398/3/2, Seafield CCC, 4 June 1985.

90 Neilson, Interview with Thompson; Willie Clarke, Interview; Chalmers, Interview.

91 Coulter, Interview with Thompson.

92 McCaig, Interview with Thompson; Mylchreest, Interview with Thompson; Billy McLean, Kelty, in Owens, Miners, pp. 61–2.

93 McCormack, in Owens, Miners, pp. 117–18.

94 NAS, CB 221/3/4, Barony CCC, 30 April 1985.

95 NAS, CB 328/3/4, Killoch CCC, 16 May 1985.

96 Karen Legge, Human Resource Management: Rhetoric and Realities (Basingstoke, 2005), pp. 303–11.

97 George Bolton, Interview with Thompson; Mylchreest, Interview with Thompson.

98 NAS, CB 229/3/1, Bilston Glen CCC, 14 May 1985 and 18 March 1986.

99 Leys, in Owens, Miners, pp. 75–6.

100 NAS, CB 229/3/1, Bilston Glen CCC, 30 July and 10 September 1985.

101 Fife Pits: www.users.zetnet.co.uk/mmartin/fifepits/starter/east/pits/s/pit-6.htm; accessed 1 December 2010.

102 Amos, Interview; Hamilton, Interview.

103 Hamilton, Interview.

104 Amos, Interview.

105 Winterton and Winterton, Coal, Crisis and Conflict, pp. 171–8.

106 Eric Clarke, Interview; Moffat, Interview with Thompson.

107 Taylor, NUM and British Politics. Volume 2, pp. 281–97; Wrigley, 'The 1984–5 miners' strike', pp. 223–4.

108 NAS, CB 363/17/8, Handwritten (NCB) account of NCB–NUM meeting, Monktonhall Colliery, 2 December 1985.

109 Amos, Interview.
110 STUC, *88th Annual Report*, pp. 223–5.
111 NAS, SOE 12/573, Note of a Meeting Held at the House of Commons, 17 April 1985:
    Coal Board Dismissals.
112 Hamilton, Interview.
113 *One Year On. Sacked Polmaise Miners Speak Out* (Airth, 1986), edited by Steve
    McGrail.
114 *Scottish Miner*, May 1985.

6

Legacy and conclusion

In Loanhead there is a memorial to the fifteen miners who died in accidents at Bilston Glen between 1957 and 1986. The youngest was William Smith, killed at the age of 31, on 8 April 1985, just weeks after the end of the great strike. The Loanhead memorial is one of several established in Midlothian by the NUM in the 2000s. Each lists the names of the dead above the words, 'THE TRUE PRICE OF COAL'. This is a significant phrase. It implicitly but powerfully challenges the Thatcherite narrative that dwelt on the supposedly high costs of coal extraction in the UK, compounded by the allegedly privileged position of workers and unions in the industry. This narrative, focusing on the narrow economic price of coal, shaped the 1984–85 strike.

The strike was also conditioned by the miners' desire to defend the work culture of the coalfields. But there was a tension within this culture which 'The True Price of Coal' memorials highlight. Mining was rewarding, in social and cultural as well as material terms, but it was also highly dangerous. The hazards, it should be emphasised, tended to increase rather than negate the rewards. Miners, like workers in other heavy industries, traded risk for money and social esteem.[1] They were also compelled by the constant presence of potential catastrophe to rely utterly on their fellows underground. The bonds and necessities of personal inter-dependence shaped a highly distinctive work culture and a pattern of social relations that were intensely communal. *Coal Is Our Life*, the study of Yorkshire miners, originally written and published in the 1950s, was aptly named, capturing the pervasive reach of the industry.[2] Alex Nicholson, born in 1957, recalls his childhood in East Wemyss, Fife, adjacent to the mighty Michael, then Scotland's largest colliery with more than 2,000 employees. Alex and other children were fascinated by the pit, where his father and so many neighbours worked. The youngsters gathered by the gates on pay day, receiving threepenny bits from miners finishing their shifts for the week, or clustered at the canteen, where the women gave them chips, steamed pudding and other treats. The pit intruded on the children's play, their mothers scolding them away from houses where nightshift men were sleeping. Nicholson entered the industry gladly, despite the dangers, so strongly evident in his community with the

1967 disaster that killed nine men and permanently closed the pit. He started at Frances in January 1974 and then moved to Seafield in 1977, to pursue his ambition of working as 'one of the boys' on the face. His father, Dave, was also a Seafield face-worker at this point. When both were on the early shift, starting at 6 a.m., they would spend each evening discussing the events of the day, comparing production levels on different faces.[3]

This was the work culture of the Scottish coalfields, familial as well as communal, and emphasising the social worth of physical endeavour and the economic value of material production. It was also, of course, highly gendered: Nicholson was 'one of the boys', and coal certainly provided a form of heavy industrial employment that privileged the interests of men, and placed fetters on the lives of women. For this reason the dwindling of employment in coal and other heavy industrial sectors in western societies in the late twentieth and early twenty-first centuries has not been universally mourned. Guy Standing, for example, argues that 'industrial citizenship' – shaped by the imperatives of manufacturing and heavy industry – was a key but problematic feature of western political economy in the twentieth century. Citizenship, he writes, was contingent, more or less, on formal, paid employment. Those not engaged in this activity, including a disproportionately large number of women, particularly married women, experienced a lesser form of citizenship.[4]

Economic and industrial restructuring from the late twentieth century onwards may subsequently have contributed to the development of less inequitable gender relations in western societies. It would be difficult to argue, however, that this restructuring has not come at a very heavy human, social and economic cost, which has been borne by women as much as men. This is especially true of the coalfields, and not just in the UK, as Portelli's study of Harlan County in Kentucky amply demonstrates, with elevated levels of poverty, and alcohol and drug dependency, accompanying the transition from stable industrial employment to insecure and low-wage service sector employment.[5] The core issue was pithily summarised by Jonathan Meades, in his memorable tour of 'The Football Pool Towns' of Scotland, originally broadcast on BBC4 in September 2009. This took him through Dunfermline, Cowdenbeath, Methil and Kirkcaldy, where he stood below the winding gear that survives on the site of Frances Colliery and said, 'Mining might, just might, have been economically exhausted, but it was socially cohesive. Jobs ferment pride [and] inculcate a sense of self-worth.'[6] The detailed implications of this, the loss especially of male employment, have been scrutinised by Huw Beynon, Ray Hudson and Tim Strangleman, exploring the economic, industrial and social dislocation experienced by ex-miners in the English and Welsh coalfields. In South Wales 'regeneration' was a chimera, at least in the 1990s: ex-miners were burdened by the loss of employment and social status, and younger people, without the direction and discipline of full-time employment, were adrift and demoralised.[7] In Durham ex-miners also lost income and job satisfaction in the 1990s, even where they acquired new jobs in different economic sectors: the extrinsic and intrinsic rewards of work, to borrow from the famous *Affluent Worker* study of

the 1960s, were both diminished.[8] There were, it is true, some new job opportunities for women, including married women, but these were relatively low
paid when measured against the positions lost in the coal industry, and were of
necessity supplemented in many households by male earnings from similarly
low status employment.[9]

This pattern was observable too in Scotland, where coal industry employment
fell steadily after the strike. Polkemmet and Bogside, flooded in 1984–85, shut
in 1986, along with Comrie. Killoch and Polmaise closed in 1987, Seafield,
Frances and the Cowdenbeath workshops in 1988,[10] and Barony in 1989 along
with Bilston Glen, where arguments between management and union representatives continued until the end, the former complaining about poor worker
commitment and effort, and the latter insisting that low managerial ambition
and financial disinvestment were the real source of the pit's enduring problems.[11] Solsgirth and Castlehill, servicing the power station at Longannet, closed
in 1990. Production ceased at Monktonhall in 1988, and the vast majority of its
employees were made redundant, although 30 were retained on a care and
maintenance basis, enabling the pit to re-open briefly as a workers' cooperative
in the mid-1990s, before its ultimate closure and destruction in 1998.[12]
Longannet continued to burn locally mined coal, from a small pit immediately
adjacent to the power station, which flooded and closed in 2002, and
Castlebridge in Clackmannan, where production commenced shortly after the
strike, and ended in 1999.[13]

The timing and sequence of this rundown, commencing in 1985 and largely
concluded by 1990, is significant. 'Deindustrialization does not just happen,'
wrote Barry Bluestone and Bennett Harrison in their 1982 analysis of plant
closures in the USA. In practice, they contend, it is generally the consequence of
political and business decisions, taken in the context of social relationships and
tensions.[14] So it was with deindustrialisation in the Scottish coalfields, which
was the legacy of the strikers' defeat in 1984–85, rather than the inevitable
working out of structural economic change. Chapter 1 of this book showed that
there was restructuring after nationalisation in 1947, with major closures and
job losses experienced in Scotland in the 1960s especially. The closures after the
1984–85 strike were not a delayed or linear extension of this process. Here the
existence and importance of the moral economy of the coalfields must be
restated. The closures of the 1960s were, by agreement, part of – Willie Clarke's
phrase – the necessary 'retooling' of the industry, allowing human and financial
resources to be concentrated in a smaller number of larger and more highly
mechanised pits.[15] Miners at pits that closed were able to enjoy continuing
economic security, either by transfer to one of the new 'cosmopolitan' collieries,
or by obtaining work of more or less equal value that was available elsewhere.
These factors did not apply in the early 1980s, when pits were closed by the NCB
in Scotland against workforce and union opposition, in a period of rapidly
rising unemployment, amid radically declining industrial activity. Nor did they
apply between 1985 and 1990, when the majority of the remaining pits were
closed.

The changing industrial and employment position for men and women in the coalfields is summarised in Table 6.1. This uses the methodology deployed in Chapter 4 to establish pit-level Married Women in Employment data. The approach here is slightly different, identifying all persons – not just married women – in work, but in the same manner shows variations of experience according to colliery employment area.

Table 6.1 Persons in employment, part-time and full-time combined (percentages), by colliery employment area in Scotland, 1981 and 1991

Colliery employment area	1981		1991	
	Men, aged 16–64	Women, aged 16–59	Men, aged 16–64	Women, aged 16–59
Frances/Seafield	80.3	55.5	66.4	54.1
Comrie	82.9	54.8	68.6	58.0
Bogside/Castlehill/Solsgirth	81.6	54.6	67.1	57.5
Polmaise	78.6	56.0	61.4	56.6
Bilston Glen	83.9	62.0	67.0	64.7
Monktonhall	82.8	60.4	67.0	63.4
Polkemmet	78.6	55.8	69.1	63.2
Barony/Killoch	71.8	49.7	56.9	42.6
Scotland	77.6	55.7	63.0	57.7

Sources: Registrar General Scotland, *Census 1981 Scotland. Scottish Summary, Volume 2; Report for Central Region. Volume 1; Report for Fife Region. Volume 1; Report for Lothian Region. Volume 1; Report for Strathclyde Region. Volume 1;* General Registry Office for Scotland, *1991 Census. Report For Scotland, Part 1, Volume 1; Central Region, Part 1; Fife Region, Part 1; Lothian Region, Part 1; Strathclyde Region, Part 2.*

This data highlights in vivid form the unambiguously negative outcome of the strike: the reduction of stable manual employment for men. In all colliery employment areas this fell significantly between the Census years of 1981 and 1991, by a median of roughly fourteen percentage points. This was, of course, a broader phenomenon across Scotland, as the bottom row in Table 6.1 illustrates, but the continued loss of industrial employment after 1991 appears to have worsened the relative economic and social position in the ex-coalfields. Analysis of multiple deprivation data from 2006 indicated that problems were especially pronounced in the former mining communities of Ayrshire, Fife and Lanarkshire.[16]

The broader legacy of deindustrialisation across Scotland, with economic and social hardship intensifying the 'Scottish effect' in health,[17] was arguably a gender as well as a class phenomenon. Unemployment or the loss of skilled and physically challenging manual work was resented by men in more than economic and material terms: their prestige as men was adversely affected.[18] Deindustrialisation had lasting political repercussions too, in the further erosion of support for the government, already evident in Scotland in the 1983 General Election, and confirmed in the 1987 General Election, when the

Conservative Party retained only ten of the 21 seats it was defending. Deindustrialisation, broadly unwelcomed in Scotland, was understood by many to be the direct consequence of the government's economic policies.[19] These policies, unpopular as they were in Scotland, were nevertheless 'imposed' through the 'remote' administration of power from Whitehall and Westminster. In this way deindustrialisation generally, and the outcome of the miners' strike in particular, contributed to renewed enthusiasm in Scotland for political devolution.[20]

In the context of deindustrialisation it is perhaps unsurprising that each of the men interviewed for this book who were employed as miners immediately before the strike, and who left the industry afterwards, report experiencing a loss of income, status and satisfaction when they did so. Rab Amos worked briefly after redundancy from Monktonhall for a heavy engineering firm on the south side of Edinburgh, but bridled against the absence of meaningful joint industrial regulation in his new environment. He was sacked for 'challenging management's right to manage'. Iain Chalmers left the coal industry in 1994, finishing at Castlebridge, and worked in a variety of environments thereafter, but without experiencing the same intrinsic pleasures that he encountered as a miner. He retained in 2009 a deep commitment to the coal industry, reflected in his desire to preserve its history through seeking out and collecting its memorabilia, bequeathing much of this to Kirkcaldy Art Gallery and Museum. Willie Clarke thought about leaving the industry after the strike but kept going until Seafield closed in 1988, bound by his obligations to the men and women who had endured the thirteen months without pay in 1984–85. David Hamilton was unemployed for almost three years after his dismissal during the strike, blacklisted, he is convinced, by private sector employers because of his trade union activism. Interviewed in September 2009, he said there was 'a computer in Manchester wi all oor names oan it'. This was an allusion to the activities of an individual named in the *Guardian* four months earlier as selling intelligence on trade unionists to private sector employers, including major construction firms, since the 1970s.[21] Hamilton eventually secured employment with Midlothian District Council, in the Parks Department. Alex Nicholson left Seafield, redundant, in March 1988, and, like Hamilton, found work with his local authority's Parks Department. He enjoyed this generally, but at times disliked the work culture, which, with its gossipy 'back-stabbing', contrasted unfavourably with the open and direct honesty of the pits.

These were the experiences of only five men, but it is likely, given the data in Table 6.1, that they were not unrepresentative of the generality of male experience in the coalfields. The sense of male material and cultural loss is reinforced in the film *Finding the Seam*, a collaboration between Rab Wilson, ex-miner and poet, and Tony Grace, of the University of West of Scotland. Wilson worked underground at Barony Colliery from 1977 to 1986, and his poetry, written mainly in the Scots language, has included reflections on the strike.[22] In *Finding the Seam* he draws out the continuities from deep mining to open cast mining, a significant activity in South Ayrshire in the 2010s: the coal, 250 million years old, is still being won, to provide society with energy, and men and their families with income from employment. But the lost social world of deep mining and its major cultural infrastructure is substantially to the fore: the non-competitive fellowship of the underground miners, the workers' housing, the union banners, the colliery bands and the community memorials.[23]

Deindustrialisation has had slightly different implications for women, who in the coalfields – with the contraction of male work – came to inhabit a proportionately greater share of total employment. This is illustrated in Table 6.2. There was an almost uniform increase from 1981 to 1991 across ex-colliery employment areas of women's share of employment overall, of roughly seven percentage points. This broadly resembled the pattern across Scotland. The data on women's employment share should not, of course, obscure the substantial pit-area variations in women's overall employment levels that were summarised in Table 6.1. Employment among women in Ayrshire, already relatively low in coalfield terms, dropped significantly from 1981 to 1991, by seven percentage points, while there was a large increase, by slightly more than seven percentage points, at Polkemmet, reflecting the continuing development of services and assembly manufacturing in Livingston especially. Elsewhere there were generally small increases.

Table 6.2 Women aged 16–59 as percentage of persons in employment, by colliery employment area in Scotland, 1981 and 1991

Colliery employment area	1981	1991
Frances/Seafield	40.1	46.1
Comrie	37.4	44.1
Bogside/Castlehill/Solsgirth	37.9	44.4
Polmaise	40.5	47.3
Bilston Glen	41.1	48.1
Monktonhall	40.5	47.5
Polkemmet	40.4	47.3
Barony/Killoch	39.4	46.1
Scotland	40.1	46.6

Sources: Registrar General Scotland, *Census 1981 Scotland. Scottish Summary, Volume 2*; *Report for Central Region. Volume 1*; *Report for Fife Region. Volume 1*; *Report for Lothian Region. Volume 1*; *Report for Strathclyde Region. Volume 1*; General Registry Office for Scotland, *1991 Census. Report For Scotland, Part 1, Volume 1*; *Central Region, Part 1*; *Fife Region, Part 1*; *Lothian Region, Part 1*; *Strathclyde Region, Part 2*.

Strangleman's misgivings about the gendered adjustment of the ex-coalfields labour market, based on an analysis of Durham, have been noted: women were compelled through straitened circumstances to assume a greater share of 'bread-winning', but in relatively low paid and often unsatisfying jobs. There is no evidence that the employment experiences of women in the Scottish ex-coalfields were substantially different. Yet there is at least a sense that these altered employment roles contributed to the continuing and positive reconstruction of gender relations more broadly that was initiated by the strike. This was very strongly affirmed by the women who appeared in *Here We Go*, Margaret Wright's 2009 film of the strike. Their politicised activism was an expression of what Annmarie Hughes calls 'gendered citizenship', a fusion of class and gender consciousness.[24] The women found this personally transforming. It contributed to greater engagement in 'public' affairs, with involvement in community and local authority politics and trade unionism. For some it also led to further education and training, and higher status employment subsequently.

Relations in the home were built anew. Matilda Wilson said that her husband 'used tae get away wi murder' in the house: 'No any mair!' Anne Hunter and Ann Robertson, speaking together, acknowledged the strike's pressures on marriages and domestic relationships. These were not necessarily financial, as might be expected, but arose from the unusual experience – for young couples especially – of being alone together for extended periods. Rab Amos offers the same perspective: working class women and men were unused to the pressure of 'constant' company that they would not ordinarily have experienced until retirement.[25] Yet most relationships survived the strike, strengthened rather than diminished. This was partly a question of the moral regeneration of communities in 1984–85. The extent of this should not be exaggerated. There were substantial fissures in many coalfield communities, chiefly, of course, between the strikers and the strike-breakers. The tendency to 'composure' in participant testimony, constructing internally consistent political and personal narratives, should also be restated, as a factor in potentially de-emphasising community problems and divisions. It is nevertheless significant that several of the women in Wright's film, like a number of the men interviewed for this book, said that the strike restored the connection between the industry and its communities that had been weakened in the 1960s with the move from village pits to cosmopolitan collieries. Lesley McGuinness of Oakley, whose husband Jim worked at Comrie and then Solsgirth, put it this way: the men were defeated in the pits but decidedly not broken in the communities. In this connection several of the women remembered the importance of their marching to the colliery gates with the men on the first day back after the strike, demonstrating their togetherness. These communities have gradually become fragmented again, under the weight of further economic restructuring and subsequent generational change, but they remain intact. 'You can't live an isolated exis- tence,' said Cath Cunningham in *Here We Go*: 'You need people around you.'

These lived coalfield experiences, in collieries and communities, have been central to this book. The strike clearly involved and was shaped by the high political personalities and questions that have tended to dominate the literature: the changing political economy of coal examined in Chapter 1; the anti-union 'Stepping Stones' Thatcherite political strategy analysed in Chapters 1 and 3; the victimisation of pickets and union activists by police, courts and NCB managers detailed in Chapters 3 and 5; and the transgression by NCB management in Scotland of the moral economy, explored across the book. Yet high political factors alone cannot explain the key feature of the strike in Scotland: the varieties of pit-level endurance within a broader pattern of impressive solidarity. This is explicable only with reference to the factors of workplace and community. Chapter 1 located the strike's deep origins in the workplace and communal responses to the restructuring of the 1960s. This amounted to a revival of militancy in the Scottish coalfields after the relative quiescence of the late 1940s and 1950s. Michael McGahey was elected NUMSA President in 1967 chiefly on the basis of his opposition to further closures. NUMSA's politics were devolutionary as well as militant. McGahey and other union officials argued that the pit closures exemplified the damaging economic and social effects in Scotland of centralised governance from London. The confluence of industrial and devolutionary politics was vividly illustrated, it will be remembered, during the 1972 strike, when miners intensified the pressure on Heath's Conservative government by blockading Longannet and participating in the cross-party but STUC-convened Scottish Assembly on Unemployment.

A number of pits were closed in the 1970s, but, as has been stressed here already, through agreement between unions and managers. The position was then transformed in the early 1980s by Thatcherism, which characterised coal as a high-cost prisoner of trade unionism, and the related changes in approach by the industry's management in Scotland. These were analysed in Chapter 2. Albert Wheeler, responding to cost pressures that were perhaps particularly acute in Scotland, breached the assumptions and expectations of the coalfield moral economy. He and his officials sought and obtained closures against union and workforce opposition, and attacked workplace trade unionism, harassing worker representatives and unilaterally altering work practices. This process was consolidated and indeed greatly extended immediately after the strike in 1985, as Chapter 5 demonstrated, with sackings of union officials and activists, as well as the serial abandonment of pre-strike workplace agreements. Managerial actions before the strike provoked a sequence of pit-level disputes, notably at Seafield and Monktonhall, with effects too in West Fife and Ayrshire and at Polmaise, threatened with closure early in 1984. The analysis presented in Chapter 2 confirmed an earlier observation, offered by Terry Brotherstone and Simon Pirani, that some 50 per cent of miners in Scotland were engaged in a serious dispute with their pit-level managers before the national strike commenced on 12 March 1984.[26] There were doubts about pursuing a strike at some pits, at Bilston Glen especially, which NUMSA and SCEBTA officials and activists responded to, carefully constructing a collective response to the crisis in January and February 1984. Contrary to NCB and Scottish Office expectations, the strike was supported – or at least respected – at every pit in Scotland.

The strike proceeded without a national ballot. This was a source of difficulty at the time, and is a powerful component of the anti-Scargill narrative that continues to dominate much of the strike's literature. The analysis in this book emphasised the difficulty of balloting miners on the issue of pit closures, which did not affect them equally, and in a situation – already reiterated here – where 50 per cent of the Scottish workforce was already in dispute with its management. Lockouts were under way at Frances and Seafield, strikes were imminent at the Longannet complex, in response to the threatened closure of Bogside as well as Polmaise, and troubles were emerging in Ayrshire and re-emerging at Monktonhall. Joint industrial procedures at several pits had been unilaterally abandoned by management. The strategy adopted by the mining unions, securing the legitimacy of collective action against closures through pit-head and delegate meetings, was pragmatic, and maintained the unity of their members, precarious as this was.

This book has challenged two other received wisdoms that appear frequently in the literature in relation to strike strategy and leadership: the 'siege' of Ravenscraig, which is said to have damaged unnecessarily the solidarity of labour, with miners jeopardising the jobs of steel workers; and the claim that the national dispute could have ended differently, in ways more beneficial to the majority of miners, had the NUM been led by McGahey rather than Arthur Scargill. Two points, explored in detail in Chapters 3 and 5, can be restated. There was no prospect of the strikers gaining traction in the dispute in Scotland by blockading the supply of coal to power stations. Electricity 'endurance' could have been sustained well into 1985 without any new supplies of coal, such had been the switch over in the later 1970s and early 1980s to oil and nuclear-generated provision. Ravenscraig, owing to the peculiarities of Scottish industrial and electoral politics, offered the strikers a highly compelling and logical target. Bringing steel production to a halt and, yes, threatening the survival of the plant, would have damaged the government and further weakened the Conservative Party in Scotland. The delicacy of this position, and the propinquity of the strikers to victory, was fully illustrated by the intervention of Bob Haslam, head of British Steel, after discussion with officials at the Department of Energy and the Scottish Office. This apparently compelled Strathclyde Police to effect a change in its tactics, stopping pickets on the open road many miles from Ravenscraig. This relieved the mass pressure on the plant, allowing road supplies of coal to enter. On the question of the NUM's leadership, McGahey may well have been politically more flexible and adroit than Scargill, capable of building and consolidating valuable links across and indeed beyond the labour movement. He was possibly also more substantial intellectually, and a more effective negotiator. Yet it is difficult nevertheless to accept that he could have obtained the type of settlement, acceptable to the generality of strikers as well as the NCB, which evaded Scargill. Closures were desired by the NCB on 'economic' grounds, but the strikers could not accept these, and McGahey was just as committed as Scargill to resisting them, not least because they were as likely to occur in Scotland as in any other coalfield area in the UK. The government, moreover, was clearly willing, especially from the summer of 1984 onwards, to veto any settlement that might have offered a reprieve to the threatened pits, such was its increasing confidence and desire to inflict unconditional defeat on the strikers and their unions.

Miners were returning to work in Scotland in the summer of 1984, notably at Bilston Glen. The solidarity of the strike gradually weakened at some pits in the autumn and towards Christmas, crumbling in Ayrshire as well as at Bilston Glen from late January, but commitment remained intense in East Fife into February and was completely solid in West Fife and Clackmannan until the end. Chapter 4 analysed the manner in which differential pit-level strike endurance was related to pre-strike economic variables. Three in particular were emphasised: income earned from the wages of Married Women in Employment (MWE), income saved from local authority housing rents deferred by sympathetic Labour-controlled councils (CHD), and a Militancy Index (MI), establishing the character of pre-strike industrial relations. These variables were used to develop a model for predicting relative pit-level Potential Strike Endurance (PSE). There was a fairly close match between the PSE pit-level rankings and Actual Strike Endurance (ASE) pit-level rankings, based on back to work figures compiled by the NCB and archived by the Scottish Office. Seven of the twelve pits moved just three places or less from one set of rankings to the other; and Bilston Glen, Barony and Killoch were in the bottom five of each. The analysis demonstrated a close fit also between ASE pit-level rankings and pre-strike pit-level economic performance (EP). The correlation in Scotland between performance and commitment was positive, in contrast to the position usually noted in the strike literature, where 'good' performance – notably in Nottinghamshire – is generally depicted as weakening strike willingness. Hence the collapse of the strike at Barony and Killoch was related to pre-strike performance worries in Ayrshire, which were significant, and the contrasting solidarity in West Fife and Clackmannan explained in terms of the future confidence of workers in the Longannet pits. Miners at these pits may have developed a particular reading of the dominant narrative of coal, privileging and applying the virtues of 'good' economic performance to an economically 'rational' defence of their own pits. Reinforcing this impression is the fact that Solsgirth and Castlehill were the longest-lived of the twelve pits going into the strike, only closing in 1990.

Economic variables alone, however, do not explain the distinctive pit-level strike histories. This is why pit-level, community-embedded moral factors were examined as further strike-building resources. These were not straightforward, chiefly because of the gap that opened between community and colliery with industrial restructuring in the 1960s. But the manner in which the strike closed this gap has been noted, reinvigorating moral economy arguments at a community level. The moral economy, it should be remembered, encapsulated a distinctive communal attitude to closures, and the related matters of job ownership and redundancy. Individual miners could not 'sell' resources that really belonged to the community. Those who did so 'sold' their community as well as their job. Men who broke the strike, especially the 'super scabs' who returned early, in the summer of 1984, were also regarded as abandoning their communities, as well as failing their work-mates. They were hounded from a gender and a class perspective, depicted as exhibiting a lesser or deviant form of masculinity, while the 'real' men remained on strike. The costs of strike-breaking appear to have been particularly raised when and where these communal arguments were articulated by women. Pit-level strike commitment was duly most pronounced where female involvement moved from material support to engaged participation and leadership. The strike was strongest, in other words, in communities where relatively there was a more equal – or at least a less unequal – division of labour by gender, and women enjoyed a positive economic, political and cultural role.

The centrality of these workplace and community experiences to the history of the 1984–85 strike is the main conclusion, and core original feature, of this book. The dominant emphasis on high politics and personalities, whether in historical literature, political discourse or media content, has been deeply ideological, masking the extent to which Thatcherite economic management and industrial relations 'reforms' were more than a challenge to trade unions and trade unionism. The deliberate destabilisation of industrial employment and occupational communities was, to be blunt, a consciously constructed and carefully executed assault on the collective culture and material position of the working class. No amount of anti-Scargill, anti-socialist or anti-trade union hyperbole should conceal this conclusion.

The book has also detailed the importance to the strike of developments in Scotland. The origins of the strike can be read in serial instances of workplace conflict in Scottish pits, instigated by NCB management; and the conduct of the strike in Scotland, with the Ravenscraig siege and the disproportionately punitive victimisation of union activists and officials, was highly distinctive. The strike, moreover, accelerated a broader and important trend in British politics: the disintegration of support for Conservatism and an unreconstructed United Kingdom in Scotland. The contraction of basic industries and manufacturing, accelerated by Thatcherism, stimulated renewed support for a Scottish Parliament in the 1980s. This, it was hoped, would articulate, defend and advance the interests of Scottish workers. Such has not transpired, in the neoliberal and globalised environment that has framed the work of the Scottish Parliament since its establishment in 1999. But it would be a mistake to conclude from this that the working class – which in Scotland sought to defend industrial employment and industrial communities – has been terminally defeated. The working class, it should be emphasised, is not synonymous with industrialism. Many employees in private sector services, as well as the smaller number still deployed in basic industries and manufacturing, constitute a working class with interests that are separate from and sometimes in opposition to those of their employers. Public sector employees face comparable difficulties, with the finance capital-created economic crisis leading, perversely but predictably, to government spending cuts that jeopardise valuable services and the jobs and wages of those who provide them. In these circumstances of crisis and conflict workers will continue the struggle that the miners and their supporters pursued with clarity and courage in 1984–85, for economically and socially stable communities, and fairness and dignity in employment.

Notes

1 Arthur McIvor and Ronnie Johnston, 'Voices From the Pits: Health and Safety in Scottish Coal Mining Since 1945', *Scottish Economic and Social History*, 22 (2002), 129–30.
2 Dennis, Henriques and Slaughter, *Coal is our Life*.
3 Nicholson, Interview.
4 Guy Standing, *Work After Globalization. Building Occupational Citizenship* (Cheltenham, 2009), pp. 32–56.
5 Portelli, *Harlan County*, pp. 344–65.
6 *Jonathan Meades Off-Kilter*, 'The Football Pools Towns'.
7 Huw Beynon, Ray Hudson and Tim Strangleman, 'Rebuilding the Coalfields', The Coalfields Research Programme: Discussion Paper No. 4, Economic and Social Research Council, Cardiff University and University of Durham, 1999.
8 John Goldthorpe, David Lockwood, Frank Bechhofer and Jennifer Platt, *The Affluent Worker: Industrial Attitudes and Behaviour* (Cambridge, 1968).
9 Tim Strangleman, 'Networks, Place and Identities in Post-Industrial Mining Communities', *International Journal of Urban and Regional Research* 25 (2001), 253–67.
10 Maxwell, *Chicago Tumbles*, p. 157.
11 NAS, CB 229/3/1, Bilston Glen CCC, 1 March 1988 and 15 May 1989 (final meeting).
12 Amos, Interview; *Monktonhall Colliery, 1953–1998*. Written by Susan Whiteford and Directed by Jim Dickson (Midlothian Council, 1998).
13 Oglethorpe, *Scottish Collieries*.
14 Barry Bluestone and Bennett Harrison, *The Deindustrialization of America. Plant Closings, Community Abandonment, and the Dismantling of Basic Industry* (New York, 1982), p. 15.
15 Willie Clarke, Interview.
16 EKOS, *Evaluation of the Coalfields Regeneration Trust Activity in Scotland: Report for the Coalfields Regeneration Trust* (Glasgow, 2009), pp. 69–74.
17 Chik Collins and Gerry McCartney, 'The Impact of Neoliberal "Political Attack" on Health: The Case of the "Scottish Effect"', *International Journal of Health Services*, 41 (2011), 501–23.
18 Hilary Young, 'Being a Man: Everyday Masculinities', in Lynn Abrams and Callum G. Brown, *A History of Everyday Life in Twentieth-Century Scotland* (Edinburgh, 2010), pp. 132, 143; Wight, *Workers Not Wasters*, p. 200.
19 Cameron, *Impaled Upon a Thistle*, pp. 320–40; Mitchell, *Conservatives and the Union*, pp. 102–23.
20 Phillips, *Industrial Politics of Devolution*, pp. 179–84.
21 'Man behind illegal blacklist snooped on workers for thirty years', the *Guardian*, 27 May 2009: www.guardian.co.uk/uk/2009/may/27/construction-worker-blacklist-database1, accessed 18 March 2011.
22 Rab Wilson, 'Somewhaur in the Dark. Sonnets Inspired by the Miners' Strike of 1984–85', in *Accent o the Mind* (Edinburgh, 2006), pp. 62–82.
23 *Finding the Seam. Rab Wilson's Poetic Journey*. Filmed, produced and directed by Tony Grace (2011).
24 Hughes, *Gender and Political Identities in Scotland*.
25 Amos, Interview.
26 Brotherstone and Pirani, 'Were There Alternatives?'.

Bibliography

Interviews

Unless otherwise indicated, these were conducted by the author in the homes of inter-viewees, with 1984 union position and colliery affiliation where appropriate in parenthesis.

Rab Amos (SCEBTA, Monktonhall), Roslin, 23 February 2011.
Iain Chalmers (NUM, Seafield), Cowdenbeath, 30 July 2009.
Eric Clarke (NUMSA General Secretary), Scottish Mining Museum, Newtongrange, 25 August 2009.
Councillor Willie Clarke (NUM, Seafield), Ballingry, 13 November 2009.
Charlie Goodfellow (ex-miner, Polkemmet), Whitburn, 12 August 2009.
David Hamilton MP (NUM, Monktonhall), Parliamentary Advice Office, Dalkeith, 30 September 2009.
Alex Nicholson (NUM, Seafield), Windygates, 8 March 2011.
Nicky Wilson (SCEBTA, Cardowan), Scottish Miners' Convalescent Home, Blair Castle, Culross, 18 August 2009.

Willie Thompson interviews

Willie Thompson generously provided recordings of interviews he conducted in 1985–86 with strike participants. 1984 union position and colliery affiliation where appropriate in parenthesis.

Ayrshire strike leaders (Barony and Killoch), 9 December 1985.
George Bolton (NUMSA Vice President), undated, but presumed late 1985.
Tam Coulter (NUM, Castlehill), 28 January 1986.
Ella Egan (COSA, and convenor of NUMSA Women's Support Group), 28 October 1985.
Iain McCaig (NUM, Solsgirth), 12 March 1986.
Abe Moffat (SCEBTA President), 11 February 1986.
Tam Mylchreest (NUM, Castlehill), undated, but presumed early 1986.
Jocky Neilson (NUM, Seafield), 19 May 1986.

Archive materials

Glasgow Caledonian University Archives
Scottish Trades Union Congress, General Council Papers, 1984–85.

Kirkcaldy Art Gallery and Museum
National Union of Mineworkers, Seafield and Frances Strike Committee, Dysart Strike
  Centre, Reports, March 1984 to July 1984.
Iain Chalmers, Strike Diary, 1984.
Iain Chalmers, Strike Diary, 1985.

Modern Records Centre, University of Warwick
MSS. 371 Fred Lindop, transcribed interviews with figures from port transport.

National Archives of Scotland, Edinburgh
CB 221 National Coal Board, Scottish Area, Barony Colliery.
CB 229 National Coal Board, Scottish Area, Bilston Glen Colliery.
CB 328 National Coal Board, Scottish Area, Killoch Colliery.
CB 335 National Coal Board, Scottish Area, Kinneil Colliery.
CB 363 National Coal Board, Scottish Area, Monktonhall Colliery.
CB 382 National Coal Board, Scottish Area, Polmaise Colliery.
CB 398 National Coal Board, Scottish Area, Seafield Colliery.
CB 550 National Coal Board, Scottish Area, Cardowan Colliery.
SEP 4 Department of Trade and Industry in Scotland, Papers.
SOE 12 Scottish Office and Secretary of State for Scotland, Papers.

National Library of Scotland, Edinburgh
Acc. 9805 National Union of Mineworkers, Scotland, Papers and Correspondence.

Scottish Mining Museum, Newtongrange
National Union of Mineworkers, Scottish Area, Executive Committee and Delegates'
  Conference Minutes, 1980–84.
National Union of Mineworkers, Scottish Area, Strike Committee, Minutes, 1984–85.
National Union of Mineworkers, Scottish Area, Strike Reports, 1984–85.

The National Archives, Kew
COAL 26 National Coal Board, correspondence with National Union of Mineworkers.
COAL 30 National Coal Board, Papers.
COAL 31 National Coal Board, meetings and correspondence with National Union of
  Mineworkers.
COAL 74 Coal Industry National Consultative Council.
COAL 84 National Coal Board, Bilston Glen Colliery.
COAL 89 National Coal Board, Kinneil Colliery.
PREM 15 Prime Minister's Private Office Papers.

Official publications

Department of Employment, *Employment in the Ports: The Dock Labour Scheme*, Cm. 664 (London, HMSO, 1989).

General Registry Office for Scotland, *1991 Census. Report For Scotland, Part 1, Volume 1* (Edinburgh, HMSO, 1993).

General Registry Office for Scotland, *1991 Census. Central Region, Part 1* (Edinburgh, HMSO, 1993).

General Registry Office for Scotland, *1991 Census. Fife Region, Part 1* (Edinburgh, HMSO, 1993).

General Registry Office for Scotland, *1991 Census. Lothian Region, Part 1* (Edinburgh, HMSO, 1993).

General Registry Office for Scotland, *1991 Census. Strathclyde Region, Part 2* (Edinburgh, HMSO, 1993).

Monopolies and Mergers Commission, *National Coal Board. A Report on the Efficiency and Costs in the Development, Production and Supply of Coal by the National Coal Board, Volume One and Volume Two*, Cmnd. 8920 (London, HMSO, 1983).

Parliamentary Debates, Fifth Series, Commons and Lords.

Parliamentary Debates, Sixth Series, Commons and Lords.

Registry General Scotland, *Census 1981 Scotland. Scottish Summary. Volume 1 and Volume 2* (Edinburgh, HMSO, 1983).

Registry General Scotland, *Census 1981 Scotland. Report for Central Region. Volume 1* (Edinburgh, HMSO, 1982), and *Volume 4* (Edinburgh, HMSO, 1983).

Registry General Scotland, *Census 1981 Scotland. Report for Fife Region. Volume 1* (Edinburgh, HMSO, 1982), and *Volume 4* (Edinburgh, HMSO, 1983).

Registry General Scotland, *Census 1981 Scotland. Report for Lothian Region. Volume 1* (Edinburgh, HMSO, 1982), and *Volume 4* (Edinburgh, HMSO, 1983).

Registry General Scotland, *Census 1981 Scotland. Report for Strathclyde Region. Volume 1* (Edinburgh, HMSO, 1982) and *Volume 4* (Edinburgh, HMSO, 1983).

Business and labour publications

Committee of Inquiry appointed by the Scottish Council (Development and Industry) under the Chairmanship of J.N. Toothill, *Report on the Scottish Economy* (Edinburgh, 1961).

Scottish Miner.

Scottish Trades Union Congress (STUC), *Annual Reports, 1984–85*

'James Yuill, 1934–2006', *Transport News Network*, 4 September 2006: www.tnn.co.uk /UKNews/plonearticle.2006–09–04.7892083892.

Coal communities ephemeral literature and web resources

'*A Very Hard Year*'. *1984–5 Miners' Strike in Mauchline* (Glasgow: Workers' Educational Association, 1985), compiled by Catriona Levy and Mauchline Miners' Wives.

Fife Pits: www.users.zetnet.co.uk/mmartin/fifepits/.

'*For as long as it takes!*' *Cowie Miners in the Strike, 1984–5* (Cowie, 1985), by Steve McGrail and Vicky Patterson.

The Lost Village of Glencraig: www.glencraig.org.uk.

One Year On. Sacked Polmaise Miners Speak Out (Airth, 1986), edited by Steve McGrail.

Newspapers

Courier & Advertiser.
The Economist.
Glasgow Herald and the *Herald.*
Guardian.
Scotsman.
The Times.

Television, film and DVDs

Finding the Seam. Rab Wilson's Poetic Journey. Filmed, produced and directed by Tony Grace (2011).
Here We Go. Women Living the Strike. Presented and directed by Margaret Wright (TV2DAY, Independent Video Production, 2009).
Jonathan Meades Off-Kilter, 'The Football Pools Towns' (originally broadcast BBC4, 9pm, Wednesday 23 September 2009).
Monktonhall Colliery, 1953–1998. Written by Susan Whiteford and directed by Jim Dickson (Midlothian Council, 1998).
National Coal Board Collection, Volume One, Portrait of a Miner (London, 2009).

Secondary literature

Adeney, Martin and John Lloyd, *The Miners' Strike, 1984–5: Loss Without Limit* (London, 1986).
Aitken, Keith, *The Bairns O' Adam. The Story of the STUC* (Edinburgh, 1997).
Aldcroft, Derek H. and Michael J. Oliver, *Trade Unions and the Economy: 1870–2000* (Aldershot, 2000).
Ashworth, W., *The History of the British Coal Industry, Volume 5, 1946–1982: The Nationalized Industry* (Oxford, 1986).
Barron, Hester, 'Women of the Durham Coalfield and their Reactions to the 1926 Miners' Lockout', *Historical Studies in Industrial Relations,* 22 (2006), 53–83.
Beckett, Andy, *When the Lights Went Out. What Really Happened to Britain in the Seventies* (London, 2009).
Beckett, Francis and David Hencke, *Marching to the Fault Line. The 1984 Miners' Strike and the Death of Industrial Britain* (London, 2009).
Benn, Tony, *The End of an Era. Diaries, 1980–1990,* edited by Ruth Winstone (London, 1992).
Beynon, Huw, 'Introduction', in Huw Beynon (ed.), *Digging Deeper. Issues in the Miners' Strike* (London, 1985).
Beynon, Huw, Ray Hudson and Tim Strangleman, 'Rebuilding the Coalfields', The Coalfields Research Programme: Discussion Paper No. 4, Economic and Social Research Council, Cardiff University and University of Durham, 1999.
Bluestone, Barry and Bennett Harrison, *The Deindustrialization of America. Plant Closings, Community Abandonment, and the Dismantling of Basic Industry* (New York, 1982).
Brotherstone, Terry and Simon Pirani, 'Were There Alternatives? Movements from Below in the Scottish Coalfield, the Communist Party, and Thatcherism, 1981–1985', *Critique,* 36–7 (2005), 99–124.

Bruley, Sue, 'Women', in John McIlroy, Alan Campbell and Keith Gildart (eds), *Industrial Politics and the 1926 Mining Lockout* (Cardiff, 2004), pp. 229–48.

Cameron, Ewen, *Impaled Upon a Thistle. Scotland Since 1880* (Edinburgh, 2010).

Campbell, Alan, *The Scottish Miners, 1874–1939. Volume One: Work, Industry and Community;* and *Volume Two: Trade Unions and Politics* (Aldershot, 2000).

Campbell, Alan, 'Scotland', in John McIlroy, Alan Campbell and Keith Gildart (eds), *Industrial Politics and the 1926 Mining Lockout* (Cardiff, 2004).

Campbell, Alan, 'Reflections on the 1926 Mining Lockout', *Historical Studies in Industrial Relations,* 21 (2006), 143–81.

Campbell, Beatrix, *Wigan Pier Revisited: Poverty and Politics in the Eighties* (London, 1984).

Campbell, John, *Edward Heath. A Biography* (London, 1993).

Chick, Martin, 'Time, Water and Capital: The Unintended Contribution of the North of Scotland Hydro-Electric Board to the Application of Welfare Economics in Britain, 1943–1967', *Scottish Business and Industrial History,* 25 (2009), 29–55.

Clarke, Eric with Bob McLean, 'The Mineworkers' Strike 1984–5: The Role of the Scottish Area as Banker to the Union', *Scottish Affairs,* 49 (2004), 138–50.

Collins, Chik and Gerry McCartney, 'The Impact of Neoliberal "Political Attack" on Health: The Case of the "Scottish Effect"', *International Journal of Health Services,* 41 (2011), 501–23.

Corrigan, Suzanne, Cath Cunningham and Margo Thorburn, 'Fife Women Stand Firm', written in collaboration with Vicky Seddon, in Vicky Seddon (ed.), *The Cutting Edge. Women and the Pit Strike* (London, 1986), pp. 30–49.

Crossley, Nick, *Making Sense of Social Movements* (Buckingham, 2002).

Cunningham, Cath, 'Fife', in Vicky Seddon (ed.), *The Cutting Edge. Women and the Pit Strike* (London, 1986), pp. 222–6.

Cunningham, Harry, 'Miners' Strike – 20 years on', *The Citizen:* www.thecitizen .org.uk/articles/vol3/article26f.htm.

Cutler, T., C. Haslam, J. Williams and K. Williams, 'The Aberystwyth Report on Coal', in D. Cooper and T. Hopper (eds), *Debating Coal Closures: Economic Calculation in the Coal Dispute, 1984–5* (Cambridge, 1988), pp. 161–94.

Dennis, Norman, Fernando Henriques and Clifford Slaughter, *Coal is our Life. An Analysis of a Yorkshire Mining Community* (London, 1969).

Denselow, Robin, 'MacColl, Ewan (formerly James Miller), (1915–1989)', in H.C.G. Matthew and Brian Harrison (eds), *Oxford Dictionary of National Biography* (Oxford, 2004), pp. 138–9.

Dimitratos, Pavlos, Ioanna Liouka, Duncan Ross and Stephen Young, 'The Multinational Enterprise and Subsidiary Evolution', *Business History,* 51 (2009), 401–25.

Dorey, Peter, 'Conciliation or Confrontation with the Trade Unions? The Conservative Party's "Authority of Government Group", 1975–1978', *Historical Studies in Industrial Relations,* 27/28 (2009), 135–51.

Douglass, David, 'Misunderstanding the Miners' Strike', *Weekly Worker,* 777, 9 July 2009: www.cpgb.org.uk/worker/777/misunderstanding.php.

Edgerton, David, 'The Decline of Declinism', *Business History Review,* 71 (1997), 201–7.

EKOS, *Evaluation of the Coalfields Regeneration Trust Activity in Scotland: Report for the Coalfields Regeneration Trust* (Glasgow, 2009).

England, Joe, *The Wales TUC, 1974–2004. Devolution and Industrial Politics* (Cardiff, 2004).

Foster, John, 'The Twentieth Century, 1914–1979', in R.A. Houston and W.W.J. Knox (eds), *The New Penguin History of Scotland* (London, 2001), pp. 417–93.

Foster, John and Charles Woolfson, *The Politics of the UCS Work-In: Class Alliances and the Right to Work* (London, 1986).

Fox, Alan, *Industrial Sociology and Industrial Relations. Royal Commission on Trade Unions and Employers' Associations, Research Papers, 3* (HMSO, 1966).

Francis, Hywel, *History On Our Side: Wales and the 1984–85 Miners' Strike* (Ferryside, 2009).

Fraser, W. Hamish, *A History of British Trade Unionism, 1700–1998* (London, 2000).

Gibbon, Peter and David Steyne, *Thurcroft: A Village and the Miners' Strike: An Oral History* (Nottingham, 1986).

Gilbert, David, *Class, Community and Collective Action. Social Change in Two British Coalfields, 1850–1926* (Oxford, 1992).

Gildart, Keith, *North Wales Miners: A Fragile Unity* (Cardiff, 2001).

Glyn, A., 'The Economic Case Against Pit Closures', in D. Cooper and T. Hopper (eds), *Debating Coal Closures: Economic Calculation in the Coal Dispute, 1984–5* (Cambridge, 1988), pp. 57–94.

Goldthorpe, John, David Lockwood, Frank Bechhofer and Jennifer Platt, *The Affluent Worker: Industrial Attitudes and Behaviour* (Cambridge, 1968).

Griffin, Colin, '"Notts. Have Some Very Peculiar History": Understanding the Reaction of the Nottinghamshire Miners to the 1984–85 Strike', *Historical Studies in Industrial Relations*, 19 (2005), 63–99.

Hall, Tony, *King Coal: Miners, Coal and Britain's Industrial Future* (Harmondsworth, 1981).

Hamilton, Jean, 'Give us a Future, Give us our Jobs!', written in collaboration with Vicky Seddon, in Vicky Seddon (ed.), *The Cutting Edge. Women and the Pit Strike* (London, 1986), pp. 211–21.

Harvie, Christopher, *Fool's Gold: The Story of North Sea Oil* (Harmondsworth, 1994).

Heath, Edward, *The Course of My Life. My Autobiography* (London, 1998).

Heffer, Eric S., 'Preface', in Huw Beynon (ed.), *Digging Deeper. Issues in the Miners' Strike* (London, 1985).

Heughan, Hazel, *Pit Closures at Shotts and the Migration of Miners* (Edinburgh, 1953).

Holden, Triona, *Queen Coal. Women of the Miners' Strike* (Stroud, 2005).

Howell, Chris, *Trade Unions and the State. The Construction of Industrial Relations Institutions in Britain, 1890–2000* (Princeton, 2005).

Howell, David, *A Lost Left. Three Studies in Socialism and Nationalism* (Manchester, 1986).

Howell, David, *The Politics of the NUM: A Lancashire View* (Manchester, 1989).

Hughes, Annmarie, *Gender and Political Identities in Scotland, 1919–1939* (Edinburgh, 2010).

Hutton, Guthrie, *Fife – The Mining Kingdom* (Ochiltree, 1999).

Hutton, Guthrie (compiler), *Coal Not Dole. Memories of the 1984/85 Miners' Strike* (Catine, 2005).

Hutton, Will, *The State We're In* (London, 1995).

Hyman, Richard, 'Reflections on the Mining Strike', *The Socialist Register*, 22 (1985–86), 330–54.

James, Leighton S., *The Politics of Identity and Civil Society in Britain and Germany: Miners in the Ruhr and South Wales, 1890–1926* (Manchester, 2008).

Kerevan, G. and R. Saville, 'The Economic Case for Deep-Mined Coal in Scotland', in D. Cooper and T. Hopper (eds), *Debating Coal Closures: Economic Calculation in the Coal*

Dispute, 1984–5 (Cambridge, 1988), pp. 119–60.

Kerr, Clark and Abraham Siegal, 'The Inter-Industry Propensity to Strike – An International Comparison', in A. Kornhauser, R. Dubin and A. M. Ross (eds), *Industrial Conflict* (New York, 1954), pp. 189–212.

Kirby, M.W., 'MacGregor, Sir Ian Kinloch (1912–1998)', in H.C.G. Matthew and Brian Harrison (eds), *Oxford Dictionary of National Biography* (Oxford, 2004), pp. 433–5.

Kirk, Neville (2007) *Custom and Conflict in the 'Land of the Gael': Ballachullish, 1900–1910* (London, 2007).

Knox, W., 'Class, Work and Trade Unionism in Scotland', in A. Dickson and J. H. Treble (eds), *People and Society in Scotland. Volume III, 1914–1990* (Edinburgh, 1994), pp. 108–37.

Knox, W.W., *Industrial Nation: Work, Culture and Society in Scotland, 1800–present* (Edinburgh, 1999).

Legge, Karen, *Human Resource Management: Rhetoric and Realities* (Basingstoke, 2005).

Lindop, Fred, 'The Dockers and the 1971 Industrial Relations Act, Part 1: Shop Stewards and Containerization', *Historical Studies in Industrial Relations*, 5 (1998), 33–72.

Lyddon, Dave and Ralph Darlington, *Glorious Summer. Class Struggle in Britain in 1972* (London, 2001).

McCabe, Sarah and Peter Wallington with John Alderson, Larry Gostin and Christopher Mason, *The Police, Public Order and Civil Liberties. Legacies of the Miners' Strike* (London, 1988).

MacDougall, Ian, *Voices From Work and Home* (Edinburgh, 2000).

McIlroy, John 'Police and Pickets: The Law against the Miners', in Huw Beynon (ed.), *Digging Deeper. Issues in the Miners' Strike* (London, 1985), pp. 101–22.

McIlroy, John, 'Finale: A View from a New Century', in John McIlroy, Alan Campbell and Keith Gildart (eds), *Industrial Politics and the 1926 Mining Lockout* (Cardiff, 2004).

McIlroy, John, 'Look Back in Anger: Mining Communities, the Mining Novel and the Great Miners' Strike', *Historical Studies in Industrial Relations*, 18 (2004), 65–108.

McIlroy, John and Alan Campbell, 'Beyond Betteshanger: Order 1305 in the Scottish Coalfields during the Second World War, Part 1: Politics, Prosecutions and Protest', *Historical Studies in Industrial Relations*, 15 (2003), 27–72, and 'Part 2: The Cardowan Story', *Historical Studies in Industrial Relations*, 16 (2003), 39–80.

McIlroy, John and Alan Campbell, 'McGahey, Michael (Mick), (1925–1999)', in Keith Gildart and David Howell, *Dictionary of Labour Biography. Volume XIII* (Houndmills, Basingstoke, 2010), pp. 242–51.

McIlroy, John, Alan Cambell and Keith Gildart, 'Introduction: 1926 and All That', in John McIlroy, Alan Campbell and Keith Gildart (eds), *Industrial Politics and the 1926 Mining Lockout* (Cardiff, 2004).

Macintyre, Stuart, *Little Moscows: Communism and Working-class Militancy in Inter-war Britain* (London, 1980).

McIvor, Arthur, 'Women and Work in Twentieth Century Scotland', in A. Dickson and J.H. Treble (eds), *People and Society in Scotland. Volume III, 1914–1990* (Edinburgh, 1994), pp. 138–73.

McIvor, Arthur and Hugh Patterson, 'Combating the Left: Victimisation and Anti-Labour Activities on Clydeside, 1900–1939', in Robert Duncan and Arthur McIvor (eds), *Labour and Class Conflict on the Clyde, 1900–1950* (Edinburgh, 1992).

McIvor, Arthur and Ronnie Johnston, 'Voices From the Pits: Health and Safety in Scottish Coal Mining Since 1945', *Scottish Economic and Social History*, 22 (2002), 111–33.

McIvor, Arthur and Ronald Johnston, *Miners' Lung: A History of Dust Disease in British Coal Mining* (Aldershot, 2007).

McKibbin, Ross, 'Class and Conventional Wisdom', in Ross McKibbin, *The Ideologies of Class. Social Relations in Britain, 1880–1950* (Oxford, 1990), pp. 259–93.

McKibbin, Ross, *Classes and Cultures. England 1918–1951* (Oxford, 1998).

Macpherson, Archie, *Jock Stein: The Definitive Biography* (Newbury, 2004).

McSmith, Andy, *No Such Thing as Society: A History of the 1980s* (London, 2010).

Marr, Andrew, *A History of Modern Britain* (London, 2007).

Maxwell, Alex, *Chicago Tumbles: Cowdenbeath and the Miners' Strike* (Glenrothes, 1994).

Millward, Neil and Mark Stevens, *British Workplace Industrial Relations, 1980–1984. The DE/ESRC/PSI/ACAS Surveys* (Aldershot, 1986).

Milne, Seamus, *The Enemy Within: The Secret War Against the Miners* (London, 1994).

Mitchell, James, *Conservatives and the Union. A Study of Conservative Party Attitudes to the Union* (Edinburgh, 1990).

Morgan, Kenneth O., *The People's Peace: British History, 1945–1990* (Oxford, 1992).

National Museum of Wales, *Big Pit. National Coal Museum. A Guide* (Cardiff, 2005).

Newby, Andrew, 'Scottish Coal Miners', in Mark A. Mulhern, John Beech and Elaine Thompson (eds), *Scottish Life and Society. A Compendium of Scottish Ethnology. Volume 7: The Working Life of the Scots* (Edinburgh, 2008), pp. 579–603.

Nichols, Theo, *The British Worker Question. A New Look at Workers and Productivity in Manufacturing* (London, 1986).

Offer, Avner, *The Challenge of Affluence. Self Control and Well-Being in the United States and Britain since 1950* (Oxford, 2006).

Oglethorpe, Miles K., *Scottish Collieries. An Inventory of the Scottish Coal Industry in the Nationalised Era* (Edinburgh, 2006).

Olson, Mancur, *The Logic of Collective Action. Public Goods and the Theory of Groups* (Cambridge, Mass., 1965).

Owens, Joe (ed.), *Miners, 1984–1994: A Decade of Endurance* (Edinburgh, 1994).

Passerini, Luisa, 'Work, Ideology and Consensus Under Italian Fascism', in Robert Perks and Alistair Thomson (eds), *The Oral History Reader* (London, 1998), pp. 53–62.

Payne, Peter L., *Colvilles and the Scottish Steel Industry* (Oxford, 1979).

Payne, Peter L., 'The End of Steelmaking in Scotland', *Scottish Economic and Social Hisotry*, 15 (1995), 68–84.

Peace, David, *GB84* (London, 2004).

Peden, G.C., 'The Managed Economy: Scotland, 1919–2000', in T.M. Devine, C.H. Lee and G.C. Peden (eds), *The Transformation of Scotland. The Economy Since 1700* (Edinburgh, 2005), pp. 233–65.

Perchard, Andrew, 'The Mine Management Professions and the Dust Problem in the Scottish Coal Mining Industry, c. 1930–1966', *Scottish Labour History* 40 (2005), 87–110.

Perchard, Andrew, *The Mine Management Professions in the Twentieth-Century Scottish Coal Mining Industry* (Lampeter and Lewiston, 2007).

Perchard, Andrew and Jim Phillips, 'Transgressing the Moral Economy: Wheelerism and Management of the Nationalised Coal Industry in Scotland', *Contemporary British History*, 25 (2011), 387–405.

Phillips, Jim, 'The 1972 Miners' Strike: Popular Agency and Industrial Politics in Britain', *Contemporary British History*, 20 (2006), 187–207.

Phillips, Jim, 'Industrial Relations, Historical Contingencies and Political Economy: Britain in the 1960s and 1970s', *Labour History Review*, 21 (2007), 215–33.

Phillips, Jim, *The Industrial Politics of Devolution: Scotland in the 1960s and 1970s* (Manchester, 2008).

Phillips, Jim, 'Workplace Conflict and the Origins of the 1984–5 Miners' Strike in Scotland', *Twentieth Century British History*, 20 (2009), 152–72.

Phillips, Jim, 'Collieries and Communities: The Miners' Strike in Scotland, 1984–5', *Scottish Labour History*, 45 (2010), 17–35.

Phillips, Jim, 'Material and Moral Resources: The 1984–5 Miners' Strike in Scotland', *Economic History Review*, 65, 1 (2012), 256–76.

Pitt, Malcolm, *The World on our Backs: The Kent Miners and the 1972 Miners' Strike* (London, 1979).

Portelli, Alessandro, *They Say in Harlan County. An Oral History* (Oxford, 2011).

Rafeek, Neil, *Communist Women in Scotland: Red Clydeside from the Russian Revolution to the End of the Soviet Union* (London, 2008).

Reid, Alastair J., *United We Stand. A History of Britain's Trade Unions* (Harmondsworth, 2004).

Reid, Alastair J., *The Tide of Democracy. Shipyard Workers and Social Relations in Britain, 1870–1950* (Manchester, 2010).

Richards, Andrew J., *Miners on Strike. Class Solidarity and Division in Britain* (Oxford, 1996).

Robens, Alf, *Ten Year Stint* (London, 1972).

Robinson, Colin and Eileen Marshall, *What Future for British Coal? Optimism or Realism on the Prospects to the Year 2000* (London, 1981).

Routledge, Paul, *Scargill. The Unauthorized Biography* (London, 1993).

Samuel, Raphael, 'Preface', in Raphael Samuel, B. Bloomfield and G. Bonas (eds), *The Enemies Within: Pit Villages and the Miners' Strike of 1984–5* (London, 1986).

Saville, John, 'An Open Conspiracy: Conservative Politics and the Miners' Strike, 1984–5', *The Socialist Register*, 22 (1985–86), 295–329.

Sen, Amartya, *Rationality and Freedom* (London, 1992).

Seddon, Vicky (ed.), *The Cutting Edge. Women and the Pit Strike* (London, 1986).

Smith, Ned, *The 1984 Miners' Strike. The Actual Account* (Whitstable, 1997).

Smith, Paul and Gary Morton, 'The Conservative Governments' Reform of Employment Law, 1979–97: "Stepping Stones" and the "New Right" Agenda', *Historical Studies in Industrial Relations*, 12 (2001), 131–47.

Standing, Guy, *Work After Globalization. Building Occupational Citizenship* (Cheltenham, 2009).

Stead, Jean, *Never the Same Again. Women and the Miners' Strike, 1984–5* (London, 1987).

Steel, Mark, *Reasons to be Cheerful. From Punk to New Labour through the Eyes of a Dedicated Troublemaker* (London, 2001).

Stewart, David, 'Fighting for Survival: The 1980s Campaign to Save Ravenscraig Steelworks', *Journal of Scottish Historical Studies*, 25 (2005), 40–57.

Stewart, David, 'A Tragic "Fiasco"? The 1984–5 Miners' Strike in Scotland', *Scottish Labour History*, 41 (2006), 34–50.

Stewart, David, *The Path to Devolution and Change. A Political History of Scotland under Margaret Thatcher* (London, 2009).

Strangleman, Tim, 'Networks, Place and Identities in Post-Industrial Mining Communities', *International Journal of Urban and Regional Research*, 25 (2001), 253–67.

Summerfield, Penny, 'Culture and Composure: Creating Narratives of the Gendered Self in Oral History Interviews', *Cultural and Social History*, 1 (2004), 65–93.

Summerfield, Penny, 'Dis/composing the Subject: Inter-subjectivities in Oral History', in Tess Cosslett, Celia Lury and Penny Summerfield (eds), *Feminism and Autobiography: Texts, Theories, Methods* (London, 2000).

Taylor, Andrew, 'The "Stepping Stones" Programme: Conservative Party Thinking on Trade Unions, 1975–9', *Historical Studies in Industrial Relations*, 11 (2001), 109–25.

Taylor, Andrew, *The NUM and British Politics. Volume 1: 1944–1968* (Aldershot, 2003); and *Volume 2: 1969–1995* (Aldershot, 2005).

Taylor, Robert, *The Trade Union Question in British Politics* (Oxford, 1993).

Taylor, Robert, 'The Heath Government and Industrial Relations: Myth and Reality', in Stuart Ball and Anthony Seldon (eds), *The Heath Government, 1970–1974: a Reappraisal* (London, 1996), 161–190.

Taylor, Robert, 'McGahey, Michael (Mick), (1925–1999)', in H. C. G. Matthew and Brian Harrison (eds), *Oxford Dictionary of National Biography* (Oxford, 2004), 390–1.

Terris, Ian, *Twenty Years Down the Mines* (Ochiltree, 2001).

Thatcher, Margaret, *The Downing Street Years* (London, 1993).

Thatcher, Margaret, *The Path to Power* (London, 1995).

Thompson, E.P., 'The Moral Economy of the English Crowd in the Eighteenth Century', *Past and Present*, 50 (1971), 76–136.

Thompson, William, 'The New Left in Scotland', in Ian MacDougall (ed.), *Essays in Scottish Labour History* (Edinburgh, 1978), pp. 207–24.

Thompson, Willie, *The Good Old Cause. British Communism, 1920–1991* (London, 1992).

Thompson, Willie, 'The Miners' Strike in Scotland, 1984–1985', unpublished manuscript.

Thomson, Alistair, 'Anzac Memories: Putting Popular Memory Theory into Practice in Australia', in Robert Perks and Alistair Thomson (eds), *The Oral History Reader* (London, 1998), pp. 300–10.

Tomlinson, Jim, *The Politics of Decline: Understanding Post-war Britain* (Harlow, 2000).

Torrance, David, *'We in Scotland'. Thatcherism in a Cold Climate* (Edinburgh, 2009).

Tuckett, Angela, *The Scottish Trades Union Congress. The First Eighty Years, 1897–1977* (Edinburgh, 1986).

Turnbull, Peter, Charles Woolfson and John Kelly, *Dock Strike. Conflict and Restructuring in Britain's Ports* (Aldershot, 1992).

Whitehead, Phillip, *The Writing on the Wall. Britain in the Seventies* (London, 1985).

Wight, Daniel, *Workers Not Wasters. Masculine Respectability, Consumption and Employment in Central Scotland* (Edinburgh, 1993).

Wilson, Rab, 'Somewhaur in the Dark. Sonnets Inspired by the Miners' Strike of 1984–85', in Rab Wilson, *Accent o the Mind* (Edinburgh, 2006).

Winterton, J. and R. Winterton, *Coal, Crisis and Conflict: The 1984–85 Miners' Strike in Yorkshire* (Manchester, 1989).

Winterton, Jonathan and Ruth Winterton, 'Production, Politics and Technological Development: British Coal Mining in the Twentieth Century', in Joseph Melling and Alan McKinlay (eds), *Management, Labour and Industrial Politics in Modern Europe: The Quest for Productivity* (Cheltenham, 1998), pp. 122–44.

Wrigley, Chris, 'The 1984–5 Miners' Strike', in Andrew Charlesworth, David Gilbert, Adrian Randall, Humphrey Southall and Chris Wrigley, *An Atlas of Industrial Unrest in Britain, 1750–1990* (London, 1996), pp. 217–25.

Young, Hilary, 'Being a Man: Everyday Masculinities', in Lynn Abrams and Callum G.

Brown, *A History of Everyday Life in Twentieth-Century Scotland* (Edinburgh, 2010), pp. 131–52.

Young, Hugo, *One of Us* (London, 1990).

Zeitlin, Jonathan, 'From Labour History to the History of Industrial Relations', *Economic History Review*, 60 (1987), 159–84.

Zeitlin, Jonathan, '"Rank and Filism" in British Labour History: A Critique', *International Review of Social History*, 34 (1989), 42–61.

Index

Note: The position of individuals in the coal industry or trade unions immediately before and after the strike is denoted in parenthesis.

Aberystwyth Report on Coal 45, 129
accidents and fatalities 26, 29, 56, 97, 157–8, 165
Actual Strike Endurance (ASE) 12–13, 111, 125–9, 137, 174
Advisory, Conciliation and Arbitration Service 100, 103, 147
age profile of workforce and strikers 24, 59, 63, 135–8
Aitchison, Jackie (NUM, Bilston Glen) 135, 152
Aitchison, Robert (miner, Bilston Glen) 150
Alexander's buses 156
Amos, Rab (SCEBTA, Monktonhall) 29, 37, 62, 68, 70, 89–90, 114, 116–17, 132, 152, 158, 169, 171
Ancram, Michael 93, 97, 102, 131
Argos, cargo ship 102
Auchengeich Colliery, Lanarkshire 26
Ayr strike centre 93, 115

'ballot' controversy in strike 3–6, 9, 62, 73–4, 83–4, 103, 144–5, 154, 172–3
Barony Colliery, Ayrshire 22, 26, 29, 54, 57, 59, 63, 67, 71, 74, 83, 103, 112, 115, 121–8, 136–7, 154, 157, 167–70, 174
Barron, Hester 112, 131
Bathgate motor plant 32
Beckett, Francis and David Hencke 7–8
Bedlay Colliery, Lanarkshire 8, 11, 61
benefits system and strike 120, 134
Benn, Tony 88
Beynon, Huw 5–6, 56, 62, 166
Bilston Glen Colliery, Midlothian 1–2, 5, 13–14, 21–3, 25, 29, 54, 57–9, 62–3,
65, 67–70, 73–5, 83, 103, 114–15, 119–31, 135–7, 147–50, 152, 155–8, 160, 165, 167–8, 170, 172–4
Bloomberg, Joe 101
Bluestone, Barry and Bennett Harrison 167
Bogside Colliery, Fife 11, 21–2, 28, 39, 57, 59–60, 62–4, 72–3, 121, 123–4, 126–8, 160, 167–8, 170, 173
Bolton, George (NUMSA Vice President) 6, 23, 89–90, 103, 155, 157
Bolton, Guy 23
Bolton, John 23
Bowman, James 25
Bray, Jeremy 102
Brennan, Tommy (ISTC, Ravenscraig) 89, 91, 93–4, 104
British Association of Colliery Managers 60, 71, 125, 153
British Steel Corporation 6, 12, 22, 41, 45, 76, 83–6, 89–91, 93, 95–104
Brotherstone, Terry and Simon Pirani 6, 61–2, 69, 172
Buchan, Norman 93

Caldow, George (NCB, Seafield) 66–8, 72
Cameron, Donald (NCB, Polmaise) 71
Campbell, Alan 8, 23, 31, 118
Campbell, Beatrix 132
Cardowan Colliery, Lanarkshire 8, 10–11, 21–3, 29, 43–4, 56–7, 59, 62–4, 71–2, 114, 130, 134–5
Cardowan strike centre 93, 115, 117
Castlebridge Colliery, Fife 39, 167, 169
Castlehill Colliery, Fife 11, 21–2, 28, 56–7, 62–4, 115, 121, 123–4, 126–8, 135, 151, 154, 156–7, 167–8, 170, 174

Chalmers, Iain (NUM, Seafield) 10, 23–4,
    27–8, 65, 86, 89–90, 114–15, 118–19,
    136, 154, 156, 169
children in the strike 116–17, 130
Clarke, Eric (NUMSA Secretary) 6, 24–5,
    37, 55–6, 60, 74, 83, 85–6, 90, 93–4,
    104, 114, 133, 151, 153–6
Clarke, Willie (NUM Seafield) 10, 14, 28,
    36–7, 66–7, 86, 89–90, 118–19, 130,
    134, 144, 148, 154–5, 167, 169
Clyde Port Authority 100–1
coal imports 22, 43–4, 86, 89, 99, 104
Coal Industry Act, 1980 6, 41–3, 54, 124,
    136
coal industry finances 44–6, 63, 129, 148
Coal Is Our Life, by Norman, Henriques
    and Slaughter 30, 132, 165
Colliery Officials' Staff Association 60
Colvilles 35–6, 83
Communism in coalfield communities
    and politics 3, 5–9, 14, 23, 26–8,
    37–8, 61, 86–8, 90, 119, 130, 133, 135
Community and communities 8–14,
    27–33, 46, 110–19, 129–38, 149, 151,
    153, 170–5
Comrie Colliery, Fife 22, 57, 63, 66, 72,
    74, 115, 121, 123–4, 126–30, 134,
    137, 143, 156, 160, 168, 170–1
Confederation of British Industry 92
Cortonwood Colliery, Yorkshire 73–4, 144
'cosmopolitan' collieries 11, 25, 28–9, 46,
    110, 115, 120, 132, 167, 171
Coulter, Tam (NUM, Castlehill) 22, 56,
    64, 96, 118, 135, 150, 156
Council Housing Density (CHD) 12,
    110–11, 119–24, 127, 129,137, 174
Cowan, Jimmy (NCB) 39
Cowie, Sam (NUM, Castlehill) 154
Cunningham, Cath or Cathie 99, 133, 171
Cunningham, Harry (NUM,
    Cowdenbeath workshops) 115

Dalkeith strike centre 93, 115, 149
Daly, Jimmy 23
Daly, Lawrence 23–4, 28, 33–4, 60
Dempsey, W. (Monktonhall strike-
    breaker) 158–9
Dennis, Norman, Fernando Henriques
    and Clifford Slaughter 30

Derbyshire 34, 43, 56
Devolutionary politics and pressures 2, 7,
    22, 33–6, 46–7, 86–8, 169, 172
Dewar, Donald 97–8, 159
dock strikes 86, 99–102
dock workers 30, 95
    see also National Dock Labour Scheme
Dorey, Peter 39
Douglas, Dick 98
Douglass, David 7
Dunbar, Jim (BSC, Ravenscraig) 89–91,
    97, 102, 104
Dysart strike centre 8, 93–4, 114–17,
    133–4

Eadie, Alex 42, 151, 159
Easthouses Colliery, Midlothian 29
Economic Performance (EP), pit-level 63,
    124–5, 127–9, 137, 174
    see also pit-level economic performance
Egan, Ella 9, 23, 134
electricity supply position 22, 26, 34, 40,
    44, 91–2, 103, 116, 124, 129, 173
employment levels in Scottish collieries 7,
    22, 25, 39, 126, 168
ending of strike 154–6
Energy, Department of 95, 173

Fettes, Harry (Bilston Glen strike-
    breaker) 73, 114
Finding the Seam, by Rab Wilson and
    Tony Grace 169–70
Fishcross strike centre 93, 95–6, 115, 117,
    126
Fox, Alan 55, 66
Fram, John (NCB, Cardowan) 56
Frances Colliery, Fife 11, 22, 27, 39, 57,
    62–5, 70–2, 103, 114, 116–17, 121,
    123–4, 126–8, 147, 153–6, 160,
    166–7, 170, 172
Francis, Hywel 7, 9
Frater, Jim (NUM, Kinneil) 61
Frazer, Frank 92
fund-raising 13, 90, 116–17, 119, 133

Gaw, Tam (NCB, Barony) 59
gender and gender relations 5, 9, 13,
    30–2, 112, 120–2, 130–5, 138,
    165–71, 174–5

General strike, 1926 24, 43
  see also mining lockout, 1926
German coalfield politics 87
Gilbert, David 30–1, 113, 118
Gildart, Keith 5
Givens, Margie 133
Glencraig Colliery, Fife 14, 28, 120
Glyn, Andrew 45–6, 129, 148
Goodfellow, Charlie 32
Gormley, Joe 33–4, 38, 86
Gostwick, Martin (Scottish Miner editor)
  93
Graham, Bob (miner, Lochgelly) 93
Grangemouth oil refinery 95
Gray, Alasdair 117
Gray, Margaret 148
Green, Joseph (Fife-born miner, killed in
  Yorkshire) 97
Grunwick dispute 37

Hamilton, David (NUM, Monktonhall)
  10–11, 13–14, 29, 37, 55, 67–71, 86,
  90, 93–4, 114, 119, 127, 133, 136,
  144, 149, 152–5, 158, 169
Hamilton, Jean 133
Hamilton, Nancy 133
Hamilton, Robert (NUM, Monktonhall)
  133
Haslam, Bob (BSC Chairman) 12, 85,
  95–6, 98, 100, 102, 104, 173
Heath, Edward 21, 33–40, 172
Heathfield, Peter (NUM General
  Secretary) 5, 154
Heffer, Eric 5
Here We Go, by Margaret Wright 133, 171
Highhouse Colliery, Ayrshire 8, 21–2,
  43–4, 57, 59, 62–3
Hogg, Alec (NUMSA, Cardowan) 63
Hogg, Peter (NUMSA) 2, 159
Howell, David (Conservative government
  minister) 43
Howell, David (labour historian) 4
Hughes, Annmarie 133, 171
Hunter, Anne 133, 171
Hunter, Helen 117
Hunterston, coal and ore terminal 12,
  85–6, 89–103, 127, 150–1
Hunterston B, nuclear power station 92
Hutton, Guthrie 96

Institute of Economic Affairs 44
Invergordon aluminium smelter 83, 92
Iron and Steel Trades Confederation 41,
  43, 88–91, 96–7, 102, 117

James, Leighton S. 87
joint industrial procedures in coal 8, 24,
  39, 47, 53, 56, 58, 64–7, 72, 135, 143,
  157, 160–1, 169, 173
judiciary's role in strike 4, 73, 76, 114,
  151–4

Kennedy, Charles 84
Kennedy, William (NCB, Monktonhall)
  67–8, 70
Kent 23, 34, 42–5, 57, 74, 87, 125, 160
Kerevan, George and Richard Saville 46
Kerr, Clark and Abraham Siegel 30
Kerr, Willie (NCB, Monktonhall) 158–9
Keys, Bill 7
Killoch Colliery, Ayrshire 21–2, 29, 44,
  54, 57, 59, 62–3, 67, 69, 71–2, 74,
  103, 112, 115, 121–8, 136–7, 150,
  154, 157, 167–8, 170, 174
Kinglassie Colliery, Fife 27
Kinneil Colliery, West Lothian 6, 8, 11,
  21–2, 39, 44, 57, 59–62, 64, 70–2, 136
Kirby, Anne 133
Kirk, Neville 113
Kitson, Alex (TGWU Deputy General
  Secretary) 96
Knochshinnoch Colliery, Ayrshire 26

Labour Party 2, 5, 7–8, 21, 25, 38–42, 55,
  64, 84–5, 87–8, 90, 92, 97–8, 100,
  102, 111, 119, 133–4, 151, 159, 174
Lady Victoria Colliery, Midlothian 25, 56
Lawson, Nigel 37, 43, 146
legality of strike 3–4, 6, 73–4, 76, 114
Leishman, Jim 118
Lewis, Clive (ISTC, Scotland) 43, 89–91
Lindop, Fred 101
Lingerwood Colliery, Midlothian 24
Linwood car plant 2, 36, 83–4
Lithgow, Sir James 45
'Little Moscows' 27–8, 33
local authorities and the strike 35, 46, 84,
  111, 116, 119–22, 122, 152, 169, 171,
  174

Longannet mining 'complex' and power station 11, 22, 29, 34, 39, 46, 59, 61, 63–4, 67, 71–2, 91, 103, 111, 114–15, 118, 124–5, 127, 129–31, 137, 143, 156, 167, 172–4
Lothian and Borders Police 149
see also policing of the strike

McCaig, Iain (NUM, Solsgirth) 22, 96, 118, 130, 132
McCallum, Alex (miner, Polmaise) 159–60
McCallum, Jim (NUM, Bogside) 60–1, 72–3
MacColl, Ewan 26
McCormack, John (NUM, Polmaise) 37, 70–2, 96
McGahey, Jimmy 23
McGahey Michael (NUM, Bilston Glen) 23, 150–2
McGahey, Michael (NUMSA President) 2–3, 5, 7–10, 14, 23–4, 33–4, 36–8, 42–7, 60–4, 67, 69, 72, 74, 85–9, 91, 93–5, 97, 103, 110–11, 117, 135, 144–7, 149, 155–6, 159–60, 172–3
MacGregor (NCB Chairman) 3, 41, 45, 59, 64–5, 68–9, 88, 90, 128, 132,145–7
McGuinness, Lesley 133, 171
McKay, K. W. 89–91, 93
Macmillan, Harold 36–7, 83
McNamara, Anne Kay 133
male chauvinism in the coalfields 5, 134
management and managers 1–2, 8–9, 11, 13, 25–7, 44–7, 53–76, 159–61, 167, 171–5
Marr, Andrew 91–2
Married Women in Employment (MWE) 12, 110–11, 119–24, 127, 129, 137, 174
Maxton, John 97
Maxwell, Alex (NCB, Cowdenbeath workshops) 6, 133,
Meades, Jonathan 4, 166
mechanisation of production in coal 21, 25–8, 31–2, 36, 55, 63, 65–7, 69, 167
Michael Colliery, Fife 26–8, 119, 165
Militancy Index (MI) 12, 110–11, 119–24, 129, 137, 174

Miller, Tam (victimised miner, Monktonhall) 158–9
Milne, Jimmy (STUC President) 96, 148
Milne, Seamus 3
miners' strikes of 1972 and 1974 2–3, 5, 11, 21, 23, 25, 29, 31, 33–9, 75, 92, 95, 172
mining lockout, 1926 12, 23, 33, 43, 112, 119–20, 131
see also General Strike, 1926
Mitchell, John (NUM, Frances) 70
Moffat, Abe 23
Moffat, Abe (SCEBTA President) 8, 88–9
Moffat, Alex 23
Monktonhall Colliery, Midlothian 10–11, 13, 22, 29, 54–5, 57–9, 62, 65, 67–72, 75, 86, 89, 103, 114–15, 119, 121, 123–4, 126–9, 131–7, 148–50, 152, 156, 158–60
Monopoly and Mergers Commission 44–5, 59, 63
Moodie, William 131
moral economy of the coalfields 10–11, 13, 32–3, 39, 44, 47, 53–5, 60, 64, 75–6, 110–13, 129–38, 143, 153, 159, 161, 167, 171–2, 174
Mylchreest, Tam (NUM, Castlehill) 115, 134, 154

National Association of Colliery Overmen, Deputies and Shotfirers 6, 13, 60, 71, 103, 125, 146–9
National Coal Board
in 1950s and 1960s 25–9, 36
post-1980 6–7, 41–5, 53–4, 56–7, 173
strike-breaking strategy 85–6, 116, 127, 131–2, 136–7, 143–54
working miners data 111, 125–7
National Coal Board Scottish Area management and managers 39, 58–9, 65–73, 156–60, 167–8
see also Wheeler, Albert
National Coal Board workshops 114–15, 133
National Dock Labour Scheme 99–102
see also dock strikes *and* dock workers
nationalisation of coal, 1947 21, 24–5, 65, 132, 159
National Union of Mineworkers

leadership and politics 2–8, 33–4, 37–9, 42, 53, 56, 171–2
relations with NCB 6–7, 44–5
strike ballots 38, 42, 44, 56–7, 59, 61–2, 122–3
National Union of Mineworkers Scottish Area
ending the strike 13–14, 154–6
mobilising against closures 42–3, 54–5, 57, 59–64, 73–5
politics 2, 33–4, 36–7, 46–7, 86–8
strike committee 8, 83, 91, 97, 103, 125, 136–7, 144–7, 149
strike strategy and tactics 88–97
women 5, 135
negotiations in pursuit of settlement 144–6
Neilson, Jocky (NUM, Seafield) 25, 28, 65–7, 72, 119, 155
Nelly Colliery, Fife 25, 28
Nicholson, Alex (NUM, Seafield) 24, 28, 66, 118–19, 165–6, 169
North Sea Oil 41
North Wales 5
Not Just Tea and Sandwiches 134
Nottinghamshire 5, 13, 30, 42–3, 45, 57, 111–12, 124, 128, 159, 174

Obo King, cargo ship 91, 94–6
Offer, Avner 113
Olson, Mancur 112–13
OPEC 38
oral history theory 9–10, 28, 55, 116
Orgreave, BSC coke works 96–7, 99
Ostia, cargo ship 100–2
Output per Manshift 12, 63, 67, 124, 129
Owen, David 42
Owens, Joe (NUM, Polkemmet) 6, 155

Park's buses 156
Peace, David 74
Pearson, Jim (strike-breaker, Longannet complex) 131–2
pickets and picketing 34, 40–1, 43, 66, 70, 74, 83–6, 89–90, 93–9, 103, 111–12, 114–16, 120, 126–7, 130–2, 143–4, 147, 149–52, 154, 156, 160, 171, 173
pit closures and job losses 1–12, 21, 24–7, 32–4, 36, 39, 42–4, 54–64, 72–4,

122–3, 125, 128–9, 135–7, 144–9, 167–9, 172–4
pit-level economic performance 12–13, 46, 58, 63–5, 111, 124–5, 127–30, 137, 174
see also Economic Performance (EP)
pit-level industrial relations 57–9, 65–73, 122–3, 156–60
Plan For Coal 39, 41
Perchard, Andrew 25
policing of the strike 3, 10, 12, 40, 43, 72, 74, 85–6, 90, 93–9, 103–4, 114, 131, 143, 149–54
Polkemmet Colliery, West Lothian 6, 21–2, 32, 57, 62–4, 67, 74–5, 89, 103, 115, 120–1, 123–4, 126–8, 147, 153–4, 156, 158, 160, 167–8, 170
Polmaise Colliery, Stirlingshire 46, 57–8, 62–4, 70–5, 96, 115, 118, 121–4, 126–30, 135, 143–4, 156–7, 160, 167–8, 170, 172–3
Popular Front 88
Portelli, Alessandro 9, 166
Potential Strike Endurance (PSE) 12–13, 111, 123–4, 127–9, 137
Prentice, Reg 38
Prescott, John 100, 102
Prior, Jim 40

Ravenscraig, BSC steel works 6, 10, 12, 35–6, 40, 76, 83–104, 116–17, 127, 146, 149–51, 173, 175
'Red Friday', 1925 43
Reid, Alastair 3, 85
Reid, Jimmy 4, 23, 36–7, 145
Richards, Andrew 5
Ridley, Nicholas 39–40, 43, 99–100
Robens, Alf 25
Robertson, Ann 133, 171
Roslin Colliery, Midlothian 24, 29
Rothes Colliery, Fife 27
'rough music' crowd protest 131
Russell, Margot 118, 133–4
Russell, Muir 92, 148, 153

safety work and its problems 71–2, 103, 125, 132, 146–7, 153–4
Samuel, Raphael 4–5
Scargill, Arthur (NUM President) 3–7, 10,

33–4, 37, 42–7, 56, 60–1, 72–5, 86–8,
144–7, 154, 160, 172–3
Scotsman, The 68, 70, 91–2, 95
Scottish Colliery, Enginemen, Boilermen
and Tradesmen's Association
membership and politics 8, 23, 37, 43,
55, 73, 76
Scottish Council for Development and
Industry 35
Scottish Home Rule
see Devolutionary politics and
pressures
Scottish Miner 93, 132
Scottish Office 8, 35, 75, 85, 89–92, 95,
97–9, 102–4, 111, 113, 125, 127, 131,
148, 153, 159, 172–4
Scottish Trades Union Congress 8, 34, 36,
84, 87–8, 90, 93, 96, 117, 148, 159,
172
Seafield Colliery, Fife 10–11, 21–8, 39, 54,
57–8, 63, 65–8, 72, 75, 86, 89, 103,
114–17, 119, 121, 123–8, 130, 136–7,
147, 153–6, 158, 166–70, 172
Sen, Amartya 113
Siddall, Norman 44
Smith, John 64
Smith, Ned (NCB Industrial Relations
Director) 136, 145–6, 148
Smith, William (miner, Bilston Glen) 165
Sneddon, Bill (SCEBTA, Kinneil) 61
SOGAT, print workers' union 7, 117
Solsgirth Colliery, Clackmannan 11, 21,
28, 57, 62–3, 72, 96, 121, 123–8,
156–7, 167–8, 170–1, 174
Sorn Colliery, Ayrshire 8, 21, 43–4, 57,
59, 63
South of Scotland Electricity Board 22,
29, 91–2, 129
South Wales 1, 5, 7, 33–4, 42, 44–5, 57,
62, 74, 87, 89, 91, 125–6, 155,
159–60, 166
Standing, Guy 166
Stead, Jean 96, 134
Steel, Mark 4
steel industry and workers *see* Ravenscraig
Stein, Jock 86
'Stepping Stones', Conservative Party
anti-union strategy 39–41, 99–102,
104, 147, 171

Stewart, Allan 113, 159
Stewart, David 6, 84, 90
Strangleman, Tim 166, 170
Strathclyde Police 12, 85, 90, 95–8, 150–1,
173
see also policing of the strike
strike-breakers and strike-breaking 4,
112–14, 124–38, 143–4, 146–52,
154–60, 171, 174
strike solidarity 83, 87, 116–19, 125–7,
130–2, 174
Sunday Post 153
Sykes, Homer 37

Tebbit, Norman 100–2, 104, 146
Thatcher, Margaret 3–4, 7, 21, 33, 40–1,
43, 84, 88, 101, 146–8
Thatcherism 1–3, 12, 22, 38–41, 46–7, 54,
85, 100, 102, 165, 171–2, 175
Thompson, E. P. 10–11, 32
Thompson, Willie 9, 65, 72, 88, 96, 116,
118, 130, 132, 134, 150
Thomson, Alistair 56
Todd, Ron (TGWU General Secretary) 114
Toothill Report, 1961 35
Torrance, David 84
Trades Union Congress 7, 38, 154–5
Transport and General Workers' Union
93, 95–6, 99–102, 156
Triple Alliance 43–4, 69, 87–91, 96, 100,
102, 104

unemployment 2, 11, 32, 34, 41–2, 44,
46–7, 55, 83, 148, 167–8, 172
United Democratic Mineworkers 158–9
Upper Clyde Shipbuilders 4, 36–7

Valentine, Neil (NUM, Ayrshire) 94
Valleyfield Colliery, Fife 39
victimisation of strikers 6, 13, 23, 43, 70,
143–4, 152, 155, 157, 159–60, 171,
175

wages and wage disputes in coal industry
25, 34, 37, 41–2, 45, 57, 71, 114
Walker, Peter 3, 90, 98, 100
Wallace, James 85
Wegg, Margaret 133–4
Wheeler, Albert 1, 6, 9, 26–7, 39, 43–4,

47, 54–6, 59–61, 63–5, 67, 69–72,
74–5, 128, 130, 135, 137, 152–4, 172
see also NCB Scottish Area,
Management and managers
Whitburn strike centre 93, 115
Whitelaw, William 7, 38
Wight, Daniel 31–2, 131
Wilson, Brian 4
Wilson, Matilda 133, 171
Wilson, Nicky (SCEBTA, Cardowan)
9–10, 29, 56, 90, 94, 98, 114–15, 132,
151, 153
Wilson, Rab (miner, Barony) 169–70
'Winter of Discontent', 1978–9 40
Winterton, Jonathan and Ruth Winterton
4–5

women and the strike 5, 7, 9, 12–13, 23,
32–3, 46, 110–12, 116–24, 130–5,
137–8, 148–9, 153–4, 165–71, 174–5
Wright, Margaret 133–4, 171
Wyper, Hugh (TGWU, Scotland) 93

Yorkshire 1, 4–5, 7, 30, 33–4, 37, 42–5,
57, 69, 73–5, 87–8, 97, 125, 132, 144,
151, 160, 165
Yuill, James 92–3
Yuill and Dodds, road haulier 85, 92–5,
97, 150

Zeitlin, Jonathan 85